WHERE ARE THE UNIONS?

About the editor

Sian Lazar is a lecturer in the Division of Social Anthropology at the University of Cambridge. She is the author of *El Alto, Rebel City: Self and Citizenship in Andean Bolivia* (2008) and the editor of *The Anthropology of Citizenship: A Reader* (2013). She has conducted field research in Bolivia and Argentina, with a focus on collective politics and political subjectivity.

WHERE ARE THE UNIONS?

WORKERS AND SOCIAL MOVEMENTS IN LATIN AMERICA, THE MIDDLE EAST AND EUROPE

edited by Sian Lazar

ZED
Zed Books
London

Where Are The Unions? Workers and Social Movements in Latin America, the Middle East and Europe was first published in 2017 by Zed Books Ltd, The Foundry, 17 Oval Way, London SE11 5RR, UK.

www.zedbooks.net

Typeset in Plantin and Kievit by Swales & Willis Ltd, Exeter, Devon
Index by ed.emery@thefreeuniversity.net
Cover design by Alice Marwick

ISBN 978-1-78360-990-1 hb
ISBN 978-1-78360-989-5 pb
ISBN 978-1-78360-992-5 pdf
ISBN 978-1-78360-991-8 epub
ISBN 978-1-78360-993-2 mobi

CONTENTS

ACKNOWLEDGEMENTS

This collection began life as a conference in Cambridge, called 'Bread, Freedom and Social Justice: Organized workers and mass mobilisations in the Arab World, Europe and Latin America', which I co-organised with Anne Alexander in 2014. I am immensely grateful to Anne for all her hard work in organising that conference, bringing in many of the contributors, translating between Arabic and English (often simultaneously) and, not least, for her intellectual input in framing the conference and subsequent analysis. The conference was supported by the Centre for Research in the Arts, Social Sciences and Humanities (CRASSH) and the Division of Social Anthropology at the University of Cambridge, and the Institute of Latin American Studies of the University of London, and I am very thankful to those institutions for their financial and administrative support. A British Academy Mid-Career Fellowship provided me with the time to prepare this collection and some financial assistance for the translators, Yassmin Ahmed, Lucy McMahon and Patrick O'Hare. I am grateful to them for their sterling work, sometimes at short notice. I thank the authors of the chapters, and pay tribute to them for their ability to live a life consistent with their politics, often combining activism with academic work, but without sacrificing intellectual rigour.

INTRODUCTION

Sian Lazar

2011 was a remarkable year for spectacular mass protest. A tragic act of self-immolation by the street vendor Mohamed Bouazizi in front of the provincial headquarters of a Tunisian town sparked off protests that led to the resignation and flight of President Ben Ali four weeks later, on 14 January 2011. The effects of those mobilisations spread out of Tunisia, eventually to cross the Middle East and North African (MENA) region, including the countries of Egypt, Libya, Syria, Bahrain and Yemen. Most famously, the 18-day occupation of Tahrir Square in Cairo led to the resignation of President Hosni Mubarak in February 2011. Then, inspired by the Tahrir Square occupation, Spanish groups occupied city squares from 15 May until early August in some cases. Inspired by all these, in September, young people in New York occupied Zuccotti Park in the centre of the financial district and called themselves Occupy Wall Street. Similar groups developed in other US cities, and the protest expanded and crossed (back) into Europe on 15 October, when mobilisations occurred globally in support of the Occupy movement. Occupations developed in multiple cities, especially in the US and Canada, Europe and Australia. Many felt it at the time to be a global movement, with a unified slogan – 'we are the 99%' – and common symbols such as the tents and the Anonymous mask.

The first wave of academic and journalistic commentary often partook of the euphoria of the protests themselves, emphasising elements such as the youth of the occupiers, the role of social media in calling people to the squares in Cairo as much as in Madrid or New York, the practices of creativity, performance and democratic prefiguration to be found in the occupations themselves, and the challenge of the occupiers to politics as usual. In this space of 'politics as usual' protesters and commentators lumped together traditional political parties or governing regimes, dictatorial presidents, trade unions, corporate interests and other governing elites. They were all, it seems, characterised by verticalist forms of leadership, corruption, bureaucracy, age and irrelevance.

By December, many of the Occupy camps had disappeared, either as a direct result of state repression or because they gradually fizzled out and protesters turned to more localised forms of action, such as neighbourhood activism. Those of us who had been observing the protests or participating in them (or both) turned to questions of how to understand the mobilisations, and think about what might come next. Some of us worried that the Occupy mode of protest itself exemplified the ephemerality of spectacular protest, and confirmed the worst fears of those who had criticised the leaderless protesters for being impractical, utopic, without a programme or overly idealistic about the possibility of social change through horizontally organised collective action.

We had been here before: in what has come to be known as the global justice movement, moments of spectacular effervescence included the Zapatista uprising of January 1994, the battle of Seattle in 1999, protests against the G8 in Genoa in 2001, and the World Social Forums and their spin-offs in the 2000s. In Latin America, spectacular protests against corrupt governing regimes took place in Venezuela in 1989, Bolivia in 2000–2005, Argentina in 2001 and Ecuador in the 1990s. Yet, curiously, the effects in these countries seemed not to be quite so ephemeral, as leftist regimes were elected to state power in Venezuela in 1998, Bolivia in 2005, Ecuador in 2006, Argentina in 2003 and Brazil in 2002, in direct relation to mass protests and social movement action more broadly, to create what has become known as the 'pink tide', or 'turn to the left' in the region.

With some distance from the 2011 wave of protests, we can see similarities and differences between them and earlier waves, in Europe, North America and Latin America. One of the most important similarities between the Latin American uprisings, the Arab revolutions and the contemporary European movements of the *indignados* has been onlookers' tendency to underplay the role of organised labour in the mobilisations and their aftermath.[1] And yet, workers' strikes and protests played a critical role in propelling the mass movements in Latin America into state power, destabilised dictatorships in Tunisia and Egypt, and continue to challenge austerity governments across Europe.

Still, their role is significantly underestimated in narratives of these events. This book redresses that oversight and explores the prospects for worker mobilisation and the production of alternative worlds in the aftermath of the spectacular uprisings; as workers, migrants, the unemployed and students try to define political and social alternatives to neoliberalism and austerity. We acknowledge also the importance of taking a longer historical narrative approach than was common in the immediate aftermath of the Occupy movements in particular. This in turn enables us to overcome concerns about ephemerality: from almost spontaneous uprisings of youth discontent brought into effervescent practice by calls on social media, occupations start to look like one event in a long trajectory of day to day organisation, strikes and protest culture in the longer term. Tahrir Square is the outcome of not only the 'We Are All Khaled Said' Facebook page, but also the wave of strikes that began in 2005 (Alexander and Bassiouny, this volume); the Argentine crisis of December 2001 was immediately provoked by bank controls and food riots, but was also an outcome of longer-term organisation at the level of the neighbourhood, as unionists and local residents formed *piquetero* communities and action groups (Manzano), and so on.

The role played by organised labour in the three regions over the last two decades or so has been anything but simple; nor was it always even supportive of demands for change. Organised labour took advantage of protest situations to strengthen its own position, as in Tunisia (Omri); or traditional trade unionists retreated into their comfort zones and refused to engage with the young people in the squares, as in Greece and Spain (Anagnostopoulos and Evangelinidis, Martí i Puig and Aparicio Wilhelmi). Meanwhile, new unionist initiatives developed, sometimes as an outcome of, or at least related to, student activism (Anagnostopoulos and Evangelinidis, Moyer-Lee and Chango Lopez), sometimes as a response to inertia in trade union hierarchies (Moyer-Lee and Chango Lopez, Compton), sometimes in relationship to NGO organisational forms (McMahon). And in one case described in this book, organised labour effectively took state power after mass mobilisation (Grisaffi).

Our comparative and historical perspective also enables us to move beyond an analysis of ephemerality in a different way, to explore the 'what next?' question in greater depth. With the examples from Latin America, for example, we can examine the difficulties of gaining access to state power, directly or indirectly in the sense of relating to supposedly progressive governing regimes. In MENA, we see the dangers confronted by organised labour, as co-optation or military clamp-down lead to a reassertion of longer-term patterns of weakness or sectarianism. In Europe, strategies have varied from a turn to electoral politics in Spain and Greece; to a retreat into localised struggles in the face of victorious 'austerity' regimes, such as in the UK; to the confrontation of EU-wide issues, albeit localised into specific places, as in Italy.

This shows how difficult it is to mobilise. In Europe and MENA, it seems as though the common enemy – of corrupt governments, neoliberal economic policies, corporate interests – has returned stronger than ever, despite seeming so shaky at the time of the recent financial crisis and subsequent Occupy protests. The UK and German governments for example proclaim ever stronger notions of austerity, and through debt and bailout negotiations European finance ministers attempt to force those policies on others. The European Union seeks to limit the flow of refugees across its borders, and governments stand by while migrant workers drown in the Mediterranean. Meanwhile racial tensions intensify in countries where workers both migrant and 'native' struggle to make a living. Newly powerful military regimes in Egypt co-opt independent trade unionists, condemn activists and journalists to death, and continue neoliberal policies; in Libya and Syria, the Arab Spring rapidly became deadly civil wars, while in other countries mobilisations were brutally repressed. Only in some parts of Latin America do governing regimes proclaim a kind of 'post-neoliberal' identity and seek explicitly to combat inequality, albeit at the cost of increasing reliance upon environmentally destructive extractive industries.

It is evident that the struggle against a common enemy that might be defined very simply as government in favour of the rich requires a much longer time frame than that of a street occupation, single protest or even wave of protests. The authors of the chapters in this book are not disheartened by this realisation, but write precisely from a longer sense of ongoing struggle. This is especially the case for those who are activists themselves, but is shared also by those from journalist and academic backgrounds. Those of us who are primarily academics come from the disciplines of anthropology, history, literature, labour studies and sociology, and so this collection is ambitious in the scope of its interdisciplinarity as much as in its comparative and historical perspective. We are a collective of different voices in another sense, as we try to speak in activist registers as well as in academic ones, and mediate between the two. Our cases cover Argentina, Bolivia, Brazil, Egypt, Greece, Italy, Mexico, Spain, Tunisia and the UK, and all consider the themes of labour and mobilisation in these diverse contexts. In the remainder of my introduction, I first contextualise this book within a discussion of the relationship between labour movements and academic studies of social movements. Then I summarise the main common themes that emerge from a comparison of the case studies, and finally, I give an outline of the structure of the book.

Social movements and labour in academic studies

Historians of Europe and the US give great prominence to the labour movements of the late nineteenth and early twentieth centuries in their discussions of social movements (Tilly and Wood 2012). Yet, from about the 1970s onwards, there has been a significant decline both in labour movements themselves and in academic discussion of them, at least in some parts of the world.

Undoubtedly there has been a decline in union density in many countries across the world, particularly in the Global North.[2] This has been exacerbated by trends such as the increasing freedom of productive capital to move to locations where labour was cheaper and less well-organised, as tracked by Beverly Silver (2003). In the Global North there has been a move away from manufacturing towards forms of labour that are less amenable to the kind of trade union organising familiar from the early to mid-twentieth century. New worker identities have emerged, but many unions have not been able to appeal to them. Without significant willingness of unions to change, the usual story is that this represented something of a crisis for organised labour, as it reduced its scope and did not replace the lost members with new ones from growing sectors of exploited employees.

Counter-narratives do exist, as with that of the reinvigoration of unionism in parts of the Global North with the development of 'social movement unionism', also sometimes known as 'community unionism' (Collins 2012; Devinatz 2008; Fairbrother 2008; Fantasia and Voss 2004; Johnston 1994; Lopez 2004; Mollona 2009; Moody

1997; Robinson 2000; Turner and Hurd 2001). Community unionism is associated with a political project that stretches beyond the workplace, where unions incorporate wide community-based concerns in their campaigning activities. It developed first in countries of the Global South like Brazil and South Africa, and there is some debate about whether it has translated to the North at all. Nonetheless, some of the pioneers of this kind of organising in the US have been (some local branches of) the American Service Employees International Union, as Stephen Lopez (2004) shows for the case of health workers in postindustrial Pittsburgh (see also Durrenberger and Erem 2005). The public sector has been key for community unionist mobilisation, as in the Wisconsin protests against the attack on unions by governor Scott Walker in 2011 (Collins 2012). In the UK, some public sector unions have begun to explore ways of developing social movement unionist approaches; for example, UNITE has developed a category of 'community membership' for those currently out of work, not dissimilar to the CTA in Argentina (see Manzano, this volume).

In the Global South, community unionism has a strong trajectory, and public sector workers have also been one site for an invigorated unionism in some places, as with the case of the manual workers' union in Botswana studied by Pnina Werbner (2014). Other spaces of community union activity include among garment workers in Mexico and Central America (Collins 2007); and in the garment industry more generally local unions have linked up with global garment unions for campaigns about labour conditions in Bangladesh and other parts of South Asia.[3] Almost everywhere, workers organise in some way to make collective demands of their employers, even under highly repressive labour and governmental regimes such as in China (Kwan Lee 2007). In both South and North, new forms of syndicalist and autonomist unionism have also been a response to the decline of traditional unionism (Ness 2014).

Despite this complex picture of the reality of labour organising, since the 1970s labour unions have moved to the background of much scholarly theorising about social movements. From the 1980s onwards, academic studies tended to highlight movements based upon shared identity – on the basis of ethnicity, gender, sexuality and so on; with some of the more extreme positions almost appearing to vacate the material aspects from all social movement practices and demands in favour of their cultural and social claims.

In the 1990s, theorists' gaze was diverted away from labour movements by an increasing (and necessary) focus on globalisation, for example with the discussion of globally networked anti-capitalist movements. That 'global justice movement', also often known as the alter-globalisation movement, is a loose coalition of groups and actions that came to coalesce around anti-G7/G8 summit protests, and the World Social Forums and related regional forums (see Flesher Fominaya 2014; Juris 2008; Juris and Khasnabish 2013; Maeckelbergh 2009). There was considerable union participation in the first wave, but that was not without tension, and it appears to have fallen away in recent years. It could convincingly be argued that the Occupy protests were the latest example of the alterglobalisation movement of movements, and certainly a number of occupiers had previous experience in those networks (Graeber 2013). Activists from these movements, especially their more anarchist wings, strongly insist that they are different from more traditional social movements, a discourse that manifests as a fierce critique of establishment actors, into which category is included both traditional trade unions and political parties.

In a mirror image of the emphasis on the global, scholars have recently returned to the study of local activism, especially that focused on the demands of social reproduction in the city. Manuel Castells was one of the first theorists to propose these as a source of mobilisational force (1983); and feminists have examined women's neighbourhood mobilisation around the needs of reproduction since the 1970s. Some recent work has articulated this range of practices as ones that emphasise the desire to live a good and collective life in the city, and thus claim the right to the city (Harvey 2012), and for urban commons (Susser and Tonnelat 2013).[4]

These activists and the scholars that study them do not deny the very real material effects of the capitalist processes that are being resisted; indeed, quite the opposite. However, they do have a tendency to filter out *class* as an explicit category of identity that is the source of mobilisational energy. At one point, class seemed to be all there was for most social movements theorists and actors; and the social movements theories of the 1980s on were an attempt to get away from that 'economic reductionism' (Lagalisse 2013: 132). But the understandable urge to seek alternatives to normative versions of political mobilisation has meant that organised class-based resistance to capitalism has slipped out of view in both scholarly work and political commentary. An example of this is, ironically, David Harvey's book *Rebel Cities* (2012), in which he produces a brilliant Marxian discussion of capitalist accumulation by dispossession in the cities, but where almost none of the rights to the city movements he describes are based on labour.

And yet, despite global declines in union density, and despite theorists' tendency to celebrate 'emergent cultures of activism' (Pleyers 2013), organised labour has not in fact gone away. Something more complex and interesting seems to be occurring. On the one hand, some groups of traditional trade unions are closing in on themselves and becoming less and less relevant to the political situation in which they find themselves. But in other cases, newer kinds of unions are emerging, independent of traditional state structures, often informed by anarcho-syndicalism or other critical unionist positions. This is a global trend, as a collection edited by Immanuel Ness (2014) shows, and examples of this trend can be found here in the chapters on the UK, Greece and Egypt. Alternative strategies include those where more traditional union structures attempt to reinvigorate themselves, and reach out to new members. One case of top-down reform is that of the SEIU in the US, which has led most recently to the rather remarkable campaigns in the US for Walmart and McDonalds workers to be paid a living wage.[5] It is possible that large unions in the UK may be open to similar reform initiatives, as suggested here by Mary Compton for the NUT. Her chapter also illustrates an alternative possibility, where rank and file members fight their own bureaucracies and attempt to change their union from within, as with the teachers' union in Mexico. In still other cases, progressive reform of traditional unions seems all but impossible.

Given all these rich possibilities for labour movements, in this book we seek to reinvigorate study of organised labour as an important subgenre of social movements, albeit while retaining a critical approach. The shifting of attention away from organised labour over the last three decades or so has proved characteristic of – or at the very least good for – neoliberal politics, and in this collection we bring attention back to mobilisation based upon labouring identity. What that does *not* mean is re-invigoration as merely repetition of traditional notions of working-class identity imagined as formal sector, industrial and male. Instead, we take a much more expansive view of labour and of organisation, and explore how mobilisation based upon work articulates with forms of mobilisation based on alternative identities and needs.

Organised labour and the state

The chapters collected here show that unions of all kinds can be co-opted into different political projects, whether these are of the state, directly oppositional to the state, or positioned as alternatives completely outside the state. In this section I discuss that question of co-optation, while in the following section I move to address the impact of new forms of mobilisation on unions as political projects themselves.

State influence over unions of course varies. Evident in all of the chapters is how governance shapes the conditions of possibility for the mobilisation of workers. Different governing regimes at national and international scales create the need for organisation in the ways that they encourage or allow labour exploitation, but in a more positive sense they can also create spaces for organisation and mobilisation. So, for example, Mary Compton describes how educational reforms operate at both national and global scales to shape teachers' identities, often provoking significant levels of stress and distress; but also provoking outrage and mobilisation. In neighbourhoods of Buenos Aires, Argentina, governance techniques – specifically, census-taking – provided an opportunity for unions and residents' organisations to collaborate in order to gain access for residents to government social programmes, and build themselves as a movement.

International governance regimes also shape conditions of labour and possibilities for organisation, as in the example of migration. Migration can have contrasting effects: for example in Italy (Peano, this volume), migrant workers are currently suffering from increased EU regulation of freedom of movement, which takes the form of increased militarisation of migration control, especially when migrants attempt to cross borders. Once in the EU, after often highly dangerous journeys, they are as a consequence vulnerable to poor labour and housing conditions and racist attacks. Yet international regimes can also operate to the benefit of migrants. For example, workers who migrated initially from Ecuador and Colombia to Spain, then gained Spanish citizenship and subsequently migrated to London, were able to mobilise to improve their employment conditions in the UK, because due to EU legislation their right to work was not in doubt (Moyer-Lee and Chango Lopez, this volume).

Governance in a more direct and often brutal sense also shapes the possibilities for labour organisation, as repressive regimes attack, imprison and murder unionists. This is a problem across the globe, as work by Gill (2007) shows for the case of Colombia. In this volume the chapters on Egypt and Brazil in particular highlight this problem. In Egypt, organised workers have been attacked by the military and imprisoned for protesting (Alexander and Bassiouny), and in Brazil, some protesters' lives are deemed less grievable than others when victimised by the police (McMahon). In many countries political opposition, including in unionism, is life-threatening, today as in the past.

However, relations between labour organisations and governments do not always consist only of power versus resistance. There are multiple responses to state power, including accommodation and arrangements for co-government. In the case of Bolivia, the coca growers' union actually captured the state in 2005, with the election to the presidency of union leader Evo Morales (Grisaffi, this volume). Other forms of co-government include more standard corporatist models of an official union federation that forms a structure of government and power parallel to the state – albeit usually dependent on the state – such as in twentieth-century Egypt and Tunisia (Bassiouny and Alexander, and Omri, this volume), Argentina from the 1940s to the 1990s, and in other countries in Latin America in the mid-late twentieth century, prior to neoliberal structural adjustment. A number of those countries retain the legacy of union co-government in the form of powerful central federations with significant influence over government regimes, remnants of which can also be seen in some parts of Europe such as France and Italy, and other parts of the world such as post-1994 South Africa. As the chapters on Egypt and Tunisia show, the powerful state-dependent central union federations often grew as part of a nationalist project in the immediate postcolonial era of the mid-twentieth century.

From some perspectives, these kinds of 'traditional' trade unions appear to have been co-opted by the state. That was certainly the charge levelled against the Egyptian Trade Union Federation by the alternative Egyptian Independent Trade Union Federation (EITUF) formed in Tahrir Square in January 2011; and it is the charge levelled against traditional unions in Spain and Greece by activists who accuse them of being merely part of the political establishment. In Lebanon, similarly, the traditional unions are accused of having very close relations with the militia. Such a relationship, Walid Daou argues in his chapter, leaves them unable to make truly contentious demands of governments and employers, and beholden to government wishes for docile labour relations. Curiously, the EITUF also appears to have become co-opted by the new military regime in Egypt in the years since its foundation in 2011 (Alexander and Bassiouny, this volume).

The range of possible relationships between unions and political parties adds another complication. Independent unionists or activists may almost entirely reject political parties, but some seek connections with new political formations, such as Podemos in Spain, or Syriza in Greece. However, Thomas Grisaffi's chapter shows one of the dangers of this, as the Bolivian coca growers developed their own very successful political party and yet still found that once in government, the leadership acted more like a (conventional) party and less like a social movement. In Argentina, activists from small leftist political parties provided much of the energy for union and neighbourhood mobilisation, but the associations still found themselves engaging closely with governing regimes and therefore conventional political parties. In the UK, unions closely associated with the Labour Party have proven difficult to influence from below, such that in one case described here (Moyer-Lee and Chango Lopez), the answer was to split off and join a more independent union. However, this did not preclude making connections between the campaign and the Green Party leadership, or sympathetic Labour MPs. In still other places, such as Greece and Lebanon, traditional unionist leaderships had such a strong connection to particular political parties that it became one of the reasons to reject them completely from a more radical and grassroots perspective. Yet in Tunisia, the union federation is almost able to act as if it were something more than either a union or a party, but rather a movement able to influence cultural as well as political life. This may also have been the case in twentieth-century Egypt.

Clearly, the relationship between repression and co-optation is complex, and varies according to specific contexts. For many theorists of social movements, the danger of co-optation (whether forced or entered into willingly) is associated with a weakening of the ability to make change. That tension runs throughout most of the chapters in this collection, and it means that the issue of state and party-political co-optation begs at least two questions. First, to what extent is a close relationship with the state or a formal political party a *problem*: do any spaces of power remain, or do unions merely become representatives of the state to the workers, rather than the other way round? Second, what leads to co-optation? One reason of course might be attributed to the self-interest of those at the higher levels of union leadership, especially where personal incentives might be granted to individual leaders. Where unions lack internal democracy, the hierarchy is unaccountable to rank and file members who might wish to take a more combative position. That said, motives might not be quite so clear cut. Leaders risk high levels of personal danger when they stay in a position of combative opposition to government, and might therefore seek to negotiate. Furthermore, some unionist leaderships might consider it to be good labour politics, the best way to achieve benefit for their members. Without a serious research engagement with 'co-opted' union leaders themselves, some of these questions need to remain open for now. However, we should not take co-optation for granted as either inevitable or inevitably bad for workers and union members.

Relation to existing unions

Is there something about the union form itself that leads to co-optation? Some autonomists might argue that this is the case; and one of the effects of the different waves of mobilisation described here has been to launch fierce critiques of conventional unions. As the chapters in this collection show, challenges to established union practice take multiple forms, which I categorise in this section as internal challenges, external challenges where there is still an attachment to the union as a form of organisation, and external challenges where alternative forms of organisation are sought and the union form is argued to be irrelevant.

Internal challenges often take the form of calls from within for the transformation of existing union structures, usually through greater democratisation. Mary Compton details the corruption of one of Mexico's most powerful unions, that of teachers, and the actions of some rank and file members to challenge both their own union bureaucracy and the education reforms proposed by the government and supported by the union leadership. Teachers from Oaxaca have been particularly critical and active, since at least 2006. Jason Moyer-Lee and Henry Chango Lopez also describe the attempts of the outsourced workers of the University of London (UoL) to gain access to UNISON structures of power by participating in local branch elections.

A more common response appears to be what I have characterised as external challenges through the development of non-traditional kinds of organisation, resulting often from radical initiatives at the grassroots. According to the chapters here, the latest wave seems to have emerged from the 1990s onwards, and has been very influenced by the effects of the neoliberal governance that really took hold then across all of the countries we discuss. Such initiatives can take the form of radical unionism, as in the case of the Greek call centre workers' unions described by Anagnostopoulos and Evangelinidis. There, the union form needed to make itself adequate to new labour conditions – or, more correctly, the new, and highly precarious, labour conditions created new forms of unionism. But the workers did not reject the notion of belonging to a union as such, they just felt that the unions on offer did not represent them adequately. Something similar happened in the UK among the UoL workers, as once they realised that they had failed to make the traditional union genuinely responsive to them and representative of them, they defected *en masse* to join a new, more radical union, more attuned to their politics and needs. In Egypt, workers formed independent labour unions in part as a critique of the traditional state-led ones, one notable example being the property tax collectors' union.

Other groups of people have simply rejected the whole notion of union politics completely, and sought to form alternative organisations, such as autonomous collectives, squatters groups, advocates for social housing and so on, as in Spain. A different strategy can be found in the case described by Lucy McMahon, where a Brazilian NGO takes on labour politics but locates them in a holistic politics of life, and their campaigns for street vendors combine labour rights with sexual and reproductive rights.

Some would argue that traditional unions should move more in this direction, and, indeed, that some are, albeit slowly. As the following section of this introduction discusses, one of the key insights of contemporary scholarship for understanding labour politics is the importance of multiple aspects of life and liveability that include *but are not limited to* employment conditions. Collective mobilisation arises to address questions of reproduction (life itself) as much as those of production for economic profit. The case of Argentina shows how one union did so, namely by allying itself with neighbourhood-based associations. In the Chapare region of Bolivia, Thomas Grisaffi argues that the coca growers' union federations were a form of community leadership with responsibilities for resolving disputes, distributing land and growing rights, even providing entertainment in the form of the radio station.

We might see a parallel between a unionism embedded in local structures of non-state governance as akin to 'community' or 'social movement unionism'. Peter Waterman (1993) provided an earlier definition of social movement unionism as one charged with a similarly holistic sense of field and purpose, articulated with other social movements and attempting to address whole life issues, associated with but also lying beyond wage labour, and incorporating demands for workplace and union democracy. As Collins (2012: 17) argues, the distinctions between 'politics of the workplace and politics of the living space' – or production and social reproduction – have never been completely clear cut, and this is borne out by all of the chapters in this volume. Nonetheless, there may be ways that unions could develop closer links with their communities. For example, Mary Compton suggests that teachers' unions might seek alliances with the parents of school pupils, to share their distress at reforms that affect both the teachers' employment conditions and the quality of education they are able to provide to their children.

The lived experience of working subjectivity

Identity and subjectivity are key to understanding how workers' movements have developed and interacted with both the state and the traditional unions. All of the contributions show how new workers' identities emerged or could emerge to become key subjects in the struggle against neoliberalism. Anagnostopoulos and Evangelinidis argue that we must understand the 'lived experience of working subjectivity' if we are to understand the movements themselves. For the authors in this collection, the newly important figures are (in no particular order): teachers, migrants, precarious graduate employees, unemployed youth, the *piqueteros*, independent unionists. Importantly, identities not only emerge through work, but also through community and life.

Strategically, as noted above this might relate to questions of community unionism, as in some cases (e.g. Argentina) unions reached out to communities in order to maintain their relevance and effectiveness; in others (e.g. Spain), 'life' or the community seems to have overtaken the unions who were not able to make this change. Politically, one of the crucial aspects of the importance of identity is how identities effect fragmentation as well as coming together; and we can see some of the effects of these in the role of sectarianism shaping labour politics as much as it shapes mainstream politics in Lebanon; and in the complexities of alliances between African migrants and the white working class in Italy.

Since the 1960s, scholars began to argue that the classical notion of the industrial proletariat as archetypal revolutionary political subject would need to change. In contemporary post-Fordist capitalism, new subjects are emerging to take up the struggle for economic and social justice. Hardt and Negri (2005) famously characterised these new subjects as the 'multitude', and made a strong argument for new formations of labour, specifically immaterial labour, as at least one set of groupings that constitute the multitude; but what might this mean in practice? One potentially key political subject is teachers, as Mary Compton argues, in part because neoliberal education reforms affect teachers' senses of themselves as creative individuals and professionals. But the very things that threaten teachers also threaten children's learning, and that, alongside the fact that teachers are often well-respected members of local communities, creates openings for action. Teachers' identities as professionals serving a community can be replicated in other parts of the public sector, and public sector workers are often both at the sharp end of government cuts and protagonists in combative labour movements, as also in the example of the property tax collectors in Egypt (Alexander and Bassiouny, this volume).

Private sector workers might be less combative in part because of increased vulnerability as a result of labour reforms associated with neoliberalism and structural adjustment. Several contributions to this book speak to this problem of precarity. In Greece, graduate workers in caller centres are employed on very short-term contracts, with complicated shift arrangements, and they are thus vulnerable to pressure not to mobilise collectively. In response, unionists have developed new methods of organisation and action, governing themselves through assemblies and using direct action activist strategies on the shop floor. In Spain, university graduates also found themselves living precarious lives, facing astronomical rates of youth unemployment, and without access to affordable housing. The only prospect for them, it seems, was to migrate to other parts of the EU.

Migrants in Italy live in similarly precarious life circumstances, but have the added vulnerability of their very presence in the country being illegal. This means that they can be ultra-exploited by unscrupulous employers and landlords (Peano, this volume). Further, they are in danger of being physically attacked as societal racism increases. Their struggle therefore becomes one of claiming full humanity. The need for a whole life struggle has parallels with feminist organising in Brazil (McMahon, this volume), where NGOs work with informal sector workers not only on labour rights, but also on other vulnerabilities and on the right to have rights more generally.

The sociologist Guy Standing has argued that these groups of people – young graduates, migrant workers, informal sector workers – constitute a class in the making, which he names the *precariat*. His analysis is mostly confined to Europe and the US, and the notion of the precariat too homogenising to accurately reflect the varying conditions of work and life across the globe. Yet, precarity itself is a condition of life for many, and its increase in Europe and the US – especially among younger generations – is a way that the Global North follows in the footsteps of the Global South. There, life and work have always been precarious for all but a very small minority: in parts of Africa and Latin America, the majority of young people will likely never work in a regular job, let alone one in the formal, regulated parts of their economies (Ferguson 2015). In the Global North, state-run welfare programmes and public sector wages are cut; workers are hired on short-term, 'flexible' contracts, with few benefits and low wages; housing is expensive and attainable only through high levels of debt; and police forces are militarised.

Globally, feminists have long linked questions of work and production with questions of reproduction. Classically, feminist scholars and campaigners have argued that women's equal participation in the labour market is impossible when they are vulnerable to violence in the home; or they have highlighted the double (or triple) shift worked by many women, as they combine domestic labour with earning a living, and often also with collective work for the community. In the current climate, we might suggest that dissent arises from the conditions of life itself. Changed conditions of labour and of life produce changing modes of collective organisation. However, as new forms of collective organisation emerge, they are accompanied by new dangers, as states collude with corporations to crush or co-opt collective initiatives.

Structure of the book

The book begins with chapters that describe relations between labour movements and the state, first in Egypt. There, independent working-class self-organisation underwent a significant revival from the mid-2000s onwards, but was subsequently co-opted by the post-2013 state, as leading figures in the independent trade union movement endorsed the regimes of direct military rule. Alexander and Bassiouny tell the story of this shift, and attempt to explain how co-optation became possible. Chapter 2 moves to Bolivia, and describes what we might consider to be one of the most successful trade union movements in recent times, that is if success is measured by the capture of state power. The Movement Towards Socialism (MAS), Bolivia's ruling party since 2006, developed out of a peasant union of coca growers, concentrated in the Chapare region. The ascent of the party was linked directly to the fight to legalise the cultivation and consumption of coca; and grounded in the unions' role in organising collective life and well-being, thus bringing out questions not only of state capture but also the importance of community unionism, a theme returned to in latter chapters.

The following chapter takes as its subject a different constellation of power, namely that of the parallel union federation that is in some sense a partner of the state. The Tunisian General Union of Labour (better known by its French acronym, UGTT), has been at the heart of the liberation movement and the construction of the nation-state since its founding in the late 1940s. Mohamed-Salah Omri shows how the UGTT has been foundational in the development of a protest culture over this time in Tunisia, one that was deeply influential in the 2011 revolution.

The next four chapters engage with the themes of identity and the development of mobilisation based upon the precarity of life and work. Their focus on some of the identitarian but also aesthetic and cultural dimensions of trade union activism helps them to contribute to current debates on the nature of new social movement unionism. The first chapter in this section studies a series of migrant struggles in Italy, focusing on the labour element within them, but placing that in the context of whole life claims. Irene Peano makes the crucial argument that we must pay attention to the relationship between struggles of citizenship, anti-racism and for better labour conditions and life more generally. Together, these political struggles amount to a struggle for humanity. The classical unions responded to these demands with initial solidarity that developed into suspicion of migrant workers.

In Spain, the mobilisations from 2011 onwards rejected traditional trade unionism, and have, Salvador Martí i Puig and Marco Aparicio Wilhelmi argue, led to a complete reconfiguration of the political system. They show how the 15M movement rejected post-dictatorship establishment politics and created a new form of activism based in questions of precarious life itself, such as housing and unemployment; also enacted through various mobilisational practices, e.g. incorporating ironic humour. Yet, although the 15M activists rejected unionist politics, one of the intriguing aspects of this case is that parts of the movement at least have not completely rejected electoral politics. Instead, with Podemos and some local civic electoral movements, older political forms (i.e. parties) have been reinterpreted, and the Spanish system of bi-partisanship has been destabilised.

The case of Lebanon provides another example of a critique of traditional trade unions, as Walid Daou argues that trade union bureaucracy and lack of internal democracy has led to a depoliticisation of trade union activism there since the 1975–1990 civil war. Apart from highly dubious relationships between union hierarchies and governing militia, leaders ignore the sectarianism, racism and gender discrimination directed against many Lebanese and foreign male and female labour groups. They are therefore unable to represent the working class as a whole, and in fact contribute to the fragmentation of identities as workers divide along lines of gender and citizenship. This significantly constrains the forms and structure of trade union struggle and labour, the construction of class-consciousness, the possibility of the expansion of the labour movement and its ability to recruit new members.

The following chapter, by Mary Compton, addresses questions of identity, of state co-optation and of changing union structures, in a discussion of teachers and their unions in the UK and Mexico. Teachers are mobilising on the basis of resistance to attacks on their professional identity and their sense of themselves as ethical human beings. Traditional unions can be co-opted into government projects, but this might have significant unexpected effects, not least a response from the grassroots to demand union democratisation, as in the case of Mexico. This challenge to the dominant structure of co-optation has been very powerful, and Compton suggests that similar moves could take place in the UK.

The third part of the book presents four chapters that discuss different strategies to engage with questions of identity, precarity and the rank and file challenge to traditional trade unions – again, giving examples of new social movement unionism. In the first case study, Lucy McMahon uses the case of a street vendors' advocacy NGO, CAMTRA, to outline alternative strategies for improving labour rights. She argues that CAMTRA's oscillation between different tactics and philosophical standpoints provides one example of how to build organisational strength from a solidity of political ethics and in respect of labour activism viewed in a holistic sense and from a feminist perspective.

The last three chapters present alternative strategies of mobilisation based more strongly around non-traditional unionism. First, in Greece, Aris Anagnostopoulos and Angelos Evangelinidis show how the precarity of working life under austerity has given rise to new kinds of unions in challenge to the traditional organisations. They describe an experiment in autonomous syndicalism, at call centres. Their chapter argues that this kind of unionism emerged not only from the activities of student militants in the call centres but from the labour conditions themselves, made all the more difficult by significant repression on the part of the employers. Nonetheless, it must also be understood as part of cycles of contention that emerged in Greece in the 2000s.

Then, Virginia Manzano describes a form of social movement unionism in the '*piqueteros*' movement in part of Buenos Aires, Argentina. These groups were one of the most important actors within the popular mobilisations that opposed neoliberalism in 2001. To many social researchers, those protests demonstrated the emergence of new political subjects that had developed in response to the crisis of traditional actors – notably labour unions and political parties. In contrast, Manzano argues that members of trade unions were also active in the organisation of a number of grassroots *piquetero* associations, eventually contributing to the development of the political movement itself. One of the mechanisms for the creation of new subjects was, paradoxically, the experience of governance and neoliberal social policy in the urban neighbourhoods.

The final chapter presents a successful story of new union mobilisation. Jason Moyer-Lee and Henry Chango Lopez describe a successful campaign by outsourced workers of the University of London, which resulted in much improved employment conditions. They attempted at first to work through UNISON (the large UK public sector union), but then turned to the Independent Workers' Union of Great Britain (IWGB). This was a small militant union that became a symbol for the 'new trade unionism', contrasting sharply with UNISON's more traditional style. The authors argue that 'new unionism' need not be restricted to 'new' unions, but do suggest some reasons why UNISON was unable to respond effectively to the new and more politicised worker subjects and their conditions of labour under outsourcing regimes. We then conclude the volume with an afterword written by the long-time labour studies researcher Peter Waterman, to bring together the various contributions and propose a way forward on a global scale.

Notes

1 The title of this book is inspired by an article in *Atlantic* magazine, which asked of the Zuccotti Park demonstrators, 'where are the unions?'. See 'Why Workers Won't Unite', by Kim Philipps-Fein, *Atlantic*, April 2015, www.theatlantic.com/magazine/archive/2015/04/why-workers-wont-unite/386228/. Retrieved 19 January 2016.

2 See OECD figures on union density, at https://stats.oecd.org/Index.aspx?DataSetCode=UN_DEN#. Retrieved 19 January 2016. Source: OECD and J. Visser, ICTWSS database (Institutional Characteristics of Trade Unions, Wage Setting, State Intervention and Social Pacts, 1960–2010), version 3.0.

3 See Rebecca Prentice, 'A Year after Rana Plaza: Still Unearthing Its Causes', *Open Democracy*, 24 April 2014. www.opendemocracy.net/opensecurity/rebecca-prentice/year-after-rana-plaza-still-unearthing-its-causes. Retrieved 1 February 2016.

4 See also work on squatters in Madrid (Corsín Jiménez and Estalella 2013), anarchists in Slovenia (Razsa 2015), migrant workers' tenant groups in Berlin (Bojadzijev 2014), drug users in New York (Zigon 2014) and the Gezi

park protesters in Istanbul (Tugal 2013), among others.

5 See www.theguardian.com/business/2015/may/21/mcdonalds-workers-protest-poverty-wages- headquarters and www.theguardian.com/us-news/live/2015/apr/15/fight-for-15-protest-workers-minimum-wage-live. Retrieved 29 June 2015.

References

Bojadzijev, Manuela (2014) 'Urban Struggles, Frontiers of Capital, and Migration in the Current Global Crisis: A Perspective from Berlin', paper presented at the 13th EASA congress, Tallinn, 31 July – 3 August.

Castells, Manuel (1983) *The City and the Grassroots: A Cross-Cultural Theory of Urban Social Movements*, London: Edward Arnold.

Collins, Jane (2007) 'The Rise of a Global Garment Industry and the Reimagination of Worker Solidarity', *Critique of Anthropology*, 27(4): 395–409.

Collins, Jane (2012) 'Theorizing Wisconsin's 2011 Protests: Community-based Unionism Confronts Accumulation by Dispossession', *American Ethnologist*, 39(1): 6–20.

Corsín Jiménez, Alberto and Estalella, Adolfo (2013) 'The Atmospheric Person: Value, Experiment, and "Making Neighbors" in Madrid's Popular Assemblies', *HAU: Journal of Ethnographic Theory*, 3(2): 119–139.

Devinatz, Victor (2008) 'Introduction to Symposium on "The Future of Social Movement Unionism"', *Employee Responsibilities and Rights Journal*, 20(3): 205.

Durrenberger, E. Paul and Erem, Suzan (2005) *Class Acts: An Anthropology of Urban Workers and their Union*, Boulder, CO: Paradigm.

Fairbrother, Peter (2008) 'Social Movement Unionism or Trade Unions as Social Movements', *Employee Responsibilities and Rights Journal*, 20(3): 213–220.

Fantasia, Rick and Voss, Kim (2004) *Hard Work: Remaking the American Labor Movement*, Berkeley, CA: University of California Press.

Ferguson, James (2015) *Give a Man a Fish: Reflections on the New Politics of Distribution*, Durham NC: Duke University Press.

Flesher Fominaya, Cristina (2014) *Social Movements and Globalization: How Protests, Occupations and Uprisings Are Changing the World*, Houndmills: Palgrave Macmillan.

Gill, Lesley (2007) '"Right There with You": Coca-Cola, Labor Restructuring and Political Violence in Colombia', *Critique of Anthropology*, 27(3): 235–260.

Graeber, David (2013) *The Democracy Project: A History, a Crisis, a Movement*, London: Random House.

Hardt, Michael and Negri, Antonio (2005) *Multitude*, London: Hamish Hamilton.

Harvey, David (2012) *Rebel Cities: From the Right to the City to the Urban Revolution*, London: Verso.

Johnston, P. (1994) *Success While Others Fail: Social Movement Unionism and the Public Workplace*, Ithaca, NY: ILR Press.

Juris, Jeffrey S. (2008) *Networking Futures: The Movements against Corporate Globalization*, Durham, NC and London: Duke University Press.

Juris, Jeffrey S. and Khasnabish, A. (2013) *Insurgent Encounters: Transnational Activism, Ethnography, and the*

Political, Durham, NC: Duke University Press.

Kwan Lee, Ching (2007) *Against the Law: Labor Protests in China's Rustbelt and Sunbelt*, Berkeley, CA: University of California Press.

Lagalisse, Erica (2013) 'Gossip as Direct Action', in Cole, S. and Phillips, L. (eds) *Contesting Publics: Feminism, Activism, Ethnography*, pp. 112–137. London: Pluto Press.

Lopez, S.H. (2004) *Reorganizing the Rust Belt: An Inside Study of the American Labor Movement*, Berkeley, CA: University of California Press.

Maeckelbergh, Marianne (2009) *The Will of the Many: How the Alterglobalisation Movement Is Changing the Face of Democracy*, London: Pluto Press.

Mollona, Massimiliano (2009) 'Community Unionism versus Business Unionism: The Return of the Moral Economy in Trade Union Studies', *American Ethnologist*, 36(4): 651–666.

Moody, Kim (1997) 'Towards an International Social-movement Unionism', *New Left Review*, I/225 (September–October).

Ness, Immanuel (ed.) (2014) *New Forms of Worker Organization: The Syndicalist and Autonomist Restoration of Class-Struggle Unionism*, Oakland, CA: PM Press.

Pleyers, Geoffrey (2013) 'From Local Ethnographies to Global Movement: Experience, Subjectivity, and Power among Four Alter-globalization Actors', in Juris, J.S. and Khasnabish, A. (eds) *Insurgent Encounters: Transnational Activism, Ethnography, and the Political*, pp. 108–128. Durham, NC: Duke University Press.

Razsa, Maple (2015) *Bastards of Utopia: Living Radical Politics after Socialism*, Bloomington, IN: Indiana University Press.

Robinson, Ian (2000) 'Neoliberal Restructuring and U.S. Unions: Toward Social Movement Unionism?', *Critical Sociology*, 26(1–2): 109–138.

Silver, Beverly (2003) *Forces of Labor: Workers' Movements and Globalization since 1870*, Cambridge: Cambridge University Press.

Susser, Ida and Tonnelat, Stéphane (2013) 'Transformative Cities: The Three Urban Commons', *Focaal*, 2013(66): 105–121.

Tilly, Charles and Wood, Lesley (2012) *Social Movements, 1768–2012*, Boulder, CO: Paradigm.

Tugal, Cihan (2013) 'Commentary: "Resistance everywhere": The Gezi Revolt in Global Perspective', *New Perspectives on Turkey*, 49: 157–172.

Turner, Lowell and Hurd, Richard W. (2001) 'Building Social Movement Unionism: The Transformation of the American Labor Movement' [Electronic Version], in Turner, L., Katz, H.C. and Hurd, R.W. (eds) *Rekindling the Movement: Labor's Quest for Relevance in the Twenty-first Century*, pp. 9–26. Ithaca, NY: Cornell University Press [Articles & Chapters, vol. 313, Cornell University ILR School. DigitalCommons@ILR].

Waterman, Peter (1993) 'Social-Movement Unionism: A New Union Model for a New World Order?', *Review* (Fernand Braudel Center), 16(3): 245–278.

Werbner, Pnina (2014) *The Making of an African Working Class: Politics, Law, and Cultural Protest in the Manual Workers Union of Botswana*, London: Pluto Press.

Zigon, Jarrett (2014) 'An Ethics of Dwelling and a Politics of World-building: A Critical Response to Ordinary Ethics', *Journal of the Royal Anthropological Institute*, 20(4): 746–764.

PART ONE

LABOUR MOVEMENTS, SOCIETY AND THE STATE

1 | THE EGYPTIAN WORKERS' MOVEMENT: PROBLEMS OF ORGANISATION AND POLITICS

Anne Alexander and Mostafa Bassiouny

The role of organised workers in the 2011 revolution in Egypt has generally received less attention from researchers than that played by youth activists, or the technologies they used to communicate. However, from the 18-day uprising that culminated in the downfall of Mubarak, to the mass mobilisations two years later against Mohamed Morsi, collective action in the workplaces was a crucial element in making Egypt at least temporarily ungovernable. The pre-history of these massive waves of strikes, sit-ins and other forms of workers' protest has also been little explored. Yet the revival of working-class self-organisation in Egypt since the mid-2000s is in many ways a remarkable feat. Since that date, a qualitative change in the composition and activity of the workers' movement has taken place, in fact it is arguable that the 'workers' movement' as *a movement* revived or was reconstituted. Workers had, of course, engaged in various forms of collective action over the previous decades, and working-class activists engaged in political and social action in different arenas (including the lower levels of the state-controlled trade union federation and through their affiliation with a variety of political currents). However, there were no independent workers' organisations of any significant size or influence, and the episodic set-piece battles within the public sector over wages or conditions left residues of personal networks and collective memories, but little that was directly usable for the next generation of activists. Moreover, these struggles took place in the context of an accelerating programme of neoliberal restructuring, which until the mid-2000s had barely been challenged by organised workers, let alone suffered any serious setbacks as a result of their collective action.

The strike wave that began in 2004–2005 and was transformed by the historic victory of textile workers in Mahalla in December 2006, was one of the factors that changed this picture. For the first time in generations, it did create the conditions for independent trade union organisation to at least temporarily mark out a space for the revival of the workers' movement as an independently organised social actor. Combined with other factors, in particular the rising curve of political discontent with the Mubarak regime that exploded in the revolutionary crisis of 2011, the strike wave also showed the potential for organised workers to become independent *political* actors on a scale few had imagined since the 1940s and early 1950s. The power of this potential dynamic of reciprocal action between the social and political aspects of workers' collective action was demonstrated by the role played by the strike wave that erupted in the last week of the uprising of 2011 and continued for several weeks afterwards, playing a critical role in securing a limited victory over the regime. Subsequent strike waves also helped to destabilise the post-Mubarak military council regime, and the government led by Mohamed Morsi who took office as president in 2012.

Yet there remains a fundamental contradiction between the power of the workers' movement and its political impact. This is not merely a serious issue, but practically a defining characteristic of the movement. In particular the successful counter-revolution of July 2013, which led to the restoration of direct military rule, exposed the political weaknesses of the workers' movement. Leading activists in the independent unions endorsed the Tamarod (Rebellion) campaign agitating for popular protests against Mohamed Morsi on 30 June 2013. In the wake of his overthrow by the military on 3 July, Kamal Abu Aita, president of the Egyptian Federation of Independent Trade Unions (EFITU), was appointed Minister of Labour. Yet the Armed Forces, led by Minister of Defence Abdelfattah al-Sisi, were able to assert their dominance over the mass movement in the streets with frightening speed.

The Minister of Defence, Abdelfattah al-Sisi, demanded a 'mandate' from the streets to 'crush terrorism', by which he meant impunity to use massacres, torture and mass arrests to break the Muslim Brotherhood's resistance to his coup.[1] The state quickly turned on workers who took strike action, sending in troops against steel workers in Suez in August 2013. Within a year it was clear that the project of neoliberal reforms that had been temporarily disrupted by the uprising in 2011 was back on track, despite continuing waves of strikes and workers' protests. Sisi's regime was able to push through fuel subsidy cuts and austerity measures in 2014. By early 2015, even the privatisation programme, which had ground to a halt in 2011 as a result of workers' protests and the popular uprising, had been revived.

In this chapter we argue that the independent workers' movement that has emerged in Egypt since the mid-2000s is shaped by interlocking weaknesses in organisation and politics, which combine to stunt its overall ability to make significant gains at either a social or political level. In terms of trade union organisation, the movement suffers from a contradiction between strong and relatively resilient organisation in the workplaces and weak, competing bureaucracies at a national level. However, the movement also faces problems of political organisation: it has been unable to translate strength in workplace-based struggles into the enforcement of collective social or political demands in the national political arena. The battle over the national minimum wage is a case in point: it took six years to win even the partial implementation of demands that were first raised on a major scale in 2008.

The ruling party's machine: the Egyptian Trade Union Federation

The decade before the uprising of 2011 saw the first major changes in the organisational composition of the Egyptian workers' movement for nearly 50 years, with the founding of the first independent trade unions since the formation of the Egyptian Trade Union Federation (ETUF) in the 1950s. However, it was only with the downfall of Mubarak and the subsequent disorientation and paralysis of the old regime that independent trade unions formed in large numbers, and independent union federations emerged to challenge ETUF for the organisational leadership of the workers' movement on a national scale.

The Egyptian Trade Union Federation dominated trade union work since its foundation by Gamal Abdel Nasser in 1957. It was completely dependent on the state, and played no role in the development or organisation of the workers' movement. On the contrary it took a position in opposition to workers' strikes and protests. The formation of the first independent union in 2008 was thus an important step on the route to breaking the monopoly of the state over trade union work, and began to fill the organisational vacuum in the heart of the workers' movement.

The important role within the Nasserist regime played by ETUF continued under his successors, despite their abandonment of many of his other policies. The federation policed the Nasserist social contract – where workers were expected to abandon any claims to independent political expression in return for a range of social goods, such as job security, stable wages, access to health, education and welfare – both in the workplace and in wider society through interventions in elections on behalf of the ruling party. Despite the fact that the federation played almost no role in representing workers' grievances to the regime, it claimed to speak on their behalf, not only in the workplace, but in the national political arena.

This role developed early in ETUF's history, reflecting the Nasserist regime's consolidation of a one-party model of politics with the creation of the Arab Socialist Union. After 1962, membership of the trade unions was conditional on membership of the ruling party. Even after Nasser's successor, Anwar Sadat, moved towards a very limited form of pluralism after 1977, the ETUF bureaucracy continued to be dominated by the ruling party. Despite the emergence of a legal left-wing party, the National Progressive Unionist Party (Al-Tagammu'), the ETUF leadership remained the almost exclusive preserve of the ruling National Democratic Party (NDP). The ETUF and Ministry of Labour were also deeply intertwined: until the mid-1980s the Minister of Labour was ETUF president and after that date the post was frequently given as a reward to senior trade union leaders.

The ETUF also oversaw the electoral quota system, by providing documentation for candidates running for the reserved 'worker' parliamentary seats.[2] The process was skewed against critics of the regime: anyone wishing to run as an independent candidate or for a party other than the NDP in the 2010 elections had to wait until after the 3,500 members of the NDP had received their nomination documents.[3] The 2010 elections reversed the limited but significant gains made by the Muslim Brotherhood in the electoral arena in 2005. That year the regime had somewhat relaxed its grip on the electoral process, with the result that for the first time the MB won a substantial number of seats. Although officially banned, the Brotherhood won 88 seats, 34 of them with 'worker' candidates under the quota system. Most of these victories were concentrated in major urban areas: seven of the Brotherhood's nine MPs in Cairo were workers, for example.[4]

By the eve of the 2011 uprising, the model of workplace and political organisation that ETUF represented was in severe crisis, however. This crisis had two principal roots. First, the adoption of neoliberal policies undid the 'Nasserist social contract'. The ETUF bureaucracy, as an integral part of the regime's apparatus for managing the public sector, was damaged by the regime's own economic policies, which transferred hundreds of thousands of public sector workers to the private sector or enforced early retirement. The ETUF leaders' complicity in this assault on their members' jobs and conditions exposed the hollowness of their claim to represent workers' interests. However, structural blockages prevented union members and activists at the bottom of the ETUF machinery from successfully reforming the federation from within. If anything, the control of the top layers of the bureaucracy over the workplace committees became stronger, rather than weaker, as neoliberal reforms advanced. Moreover, the federation's membership hollowed out, with a large proportion of ETUF's claimed membership of around four million organised in large, geographical branches that essentially existed only on paper.

The second and more important source of the crisis within ETUF was the emergence of a sustained strike wave, which spawned workplace organisation completely outside its structures. State officials were compelled to negotiate directly with strike committee leaders, who were largely elected directly by striking workers in mass meetings. This ferment of activity in the workplace was then transformed in a small number of significant cases into more permanent forms of organisation, with the successful foundation of four independent unions between December 2008 and January 2011, breaking ETUF's monopoly over workplace organisation for the first time in more than 50 years.

The rise of the independent unions

The foundation of independent trade unions, the first of which grew out of a strike committee that led one of the major civil service strikes of 2007, partially fractured one element of the regime's control over the workers' movement: ETUF's monopoly of workplace organisation. However, as we will discuss in more detail below, the independent unions proved unable to assert themselves in the political arena. Nor did other forms of workers' organisation emerge, such as political parties, which either took up workers' specific interests, or integrated these into a wider political programme.

Nevertheless, the formation of independent unions marked a significant development. The Property Tax Collectors' Union (RETAU, or Real Estate Tax Authority Union), was founded in December 2008, almost exactly a year after the successful conclusion of a strike by the tax collectors demanding parity in wages with their colleagues in the Ministry of Finance. It was both an extension of the strike committee's highly democratic and participatory forms of organisation, and a transformation of those forms. The strike was organised through mass activities – protest marches, rallies and especially sit-ins. The major sit-ins involved thousands of property tax collectors who were mobilised through elected committees based in the provincial offices. They created spaces in which very intense forms of democracy were not only possible, but for many crucial matters were expected by strike leaders and participants alike. Strike committee delegates sent out of the sit-in to conduct negotiations expected to have to report back to a mass meeting of the strikers and were on some occasions overturned by the meeting and told to return to the negotiating table to reach a more favourable deal. On 9 December 2007, at the height of the Property Tax Collectors' major sit-in outside the Ministry of Finance, elected negotiators led by Kamal Abu Aita returned to the strikers with the outlines of an agreement, only to be instructed after a vote at a mass meeting to return and seek a better one.[5] This participatory culture was carried over to a certain extent into the structures of the new union, which was declared at a mass meeting of around in December 2008 of 3,000 delegates representing nearly 30,000 property tax collectors. The meeting had been built through months of patient work by the former strike committee activists, who toured the country drumming up support for the project of forming an independent union.

Attempts by the ETUF bureaucracy to split the new union were ultimately unsuccessful. Despite being offered a 'safer' alternative, through the foundation of a union affiliated with ETUF specifically representing Property Tax Collectors, the majority of RETAU's membership preferred to run the risk of the regime's displeasure by remaining loyal to the independent union. Adding to the sense of confusion and paralysis in the ruling party, different groups of officials pursued contradictory policies towards the independent union. The ETUF hierarchy took independent union officials to court, mobilised thugs to beat them up and accused them of financial misconduct at work. Ai'sha Abd-al-Hadi, Minister of Labour, by contrast, accorded RETAU *de facto* recognition, while the Ministry of Finance was prepared to negotiate over working conditions and pay with the new union's leaders.

The democratic model of trade unionism that RETAU's leaders attempted to transmit from their experience of strike organisation faced pressure from a number of different angles, even before the revolution of 2011. The routinisation of trade union work and the lack of collective action that followed up the victory of the 2007 strike were among the important factors contributing to the bureaucratisation of RETAU's leaders. Other pressure came from interactions with international trade unions, largely mediated through the Centre for Trade Union and Workers Services (CTUWS), an NGO led by Kamal Abbas, a former steel worker. The international trade unions that RETAU activists came into contact with were almost always much larger and better-resourced than their Egyptian counterparts. Frequent international visits for a small number of leading activists helped to reinforce, rather than break down, emerging differences in lifestyle between RETAU's leaders and their colleagues in the workplace.

The workers' movement during the revolution

Although independent unions were still a new and weak phenomenon in January 2011, at the outbreak of the uprising that led to the downfall of Mubarak, the idea of independent unionism proved enormously popular during the first year of the revolution. Hundreds of independent unions were formed at a workplace level in the first few months alone. In some cases these new unions brought to light pre-existing networks of activists who had been engaged in the clandestine organisation of strikes. The Postal Workers Union and the Cairo Public Transport Authority Union are two prominent examples. In other workplaces, independent unions were created in the wake of Mubarak's fall by workplace activists who felt empowered by the momentous political events of early 2011, and encouraged by changes in legislation that provided a form of legal registration for the new unions for the first time. The most important context for the growth of independent unions after

2011 was the dramatic acceleration in the frequency and duration of strike action over the following two and a half years. Although the transmission mechanisms between strike organisation and union organisation were complex, and the two forms of organisation did not map perfectly onto each other, independent unions continued both to grow out of strike organisation and to play a key role in organising strikes.

Even taking into account the historically high levels of strike action in the half-decade before the revolution, the upsurge in the volume of strike activity from late January 2011 was astounding. More episodes of strike action took place in February 2011 than during the whole of the previous year, according to a report by the Egyptian Centre for Economic and Social Rights.[6] After a lull between March and August 2011, the strike wave returned in September, with a massive teachers' strike and other strikes that brought an estimated 500,000 out for a variety of social demands, including pay increases, improved conditions, permanent contracts and the purge of former ruling party officials from public sector institutions.

The total number of strikes in 2012 surpassed the total number of strikes that had taken place over the previous ten years, according to a report from the Egyptian Centre for Social and Economic Rights. In 2013, the number of strikes that took place during the first five months surpassed the number for the whole of 2012, according to a report from the Democracy Index, published by the Centre for Democratic Development.[7]

The formation of the Egyptian Federation of Independent Trade Unions (EFITU) in Tahrir Square on 30 January 2011 in the midst of the uprising against Mubarak for a while established the idea of independent unionism as one of the democratic gains of the revolution. The movement for independent unionism escalated in the wake of Mubarak's downfall, as hopes rose that the organisational vacuum in the movement was being filled. Yet within a few months a number of significant organisational and political problems had developed. Personal and organisational rivalry between Kamal Abu Aita of the Property Tax Collectors' Union RETAU and Kamal Abbas of CTUWS spilled over into a split in EFITU in July 2011, which saw CTUWS and its supporters leaving the nascent federation and eventually forming a separate federation. There were no obvious substantive differences at the heart of this conflict – both sides were apparently agreed on the importance of the independence of the unions from the state and its institutions. Nor were there clear conflicts over perspectives on trade unionism. Rather the dominant factor behind the rivalry seemed to be the dynamics of bureaucratic competition between two relatively similar groups of activists, who were influenced by an NGO-model of trade unionism where the role of the federations' national leadership was to act as a lobby group and a conduit to international sources of funding.[8]

The problem of fragmentation in the independent union movement was compounded by the revival of ETUF, which slowly began to recover from the damage sustained during the 2011 uprising. The implementation of a court order annulling the ETUF elections of 2010 and the installation of a caretaker executive in August 2011 had appeared at first sight to herald the collapse of ETUF. However, in reality, this intervention by then Minister of Labour Ahmad al-Borai paved the way for ETUF's revival. The caretaker executive opened ETUF's structures to the Muslim Brotherhood from the top, with the appointment of leading Brotherhood figures. It also preserved a space for elements within the old ETUF bureaucracy to re-establish their positions with the blessing of the post-Mubarak government, and specifically of Labour Minister Al-Borai, who was seen by many in the independent union movement as their ally.

Interestingly, the independent union federations, which frequently criticised the official unions for their unpopularity and their paper membership, were unable to mobilise protests behind any of their demands greater than a few hundred, despite claiming an aggregate membership of millions. Even during the uprising against Mubarak, when EFITU mobilised in order to storm the headquarters of ETUF as one of the symbols of Mubarak's regime and the usurpation of workers' interests, it was only able to muster a few dozen, and failed twice to take the building. On the ground, and in strike organisation a number of independent union branches played an important role in organisation and leading strikes, such as the Public Transport Authority strike, the railworkers' strike, the postal workers' strike, Mahalla and so on. However, at the level of the two independent union federations, the dominant picture was one of bureaucracy, fragmentation and isolation from the everyday life of workers and their demands, in addition to competition and struggle within the independent trade union movement.

The workers' movement lacked a political voice of its own, nor did its leaders find effective allies among political forces representing a range of class interests that could have incorporated workers' demands into a broader reformist programme. Attempts to build a workers' party in the wake of the revolution were limited and unsuccessful, most notably the failure of the Workers' and Peasants' Party, which initially attracted the support of a number of leading trade union activists. The electoral arena remained relatively impenetrable to worker activists for a number of reasons. While the dual-member constituency system remained in force for the 2011 parliamentary elections, the nominations for the 'worker' seats still essentially remained the gift of ETUF (which, as noted above, was beginning to revive thanks to an alliance between the Muslim Brotherhood and former ruling party figures in its reconstituted leadership). Although EFITU issued certificates of trade union membership for large numbers of worker candidates, even prominent figures such as Kamal Abu Aita had their nomination papers rejected by the courts. Some of the court decisions were successfully challenged by EFITU activists, such as Tareq Mostafa, treasurer of RETAU, who ran for a seat in Qalyubiyya on a Revolution Continues Alliance ticket.[9] Ironically, Abu Aita was unable to secure nomination for a 'workers'' seat, and was eventually elected on the Muslim Brotherhood-dominated Democratic Alliance electoral list for the 'professionals'' seat in North Giza.[10] In general, the electoral system favoured well-resourced political organisations at a national level, which helps to explain the success of the Muslim Brotherhood, as the major grouping within the pre-revolutionary opposition.

In the presidential elections of 2012, the Nasserist candidate Hamdeen Sabahy appeared to have captured the support of large numbers of activists in the independent unions. His programme expressed many of the core social demands of the workers' movement around raising wages, defending nationalised industries and the public sector and improving job security.[11] Sabahy's role as the leading figure in the Dignity (Karama) Party of which Kamal Abu Aita was also a founding member, was also an important factor. However, despite coming an unexpectedly close fourth in the first round of the elections with around five million votes, Sabahy squandered the opportunity to build a political organisation of his own in the wake of Mohamed Morsi's narrow second-round victory. The political outcome of the 2012 elections was the polarisation of politics between an Islamist coalition around the Brotherhood, and a secular coalition running from the Stalinist left to elements of the old ruling party on the right. Sabahy was a key player in the National Salvation Front, which emerged as the political leadership of this coalition in November 2012. However, rather than this acting as a route for the social demands of his supporters in the workers' movement to find expression in the political storms that shook the country during the year of Morsi's presidency, they were almost completely subsumed by other issues. The key battleground became the struggle over the role of the judiciary and the reform of the constitution, where the debates were framed in impeccably liberal terms – calling for the defence of judicial independence against meddling by the state – yet it was actually the core institutions of Mubarak's old regime that benefitted.

Workers and the counter-revolution: paradoxes of the 3 July regime

In the immediate aftermath of the mass protests on 30 June 2013 against Mohamed Morsi, and the military overthrow of his government on 3 July, there was a noticeable shift in government discourse towards the workers' movement. On the one hand, the appointment of Kamal Abu Aita, then president of EFITU as Minister of Labour, appeared aimed at convincing workers that the government was taking a serious interest in their situation and their demands. In media interviews he argued that his appointment had placed the main demands of the workers' movement on the table, such as the issuing of the long-delayed trade union freedoms law and a rise in the national minimum wage to 1,200 LE (£110) for government and public sector workers, and the opening of discussions about how to restart production in companies that had stopped functioning as a result of the political and economic crisis.

However, these apparently positive signals sent by the state to the labour movement were coupled with other signs that held a completely different meaning. The army sent troops to break up a sit-in organised by Suez Steel workers in mid-August 2013 and arrested a number of workers. During a strike by textile workers in Mahalla later that month, tanks entered the factory compound. The media agitated against workers' protests, considering them to be part of an attempt by the Muslim Brotherhood to overthrow the state. In fact, Minister of Defence Abdelfattah al-Sisi had indicated early on that he wanted a 'mandate' to confront 'terrorism' by any means necessary, and both independent and official union federations had rushed to comply, even agreeing to no-strike pledges and voluntarily renouncing collective action in the interests of national security. A minority within the EFITU executive opposed the federation's support for Sisi's mandate, and one member, Fatma Ramadan, went public with a statement condemning the majority decision.

The wave of strikes that Egypt witnessed in February 2014, and that led to the resignation of the Hazem Beblawi government, provides another example of the contradictions. These strikes were the most widespread since the downfall of Mohamed Morsi on 3 July 2013. Workers participated in the strikes from the textile companies, from the postal service, from transport, the health sector, the Ministry of Justice, in addition to dozens of strikes and workers' protests in the private sector. A report by Al Mahrousa Centre for Economic and Social Development estimates the total number of workers' protests during February to be more than 1,044, divided between strikes, protests and sit-ins, compared with only 50 protests in January and 321 in March. February's protests accounted for 45 per cent of the total protests over the course of the entire year.[12]

The importance of the strike wave cannot be measured only in the number of participants. The workers' movement went through an unprecedented rise in the first five months of 2013, with hundreds of thousands of workers taking part in protests across Egypt. However, in the wake of the overthrow of Morsi by the army on 3 July, the movement subsided with a sharp decline in the frequency of strikes. Isolated strikes still took place, but these were dealt with violently by the authorities, with some broken up by the security services and striking workers and their leaders accused of belonging to the Muslim Brotherhood, or attempting to embarrass the new government. Even the main union federations backed the new government and pledged not to organise strikes to show support for what the authorities called 'the war on terror'. Both ETUF and EFITU issued declarations supporting the 3 July regime and pledging not to organise strikes during the period of confronting terrorism. It is this context that gives the strike wave of February 2014 its special importance.

The resurgence of the workers' movement showed the potential to break down the polarisation into two camps – the state and the Brotherhood – that had been imposed on society after 3 July 2013. It was the first time that widespread popular protests mobilised against the government without being connected to the Brotherhood. The government's attempts to make a connection between the workers' movement and Brotherhood agitation failed, as the same workplaces had taken strike action against the Brotherhood when it was in power. The workers' movement was also able to expose the government's failures in the economic and social domains, raising the slogan 'the war on terror cannot postpone social demands and workers' rights'.

The February strike wave was also significant in terms of its main demand of an increase in the national minimum wage. The difference here was that the implementation of the minimum wage in a distorted fashion to a minority of workers, agitated workers rather than satisfying them. The government had taken a decision in September 2013 to set the level of the minimum wage at 1,200 LE, which workers had been demanding since 2008. However, without any consultation with workers' representatives, the government decided to apply the wage in a minority of cases, namely only to around one-third of the workers employed directly by the state. This section of the labour force is six million workers in total according to the official statistics body CAPMAS, or a quarter of the total labour force of 24 million, which includes workers employed in the public business sector and economic institutions such as the railways and in public transport in addition to workers employed directly by the state.[13] This meant that only a small proportion of workers benefitted from the decision. Workers in the private sector were excluded entirely, although they would have benefitted most from the decree, as their average weekly wages did not exceed 300 LE in 2012 according to CAPMAS. Moreover, as the implementation of the law led to a spike in prices, workers to whom it did not apply lost out twice. The key point here is that a measure that the government took in order to increase its popularity and to appear accommodating towards workers' demands actually triggered the explosion of a workers' movement that led to the collapse of the government.

This was the first time that workers had mobilised on such a scale over a united demand. It was also the first time that the workers' movement collectively demanded a radical solution to the wages problem by applying the minimum wage rather than through temporary or partial pay rises. Nor is this the only measure of the development of the movement. The movement demonstrated a higher degree of consciousness and organisation than previously. Workers across seven spinning and weaving companies in different governorates coordinated simultaneous strike action with the single demand of the minimum wage, for example. Delegations of workers from the railways and the Metro visited the public transport workers during their strike to show solidarity with them over their demand for the minimum wage, they also announced that in the event of the state taking action against the bus workers, they would take solidarity strike action.

The outcomes of the strikes did not correspond to their size, or their power, however. Perhaps the resignation of the Beblawi government is the only thing that could be considered a sweeping victory for the workers' movement. But this picture changes dramatically if we look at the government that replaced Beblawi's, composed largely of Mubarak-era politicians. The sacking of Beblawi's government did not represent a response to workers' demands, but on the contrary came as a result of its failure to control the workers' movement and prevent strikes. This is confirmed by the policies that the new government has pursued towards the workers' movement. Besides the prime minister's populist performances during visits to workplaces, the new government has offered nothing but promises in response to workers' demands, while at the same time calling on workers to be patient, to tighten their belts and put up with hard conditions until the crisis has passed.

Behind the populist rhetoric the government's machinery of repression swung into action against the workers' movement. The security forces arrested strike leaders and detained them on charges of agitation and 'damaging national security'. This began with the arrest of four leaders of the postal workers' strike in Alexandria in dawn raids on their homes on 25 March, who were then accused in security reports of planning to attack the National Democratic Party. The institutions of the state intervened in order to put pressure on the workers, threatening to coerce and torture. In one of the ceramic companies, 25 of the workers' leaders were forced to resign on charges of agitating for a strike to improve wages. Three workers from the Polypropylene Company in Port Said were arrested, ironically when they went to the police station as representatives of the workers to notify the police of the workers' intention to organise a sit-in as required under the protest law brought in by the regime itself. Workers attempting to improve their conditions or claim their delayed wages have been arrested, and workers are accused of agitation and threatening national security. This happened a few days before the celebration of workers' day on 1 May 2014 when workers were arrested for four days before being released, so they joined the strike that the workers of the company had organised in protest at the detention of their colleagues. The policies announced by the government demonstrated that it had no intention of improving workers' conditions. These have included an austerity programme that includes raising energy prices and cutting subsidies, directly affecting those on low wages. From the opposite perspective, the new government's policies confirmed its bias towards businessmen and investors through the issuing of laws protecting businessmen from judicial oversight in state contracts, which had previously led to the discovery of fraud in many of them and the cancellation of some of them. Meanwhile it refused to implement the national minimum wage according to workers' demands.

In some workplaces strikes won partial victories, but there is a clear contradiction between the size and scale and widespread nature of the workers' movement on the one hand, and its ability to win its demands and affect the general policies of the state on the other. For a movement of this scale has been unable to make any genuine progress towards its principal demand of the national minimum wage; meanwhile the escalation of repression and the policies announced by the state suggest the regime emerged victorious from that particular battle.

This picture is confirmed by the regime's progress in restarting the stalled programme of neoliberal reforms in collaboration with the regimes of the Gulf, led by Saudi Arabia and the UAE. A major economic investment conference in March 2015 also confirmed the backing of global financial institutions such as the IMF for Sisi's economic policies, despite ongoing repression of the political opposition, in particular the Muslim Brotherhood. It is a sign of the regime's relative strength and self-confidence that it has been able to resurrect a number of policies that had stalled during the last days of Mubarak's rule, or were halted by the uprising that led to his downfall. The restructuring of the fuel subsidy system in 2014 is a case in point. Despite severe knock-on effects for workers and the poor through rises in transport costs, there was no coordinated opposition to the reforms. The privatisation programme, which ran into determined opposition from the workers in state industries and retail establishments facing being sold off during Mubarak's last years, was revived in February 2015, with a cabinet decision to privatise electricity production and transmission.[14] Al-Sisi also signed into law new legislation aimed at preventing citizens' or employees' legal challenges to privatisation contracts, while agreeing a new investment law allowing the government to override court decisions to repossess privatised assets and return them to investors.[15]

A third key area for further neo-liberal restructuring is civil service employment. While the post-1991 structural adjustment reforms forced hundreds of thousands of workers out of public sector employment in manufacturing and services, the civil service has until now been spared major changes in employment patterns. Over the summer of 2015, a campaign of protests and strikes by public employees gathered momentum in August as civil servants mobilised against a new law threatening the job security of millions across the public sector.[16] On 10 August up to 5,000 civil servants working in the departments of General Taxation, Sales Taxation, Customs, the Ministry of Finance and Property Taxation rallied outside the Journalists' Union headquarters in central Cairo. They were joined by bus workers from some Public Transport Authority garages who took strike action on the same day, also in protest at the law.

The scale of the mobilisation on 10 August appeared to have caught the security forces by surprise and they did not intervene to ban or break up the protest. The demonstration was the largest rally organised by workers for two years. It was also well-organised, with delegations joining the Cairo rally from Alexandria, the Canal Zone cities, Daqahiliyya province, Fayyoum and Bani Soueif. Activists toured the provinces beforehand, organising mobilising meetings. The presence of the PTA bus workers boosted the protests. The independent union in the PTA is also strong and well-rooted.

Conclusion: the political challenge of counter-revolution

The counter-revolution led by al-Sisi since 2013 gained its first victories not in economic policy, but by successfully winning political support for a brutal security crackdown on the Muslim Brotherhood. The battle lines were drawn in the crisis of July–August 2013 over questions of national security, with the army raising the spectre of Islamist terrorism and inciting fear of collapse into civil war along the lines of the disintegration of Syria and Iraq. While a minority of independent trade union leaders opposed the government on this question, the majority supported the state's call for a 'war on terror'. However, political compromise with the government soon translated into confusion and lack of coordination in the face of mounting evidence that the new regime, far from ushering in a neo-Nasserist era of state capitalism, intended to plough on with the neoliberal reforms that had made Mubarak's rule so unpopular.

However, the support of independent union leaders for al-Sisi's call for an end to strikes created a crisis with their own rank and file. As one of the leaders of the Independent School Teachers Union (ISTU) noted in an August 2015 interview, closer relations between the independent unions and the government were seen by some union members as a step back after the gains of 2011.

> After the revolution we had rights for the first time. Now there is a real attack on the independent trade union movement. The Sisi government chose some leaders of the movement to sit in government – for instance the chair of the independent union federation is now a minister. As a result many workers have lost trust in the leaderships.[17]

Nevertheless, independent unions with a large, active membership continued to be involved in strikes and protests organised at a local level, despite their national leaders' pledge not to strike. This reflected in part the development of strong, well-rooted and largely democratic organisation for collective action in many workplaces, which was relatively poorly connected to the lobbying and campaigning efforts by the staff of independent union federations at a national level. Compromise by the leaders of the federations with the state over bans on strikes could not be enforced *internally*, it had to be enforced by the state itself *externally* through escalating repression. Thus workers' protests continued, often driven by the resilience of organisation at a local or workplace level, and faced increasing brutal attacks by the police and security services. Yet, they lacked national coordination and a political strategy to counter the new regime's intensification of the neoliberal assault. Despite the relatively large scale of workers' mobilisation in 2014, for example, the regime was able to press ahead with fuel subsidy reform, restart the privatisation programme and pass a new law restructuring civil service employment.

It is crucially important that the regime has not been able to wipe out the collective memory of more than ten years of workers' self-organisation. The scale of protests by civil servants in August 2015 demonstrated the potential to catch the police and government 'off guard'. However, the experience of the last two years underscores that in order to pose a serious threat to the stability of the military regime, workers' protests need to be open to raising wider political questions, in order to re-unite the currently separated currents of political and social opposition to the counter-revolution.

Notes

1 See www.elwatannews.com/news/details/231209 (accessed 20 October 2016) for Sisi's speech calling for protests on 26 July 2013. See www.hrw.org/news/2014/08/12/egypt-raba-killings-likely-crimes-against-humanity (accessed 20 October 2016) for details of the Raba'a Square massacre of supporters of ousted president Mohamed Morsi.

2 See Anne Alexander and Mostafa Bassiouny, *Bread, Freedom, Social Justice*, Zed, 2014, Chapter 8 for a longer discussion of the history of workers' participation in electoral politics.

3 Muhammad Al-Agrudi, 'Megawer: Nuqif Bil-Marsad Did Tazwir Shihadat Al-Sifa Al-Ummaliyya', *Al-Ahram Digital*, 10 September 2010, http://digital.ahram.org.eg/articles.aspx?Serial=249159&eid=707, accessed 19 October 2012.

4 Ikhwanonline.net, 'Murashahu Al-Ikhwan Bil-Qahira', *Ikhwanonline.net*, 2005, www.ikhwanonline.net/data/baralman2005/ikhwan3.htm, accessed 16 October 2012; Ikhwanonline.net, 'Murashahu Al-Ikhwan Fi Al-Iskandaria', *Ikhwanonline.net*, 2005, www.

ikhwanonline.net/data/baralman2005/ikhwan1.htm, accessed 8 May 2013.

5 Alexander and Bassiouny, *Bread, Freedom, Social Justice*, p. 165.

6 Mu'assisat Awlad al-Ard, Al-Markaz al-Masry lil-Huqquq al-Iqtisadiyya, *Ru'iyya Huqquqiyya: Al-'Ummal wal-Thawra al-Misriyya*, Cairo, 2011.

7 Alexander and Bassiouny, *Bread, Freedom, Social Justice*, p. 221.

8 See Alexander and Bassiouny, *Bread, Freedom, Social Justice*, Chapter 5.

9 Muhammad Faris, 'Al-Quda'a Yu'akid Ahqiyya Al-Niqabat Al-Mustaqilla Fi Manah Shihadat Al-Sifa Al-'Ummaliyya Limurashahi Al-Intikhabat', *Al-Masry Al-Youm*, 16 November 2011, www.almasryalyoum.com/node/515204, accessed 19 October 2012; Noha Mohamed Murshid, interview, 2012; Tarek Mostafa, interview, 2012.

10 Yasmin Al-Giyushi, 'Al-Karama Tataqadum Bi 15 Murashahan Lil-Intikhabat Al-Nasiri Taqdim Bi 214 Murashahan', *Al-Tahrir*, 24 October 2011, http://tinyurl.com/gp4cc79, accessed 19 October 2012; *Al-Masry Al-Youm*, 'Murashah Ikhwan Shamal Al-Giza:

Nahnu 'Aqrab Lil Nas . . . Wal-Libraliyyun Tafraghu Lmuwaghatna', 12 December 2011, www.almasryalyoum.com/news/details/133065, accessed 20 October 2016.

11 Alexander and Bassiouny, *Bread, Freedom, Social Justice*, p. 266.

12 Mahrousa Centre, n.d., 'Taqrir al-hala al-umaliyya', http://elmahrousacenter.org/?p=4419, accessed 20 October 2016.

13 See Alexander and Bassiouny, *Bread, Freedom, Social Justice.*

14 http://english.ahram.org.eg/NewsContent/3/12/123385/Business/Economy/Egypts-cabinet-approves-law-privatising-electricit.aspx, accessed 20 October 2016.

15 www.alaraby.co.uk/english/features/2015/1/27/khaled-ali-privatisation-has-stolen-egypt-from-its-people, accessed 20 October 2016.

16 http://english.ahram.org.eg/NewsContent/1/64/137520/Egypt/Politics-/Egypt-govt-insists-on-implementing-new-civil-servi.aspx, accessed 20 October 2016; www.world-psi.org/en/egypt-psi-affiliates-push-suspension-civil-service-law, accessed 20 October 2016.

17 www.teachersolidarity.com/blog/leader-of-egypts-independent-teachers-union-in-interview#sthash.jwoYnaW3.dpuf, accessed 20 October 2016.

2 | FROM THE GRASSROOTS TO THE PRESIDENTIAL PALACE: EVO MORALES AND THE COCA GROWERS' UNION IN BOLIVIA

Thomas Grisaffi

Evo Morales and the Movimiento Al Socialismo (MAS) party captured the Bolivian presidency with a majority of the popular vote in 2005, and repeated that feat in 2009 and 2014. Morales and the MAS are part of a broader process that swept Latin America in the 2000s, often referred to as the 'pink tide', when a wave of leftist leaders, parties and movements came to power in various Latin American countries. What is unique about the Bolivian case, however, is that the movements that put Morales in power have commonly been labelled 'indigenous', a depiction that Morales has encouraged. For example, every year he returns to Tiwanaku (the ruins of an ancient Aymara temple located outside the capital city La Paz) where, dressed as an Inca priest, he participates in indigenous rituals. In his public declarations Morales has decried the persistence of colonialism and pledged his commitment to protect and lead the indigenous peoples of the Americas.

Morales' rhetoric has sparked the imagination of journalists who have invoked the polarisation of Bolivian society, provoking headlines such as 'Columbus toppled as indigenous people rise up after five centuries' (Carroll and Almudevar 2007) and 'Bolivian Indians hail the swearing in of one of their own as president' (Forero 2006). The growing movement for indigenous rights in Bolivia (but also across the continent), has prompted a scholarly boom as academics focused on the timing, location and strategies of indigenous mobilisation (Lucero 2008). However, the embrace of an indigenous heritage is a relatively recent phenomenon for Bolivia's social movements. Many people previously identified as peasants or workers and mobilised along class based lines. Evo Morales embodies this process, transforming from a left-wing leader of the coca growers' union to a national indigenous leader.

The objective of this chapter is to highlight the role played by the unions in Bolivia's historic 'turn to the left'. In what follows I explain how the MAS developed from its roots in an agricultural union of coca producers (hereafter the coca union) that was criminalised under US drug war policies in the 1990s, to the contemporary moment, when it is responsible for building a government and running a country. The story of the coca union alerts us to the reconstitution of union power away from the traditional heartlands of the left in the mines and factories, towards new spaces, and invoking new strategies – including placing an emphasis on ethnic identity as a way to expand its struggles and to encompass broader social sectors. The case of the coca union also allows us to examine the contradictions and conflicts that emerge when a union transforms into a governing party – in particular the challenge of working within the pre-existing political system while trying to retain a radical identity.

A brief history of rebellion in Bolivia

Bolivia is a landlocked country in the centre of South America. The high mountain ranges and Andean plateau lie to the west and the jungle and vast tropical savannah stretch eastwards towards Brazil and Paraguay. Bolivia is home to around 10 million people, the majority of whom consider themselves to be indigenous, which is conceived of as a social as well as racial category (Canessa 2012). Most are Aymara or Quechua speakers from the sierra and high valleys, but there is also a large Guarani population located in the south eastern lowlands.[1] Around a quarter of the population self-identify as mestizo. In the strictest sense of the term 'mestizo' refers to a person of mixed Spanish and indigenous parentage; however, in Bolivia it is often used to speak about people of indigenous heritage who live in urban areas but who have abandoned their original culture. By far the smallest group (comprising around 10 per cent of the population) are the White *'criollo'* elite who have historically been the most powerful economic and political group in the country (Farthing and Kohl 2014: 20–34).

People in Bolivia have repeatedly revolted; first against Spanish colonial rule and then the republic that succeeded it, and these conflicts have left a deep imprint on Bolivian politics. The most notable national heroes are Bartolina Sisa and Tupaj Katari whose Aymara armies surrounded the city of La Paz and held it under siege for several months in the late eighteenth century. In 1952 a social revolution, fought largely by miners, peasant militias, and led by a small middle class, successfully overthrew the mining oligarchy. The Bolivian Workers Union or Central Obrera Boliviana (COB), which was created in its wake, brought together workers' unions from Bolivia's main industries including the mines and the manufacturing sector into a confederation. The COB worked with the new Movimiento Nacionalista Revolucionario (Revolutionary Nationalist Movement, MNR)-led government to institute sweeping changes including expanding citizenship rights to the indigenous majority (including the right to vote), the nationalisation of the mines, land reform and the reduction in the size of the army. The 1953 agrarian reform bill designated 'peasant unions' (as opposed to indigenous community structures known as *ayllus*) as the legitimate organisation for carrying out land distribution and for governing local affairs. Peasant unions subsequently spread throughout the Bolivian countryside.

Throughout the 1960s and 1970s the COB played an important role in the struggle for democracy against military dictatorships. The backbone of the COB were the miners' unions that represented one of the most politicised sectors of organised labour in the whole of Latin America. The miners paid dearly for their struggle; the army repeatedly crushed strike action, which resulted in various massacres. The peasants meanwhile were far more compliant – the military junta maintained peasant support by promising to uphold the agrarian reform in return for their loyalty (Dunkerley 1984). The pact between the military and peasantry contributed to the failure of Che Guevara's attempt to launch guerrilla war in Bolivia in the mid 1960s. However, in 1974 the military broke this pact, mowing down protesting peasants in the Cochabamba valleys with machine guns, an event that contributed to renewed support for independent peasant unionism (Webber 2011: 101).

As military rule gave way to democracy in the early 1980s a left leaning government found itself facing severe economic crisis, which opened the door to dramatic neoliberal economic reforms. The reforms called for fiscal austerity, the privatisation of state-owned enterprises, currency devaluation and the deregulation of the economy. These cuts were deepened throughout the 1990s with the fire sale of the few remaining state-owned enterprises, the rapid expansion of NGOs and the de-centralisation of the state. The IMF-imposed measures did famously succeed at cutting the fiscal deficit and taming inflation, but this came at a heavy social and environmental cost. Bolivia experienced a dramatic fall in real wages and an increase in poverty and unemployment as trade liberalisation wiped out local businesses and destroyed peasant livelihood strategies. Tens of thousands of state workers, including 23,000 unionised miners, lost their jobs as a result of privatisation and mine shutdowns. Thus at the turn of the millennia the picture that emerged of Bolivia was one of enduring poverty, economic retardation and high levels of inequality (Kohl and Farthing 2006).

The period from 1985 to 2000 represented a historic defeat of the left; traditional labour organisations declined in organisational strength and prominent leftist figures went to work for NGOs. Nevertheless popular social sectors succeeded in mounting resistance to contest what David Harvey (2003) calls 'accumulation by dispossession'. In 2000 discontent with the government and its market-oriented policies boiled over into full-scale social protest. The insurgent cycle of events began with the Cochabamba Water War in 2000, which opposed the privatisation of the city's water supply, and peaked in October 2003 when mass mobilisations sought to block the export of natural gas through Chile. The protestors represented a broad alliance of social movements including neighbourhood associations, students, pensioners, peasants, the landless movement and trade unions. Significantly many of these movements organised along ethnic lines – stressing a shared history of exploitation at the hands of the dominant lighter-skinned elite (Canessa 2006). The protestors demanded a more socially oriented alternative to the prevailing neoliberal model of economic development, including state control over natural resources, land rights, the end to US-backed coca eradication, and the drafting of a new constitution. These demands came to be known as the 'October Agenda' (Perreault 2006).

In 2005, against the backdrop of social turmoil and economic crisis, Bolivia elected Evo Morales, the left-wing leader of the Chapare coca growers' union, as president of Bolivia. The MAS succeeded precisely because it looked nothing like the traditional parties, which were increasingly seen as corrupt, elitist and unrepresentative. The MAS was established by a confederation of unionised peasant organisations in 1995;[2] as such it was composed of political outsiders with few links to the political establishment. The election of the MAS then expressed the popular classes' will for political change and was a clear illustration of their disgust with the neoliberal capitalist model. On coming to power Evo Morales and the MAS set out to fashion a new economy geared towards helping people to 'live well' (*vivir bien*) in harmony with nature, the nationalisation of strategic industries (most significantly the hydro-carbon sector) and the reinvention of the state through the rewriting of the constitution by a popularly elected assembly.

The Chapare

To understand the politics of the MAS, it is necessary to understand the context from which it emerged among the coca unions of the Chapare and the way they acquired hegemony in a region where the state was almost entirely absent. The tropical area of Cochabamba is located at the eastern foot of the Bolivian Andes. It covers some six million acres of lowland humid tropical forests extending over three provinces, the Chapare, Tiraque and Carrasco. In the late 1970s this largely uninhabited frontier region became the focus of an intense process of migration as coca cultivation spread throughout the region in response to rising demand for cocaine in North America and Europe. The majority of the early migrants were Quechua-speaking peasants from the Cochabamba valleys but they were soon followed by tens of thousands of miners and factory workers who lost their jobs when the government closed down nationally owned enterprises in the mid 1980s. Thus today the Chapare is inhabited by an uprooted multi-cultural population many of whom were previously engaged in urban life and trade unions. As one farmer put it 'the Chapare is cosmopolitan – we come from all over the country'.

The migrants established small family-run farms on plots ranging from between 5 to 20 hectares. Relying on manual labour they cultivate a range of crops including rice, bananas, pineapples, citrus fruit and papaya, but more than anything they are dependent on coca. The farmers grow coca because it has several advantages as a cash crop; coca grows like a weed, it provides three to four harvests per year, it is light and easy to transport, but most importantly, it commands high prices and there is always a guaranteed market for it. Even so, the farmers do not get rich from cultivating coca. Rather it complements subsistence activities, and the majority of farmers live in poverty. Away from the main road many houses are constructed from wood with roofs of either tin or thatch, and do not count on basic services like running water, electricity or sanitation.

Coca has been used for millennia by indigenous Andeans; it can be chewed or prepared as a tea and is consumed in order to supress feelings of hunger, thirst and fatigue. The most prolific users are labourers, farmers and truckers who value coca's properties as a mild stimulant. The anthropological record shows how coca also serves a range of important social and cultural functions including divination, healing rituals and offerings to earth deities such as the *pachamama* and *supay* (Carter and Mamani 1986). However, while coca might appear to be a miracle plant for producers and consumers, it is also the raw material used to process cocaine paste (an impure form of cocaine), and a great deal of the Chapare crop is used for this purpose (Grisaffi 2014).

The coca unions

I spent almost three years living in Aurora[3] over several visits between 2005 and 2015. The village was established in the mid 1950s making it one of the oldest settlements in the region; it has around 150 households and almost all of them (bar three families who are dedicated to trade) are coca growers and members of the local union or '*sindicato*'. People do not have any real choice about whether to join the union because it controls access to land. Aurora put strict conditions on membership: the community would normally only allow family members or people already known to them to join, and even then only once they had proven their commitment to the organisation. The upshot of this exclusive selection procedure is that the Aurora union is crosscut by kinship relations, old friendships and alliances between families expressed as *compadrazgo* (god-parenthood). Many people described the union as being tantamount to an extended family.

I soon came to realise that given the minimal state presence in the region the union dominated almost all aspects of life. The union was responsible for opening out penetration roads, maintaining river defences, taxing the coca trade, organising collective work parties and regulating local trade including setting taxi and bus fares. One of the most important roles of the local union, however, was to provide security and administer justice. For example, the community elects a sheriff who holds regular consultations and undertakes '*rondas*' (night patrols) with local volunteers to keep the population in check. Meanwhile on-going disputes within the community, including robbery, disagreements over boundaries or outstanding debts, are dealt with at a monthly union meeting, where the issue is debated and resolved with the participation of the entire community. The union's power extends right into the home – for instance, an aggrieved spouse can bring a case against her partner for infidelity or battery. Only low-level misdemeanours are supposed to be dealt with at the union level, more serious crimes like murder or rape should be referred to the police. However, in reality this seldom happens. Trust in the police is so low, and the justice system so slow and corrupt, that most people preferred to solve their problems internally. I was told 'the law is the law – but here we do things organically', 'when you live in an organisation you are subject to the organisation', and 'around here the union is the law'. Moreover, the local police sergeant confirmed that the unions would not allow police officers to enter their communities without prior permission.

Once a month, each base-level union holds a meeting where issues of public importance are debated. The organisation of the union is based on Andean self-governing principals such as reciprocity, consensus building and high levels of community participation, mixed with Marxist traditions inherited from the displaced miners, such as electing authorities formally rather than rotating them by age and prior experience. One of the most important elements of grassroots democracy is the emphasis that the rank and file put on holding their leaders directly accountable (Grisaffi 2013). The key to the union's strength and the way that members seem to think with one mind is rooted in the union's control over land tenure. Any coca grower who does not honour his or her commitments to the group (for instance by not turning up to a meeting or mobilisation) faces a range of sanctions, including fines or community work (such as litter picking, cutting the grass, painting or other general maintenance work) and this is backed up by the threat of the confiscation of land. Farmers often grumble that because of the fines they are 'obliged' to participate in '*vida organica*' (the organic life of the organisation). Nevertheless they also understand that sanctions are necessary to ensure that members pursue collective as opposed to individual goals; it solves the so called 'free-rider problem' (see Lazar 2008).

Aurora is one of more than 1,000 base-level unions in the Chapare. These unions are organised into six federations representing over 45,000 families. Each federation is organisationally linked to national-level workers and peasant unions. The democratic ideals of the grassroots inform the practice of the union as a whole; in theory at least, the rank and file are in control.

Radicalisation

In the mid-1980s the US launched a crop eradication campaign to tackle escalating coca and cocaine production in the Chapare; in so doing they turned the farmers into the 'enemy of the war on drugs' (Albó 2002: 75). Eradication was carried out by US-trained and -funded security forces who entered small farmsteads to uproot coca plantations manually. The immediate impact of eradication was to wipe out the farmers' main source of income, leaving them destitute and struggling to survive. Worse still, the decision to orientate the security forces towards 'internal enemies' opened the space for the violation of human rights including rape, theft, intimidation, beatings, arbitrary detention and murder (Ledebur 2005). In spite of (or some might say because of) military repression, the coca growers built a powerful union to contest the Bolivian government's anti-coca policy.

Initially the US embassy in La Paz was slow to pick up on the political significance of the Chapare coca unions. In 1982 a research mission for the US Congress concluded 'It is difficult to believe that the coca producers of the Chapare could constitute a political force; these new colonizers, the majority of whom are indigenous, are apparently humble and passive' (Gamarra 1994: 27). Indeed, in the late 1970s the colonisers were making money from the coca boom (when coca prices leapt dramatically in response to US demand for cocaine) and were content. Moreover the union was a mechanism for governmental control through corporatism (the ex-dictator Hugo Banzer was even the godfather to the children of the coca union's general secretary). One local coca farmer described the relationship between the government and unions in these terms,

there were coca unions back then, but they were tied to the government, managed by the government. The leaders were not chosen by the bases (rank and file) – they were chosen by the government! Back then there really was union dictatorship (*dictadura sindical*)!

Thus the traditional left, represented by the miners union, considered the coca producers to be a petit bourgeois anti-revolutionary element (Escobar 2008: 194).

The political apathy reversed in the late 1980s with the arrival of the miners (displaced as a result of the mine closures) who bought with them their traditions of solidarity, organisational skill and revolutionary consciousness. As one miner explained 'I was a miner, I didn't have fear, I knew how to light dynamite, I knew the union life'; he went on to say that because of people like him 'more leaders were formed here in the tropics, we strengthened the unions'. The miners were also famous for their union-owned and -operated radio stations and, on entering the tropics they made it a priority to set up a station with the idea that 'it has to be the same in the Tropics just like in the mines'. A pro-radio committee was formed in 1993, which included Evo Morales as its executive. Four years later – with assistance from technicians and radio producers from the miners' stations – the coca union established the FM station, Radio Sovereignty. Ever since Radio Sovereignty has played an essential role supporting union activity, including raising awareness, spreading messages and co-ordinating protest (Grisaffi 2009).

By the late 1980s discontent was brewing in the Chapare. Coca prices were falling and impending anti-narcotics legislation (the draconian law 1008) threatened to outlaw coca cultivation in the region altogether. What is more the state had started to show its teeth; in June 1988 government forces murdered 12 coca farmers during a violent confrontation on a bridge over the Chapare river, an event that is remembered to this day as the massacre of Villa Tunari. Don Benito, a middle-aged coca farmer, was present that day. He recalled how he had to jump into the river to avoid the bullets, he was lucky, he knew how to swim, others did not and they drowned.

At the Federation's 1988 general assembly the Frente Amplio de Masas Anti-Imperialistas (led by Evo Morales) took control of Federation Tropico, the largest and most militant Chapare union. Under Evo's control the federation radicalised: the unions' demands included the right to land, the demilitarisation of the Chapare, a break in coca eradication, the modification of anti-drug laws and increased political participation. The union's repertoire of protest included setting up camps in city plazas, blocking Bolivia's main trunk road (which runs through the Chapare) and undertaking long marches from the Tropics to the capital city, La Paz. The coca union also established limited self-defence committees with the aim to prevent the military from eradicating coca plantations. These groups were lightly armed with rifles dating back to the 1930s Chaco War (*mausers*) and homemade land mines known as *cazabobos* (fool hunters); firefights with government troops, however, were only ever isolated incidents.

Old movement with a new face

In the 1990s the coca union redefined the parameters of the coca debate. While the governments of Bolivia and the United States associated coca leaf with illegality and drug trafficking, the coca unions emphasised the long history of traditional coca use, to argue that coca represents one of the most profound expressions of Andean indigenous culture, not to mention a strategic resource that could be used to promote national development. Defending coca leaf then, became synonymous with standing up for national dignity in the face of US intervention, which had taken on increasingly imperial characteristics.

The message about the sacred status of coca is continually reiterated at union meetings and on the coca growers' radio station. Coca union leaders point out that Andean cultures have used coca for millennia and it has done them no harm whatsoever. They blame foreigners for adulterating their sacred leaf with chemicals to produce cocaine. I was told on numerous occasions 'we didn't know anything about *pichicata* (cocaine paste manufacturing) until those gringos (foreigners) came here to teach us'. The prevailing sentiment is captured in a mural painted on the wall of the coca grower-owned and -operated station Radio Sovereignty, which states: 'For us the coca leaf is the culture of our ancestors . . . to them (foreigners) it causes insanity and idiocy'. In order to make the sacred status of coca leaf explicit to the wider world the Chapare agricultural federations organise events such as coca chew-ins and fairs in the cities to celebrate coca, and the members of the union undertake public rituals in which coca plays a highly visible role. Today the coca union has a strong overarching ideology built on the defence of 'millennial' coca.

It was by no means inevitable that the Chapare farmers would mobilise around indigenous cultural difference in order to justify their oppositional politics. The majority of farmers hail from the Cochabamba Valleys – a region where *mestizaje* and class-based identities took hold early on (Rivera 1987: 150). More to the point, many of the farmers are ex-miners, who famously embraced modernity in the form of Marxism and considered indigenous demands to be irrelevant or worse still dangerous as they represented a form of 'false consciousness' (Harris and Albo 1976). Contemporary coca growers meanwhile look down on the indigenous populations (comprised of Yuracare and Yuqui ethnic minorities) who have lived in the Chapare for centuries, who they consider to be backwards, dirty and uncivilised. For the coca farmers then, indigeneity is not defined by a deep history of 'blood and soil', but, rather, it is rooted in postcolonial identities and a shared struggle against the domination of foreign and national elites (Grisaffi 2010).

Mobilising under the banner of 'sacred coca' proved useful as, by fusing the coca growers' economic demands with a broader ethno-nationalist dimension, the unions were able to reach out and form alliances with other social movements from across the country. Thus when the coca unions undertook their long marches from the tropics to the capital city La Paz, or blocked the main trunk road – they could count on the support of other social sectors. Community radio stations (including the coca growers' station, Radio Sovereignty) also played an important role as disparate movements could hear and learn about one another and came to understand that they were all fighting the same battle against neoliberal imperialism (Grisaffi 2009). Given the power vacuum left by the traditional left, the coca growers became the most powerful social force in the country, with coca leaders taking on prominent roles in national-level union organisations, and leading numerous national protests and blockades.

By the mid-1990s the astronomic political ascent of the coca growers and the national presence they developed had become a matter of concern to US policymakers, who saw critics of neoliberalism as a hemispheric security issue (Grandin 2006: 213). Thus during the second Banzer administration (1997–2002) the Bolivian government effectively outlawed the coca union. In a 2001 interview the ex-drugs tsar Oswaldo Antezana argued that as coca was illegal there was really no need for a 'coca union' (Orduna and Guzman 2001). Coca farmers told me that in the early 2000s 'politics was illegal in the Chapare'. The coca farmers were denied their civil rights; union leaders were forced to live on the run and base-level unions often had to hold their meetings in secret locations, away from the main road and hidden from the helicopters that circled above. Between 1997 and 2002 over 700 union members were arrested and held indefinitely, often without charge (Ledebur 2005). Radio Sovereignty also came under attack; in February 2002 heavily armed members of the police force confiscated the transmitter, which was only returned three months later, badly damaged.

The Bolivian government justified its heavy-handed presence in the region by presenting the coca growers as criminals, drug traffickers and terrorists. For example, in 2001, Jorge Quiroga, then president of Bolivia, drew comparisons between the coca growers in the Chapare and Al Qaeda saying that drug trafficking is the 'Siamese twin' of terrorism (La Patria 2001), meanwhile the public prosecutor's office made efforts to link coca growers with illegal armed guerrilla groups – including the Revolutionary Armed Forces of Colombia (Vegas 2002). Take the case of Doña Juana, a union leader who was arrested and charged in 2002 for 'armed uprising'. Doña Juana explained that the police framed her by planting dynamite and weapons at her house; she was then taken to the military camp where she says she was imprisoned and tortured. She told me 'They attacked us saying that the leaders are terrorists. They used bullets, they killed us, they humiliated us, (they left) orphans, they did everything to us – but still we fought back – it made us stronger'.

The Movement Towards Socialism (MAS)

In response to new political spaces opened up under the 1994 Popular Participation law (which decentralised 20 per cent of national revenues to municipal governments), the coca growers set up their own electoral vehicle, which eventually ran under the registered title of the MAS. Thus the decentralisation of the state, which is often seen as a key element of neoliberal governance, actually opened the institutional space that allowed the MAS to emerge as a national political force (Postero 2006; Kohl 2006). Union leader, and one time MAS congressman, Don Rolando, explained the motivation for setting up the party:

> We marched and thought that we could change things, but
> protests don't have any impact. The neoliberal state had all
> the power . . . . They (the elites) were playing on the football
> pitch, and we didn't even have one player, we just watched
> from the side-lines! And that's when we decided we needed our
> own political party. At first it was just a union fight but later it
> changed, we had two arms, union struggle and political struggle.
> That's when we entered the pitch. Now the person who plays
> best wins.

The MAS was indeed the best player. By 1997 the coca grower party controlled most of the town halls in the Tropics. Municipal government proved to be a good training ground for the nascent party, and by 2002 the MAS was a national political force. The path for Morales and the MAS was not always easy, however – there was considerable infighting, internal division, and as a congressman Evo Morales was even expelled from parliament.[4] Further, the MAS faced considerable opposition from the US embassy. When Morales ran for president in the 2002 elections, Manuel Rocha (the US ambassador) threatened that the US government would cut all funding to Bolivia if the electorate voted for Morales. This had the opposite effect to that intended, and actually gave Morales a last minute boost in the polls. Indeed the MAS came within a slim margin of winning the presidency. Morales later quipped that Rocha was his best campaign manager to date. Finally, in 2005, lifted by a wave of popular mobilisation, Morales took the presidency with a majority of the vote, the first time any presidential candidate had won an electoral majority since 1982.

The MAS was established not so much as a party, but rather as an extension of the union with the aim to take coca grower demands to the national arena but also to open out space so that coca union leaders could enter into positions of state power. In a 2013 interview, Rolando insisted 'the MAS is not a party – it's a social and syndicalist movement'. He went on to describe the relationship between the unions and the party as like 'husband and wife' because they 'work together' – echoing the resilience of Andean conceptions of complementarity (Harris 2000). He said 'the unions are sat above the Ministers, it is a matrix institution – we (the unions) control the government'. This view is also echoed in the writing of Alvaro

Garcia Linera (Morales' vice-president) who has held up MAS as an example of 'popular democracy' that works, the ultimate proof that a grassroots alternative to neoliberal globalisation is possible (García Linera 2006, 2014). However, not everyone concurs with this interpretation. It has been argued that since 2002 (when the MAS became a national political force) it transformed into a more traditional political party and it is increasingly characterised by vertical decision-making and centralist tendencies (Harten 2011; Zegada *et al.* 2008; Grisaffi 2013).

Shortcomings

On coming to power in 2006 Morales made a radical break with the US-backed anti-drugs strategy, which focused on the forced eradication of coca leaf and the criminalisation of coca growers. His new policy, often referred to as 'coca yes cocaine no', permitted each union member in the Chapare to cultivate a small amount of coca leaf known as a *cato* (an area covering 1,600 square metres) destined for the licit market (for traditional consumption, or to be processed into coca tea, flour and other legal coca-based products). The new approach has shrunk coca cultivation and has had various positive impacts, including dramatically cutting human rights violations and allowing coca growers to diversify their sources of income (Grisaffi and Ledebur 2016). Nevertheless not all coca growers are sanguine.

Expectations in the Chapare were unrealistically high when Morales entered the presidency and so it was inevitable that Morales would fail to meet them. Morales has had to balance coca grower demands with those of other constituencies, including the international community and its desire to keep a cap on coca production. Thus today some farmers grumble that Morales has sold out. They say that the *cato*, which generates around 200 dollars per month (equivalent to the minimum wage) does not generate enough cash to support a family. One informant complained 'if all we get is a miserable *cato*, then what did we bother fighting for?' Others follow the union's original argument to its natural conclusion to argue that as coca is not cocaine, then they should be allowed to cultivate unlimited coca (or two *catos* at the very least).

This alerts us to the problem of winning and the difficulty of maintaining a radical identity once in power. Glorifying coca as an 'indigenous shrub' was a successful strategy for building a political platform and making alliances with other social sectors while the MAS was in opposition. But the reality is that coca is a cash crop that is essential to the local economy, moreover most of the Chapare's coca production is used to process cocaine. Thus Morales has had to back-track, and at times he rhetorically tears the coca leaf apart from Andean tradition in order to justify the uprooting of coca plantations by the military (Grisaffi 2010). Restrictions on the amount of coca that can be grown and the use of troops to destroy excess coca have caused some sections of the rank and file to complain of betrayal. Some base-level unions have even faced up to soldiers on eradication missions (see Grisaffi forthcoming).

Top-down control

Morales has consistently encouraged the coca union to rally in support of MAS-sponsored bills, which has involved staging mass protests and assemblies in distant cities at the coca growers' own expense. Understandably most coca growers are fed up with these sorts of activities, they want to be left in peace to farm and to rebuild their economy after years of constant mobilisation. However many base-level members complain that they are obliged to attend pro-government marches and rallies, because if they do not then they risk heavy fines or even the loss of the right to grow coca. In this context some farmers have come to refer to the *cato* of coca as a form of blackmail or extortion (*chantaje*).

As we have seen, the union has always relied on fines to ensure compliance; what is different today is that the dictates and fines are seen to come from the top down. In other words, from the perspective of many rank and file members the MAS party is using the union's system of sanctions to ensure compliance with MAS (as opposed to union) goals. This has angered some union members – Don Jose expressed his dissatisfaction in the following way: 'what do you call it when they oblige you to go (on pro-government marches), and they have not even consulted the bases? They call it a dictatorship!'

Morales can count on the complicity of the union leadership to support MAS initatives, because many aspire to a job in a state institution. It was often said that Morales hand picks people to occupy senior positions in the union and government, thus the most surefire way to get a good job was to please superiors. I was told by one middle-level leader: 'the union leaders who get on (ascend the union career ladder) are those who are most aligned with the MAS'. Thus rank and file members frequently complain that these days 'everything comes from the top down' and 'there is no longer any debate at the meetings' and 'it's all Evo, Evo, Evo, the leaders just do propaganda for Evo'.

Given the power that the leadership have over union members, most people do not voice contrary opinions at meetings. They fear that if they do, then they will be labelled a member of the 'opposition' or 'right wing' (common denunciations against anyone who does not toe the party line). Indeed when I undertook interviews with people about their views on the government, many people either refused to speak with me, or would take me to the side and whisper discreetly in my ear. Meanwhile rank and file members who have taken a stand against Morales and the MAS have been punished. For example, during the 2015 municipal elections Morales overruled the union's choice of candidate for the position of mayor of Shinahota (one of the main Chapare towns). This caused considerable dissatisfaction amongst the rank and file who characterised Morales as an 'autocrat'. Some base-level activists who challenged the union leadership and the MAS on this issue lost their right to grow coca and some were arrested and charged with endangering the life of the president (for the part they played orchestrating a protest against Morales). Correspondingly support for the MAS party decreased significantly in Shinahota's 2015 municipal election.

Conclusion

The most important contribution of this chapter is to move the focus away from 'indigenous movements' to the role played by agricultural unions in Bolivia's shift to the left. I have argued that despite being composed of Quechua speakers, the coca union is not an ethnic movement *per se*; indeed the coca growers have never made 'ethnic' demands. Rather the union leadership has used indigeneity – captured in the image of 'millennial coca' – as a way to build a coherent political identity within the Chapare, but also to mobilise support from different constituencies to achieve the union's economic and social demands.

More broadly the case of Bolivia disrupts how we think about unions in the West. If a union was composed of extended kinship groups, who patrolled the streets at night, intervened in marital disputes, sanctioned its members and was responsible for local governance, most Europeans would label it as nepotistic, vigilante or corrupt. But these are exactly the characteristics of the coca union. From the coca growers' perspective anything less holistic just wouldn't be considered a 'union'. In this way the coca union poses a profound challenge to emergent movements like Occupy that promote the view that politics can and should be conducted through spontaneously convened direct assemblies (Hickel 2012). When I spoke about Occupy with my coca union informants they said they thought it was absurd, indicating a complete lack of organisation, solidarity and commitment. The coca union then encourages us to think of radical politics anew – transcending the role of a union as a mere vehicle for workers' demands to something much deeper and ingrained in daily life.

The case of the coca union further illustrates that we cannot assume unions are necessarily linked to traditional industries or agricultural sectors. In this case the union emerged from coca growing, which for many years was an illegal activity; moreover many members of the rank and file have at some point worked directly in the cocaine trade. This basic fact has posed distinct challenges and opportunities for the union organisation by defining its relation to the state. The union's association with coca justified oppression in the name of the 'war on drugs' throughout the 1990s, but coca also allowed the union to gain a global profile as the self-styled defenders of the nation's indigenous cultural patrimony.

This links to the following point regarding the challenges that arise when a union is successful at taking state power. The problem with winning is that it is almost impossible for unions to maintain their radical identity once in power, particularly if they opt to work within the existing political system. This in turn alerts us to the different operating logics of unions and governing parties. Unions are focused on a specific sector and they are characterised by perpetual collective action. Political parties meanwhile are supposed to be durable, representative of all citizens and driven to seek the common good. This difference inevitably generates distance between the union and the party. So, for example, since entering public office Morales has had to make alliances and seek compromise with sectors who the coca growers once considered to be enemies, and attend to the needs of other constituencies (including the international community's anti-coca agenda). In this context it is inevitable that the rank and file end up disillusioned with Morales. In short Morales and the MAS are no longer as fully representative as they could be when they only stood for the coca growers.

Finally, it seems as if Morales has taken control of the union through the co-optation of leaders and the use of sanctions to ensure the rank and file's compliance with MAS dictates. This observation alerts us to the fact that the model of bottom-up 'direct democracy' that Morales and his aides claim characterises the MAS, is no more than a rhetorical trope to legitimise the party, rather than something that they have actually operationalised in their current political practice.

Notes

1 There are 35 indigenous minorities in Bolivia.

2 The MAS was established by the National Peasants Confederation (CSUTCB), the Coca Growers Federations, the Union of Colonizers and the Peasant Women's movement 'Bartolina Sisa'.

3 This is not the real name of the village.

4 Morales was expelled from congress in 2002 for the part he allegedly played inciting protests that led to the death of two police officers.

References

Albó, X. (2002) *Pueblos Indios en la política*, La Paz: CIPCA.

Canessa, A. (2006) '"Todos Somos Indígenas": Towards a New Language of National Political Identity', *Bulletin of Latin American Research*, 25(2): 241–263.

Canessa, A. (2012) *Intimate Indigeneities: Race, Sex and History in the Small Spaces of Life*, Durham, NC and London: Duke University Press.

Carroll, R. and Almudevar, L. (2007) 'Columbus Toppled as Indigenous People Rise up after Five Centuries', *The Guardian*, 12 October.

Carter, W. and Mamani, M. (1986) *Coca en Bolivia*, La Paz: Editorial Juventud.

Dunkerley, J. (1984) *Rebellion in the Veins: Political Struggle in Bolivia, 1952–82*, London: Verso.

Escobar, F. (2008) *De la Revolución al Pachakuti. El Aprendizaje del Respecto Reciproco entre Blancos e Indianos*, La Paz: Garza Azul.

Farthing, L. and Kohl, B. (2014) *Evo's Bolivia: Continuity and Change*, Austin, TX: University of Texas Press.

Forero, J. (2006) 'Bolivian Indians Hail the Swearing In of One of Their Own as President', *The New York Times*, 23 January.

Gamarra, E. (1994) *Entre la Droga y la Democracia: La Cooperación entre Esatdos Unidos-Bolivia y la Lucha Contra el Narcotráfico*, La Paz: ILDIS.

García Linera, Á. (2006) 'El Evismo: lo nacional-popular en acción', *Revista OSAL: Observatorio Social de América Latina*, January–April, no. 19.

García Linera, Á. (2014) *Plebeian Power: Collective Action and Indigenous, Working-class and Popular Identities in Bolivia*, Leiden: Brill.

Grandin, G. (2006) *Empire's Workshop: Latin America, the United States and the Rise of the New Imperialism*, New York: Metropolitan Books.

Grisaffi, T. (2009) 'Radio Soberanía: The Sovereign Voice of the Bolivian Cocalero?', PhD Thesis, The University of Manchester.

Grisaffi, T. (2010) 'We are *Originarios* . . . We Just Aren't from Here: Coca Leaf and Identity Politics in the Chapare, Bolivia', *Bulletin of Latin American Research*, 29(4): 425–439.

Grisaffi, T. (2013) 'All of Us Are Presidents: Radical Democracy and Citizenship in the Chapare Province, Bolivia', *Critique of Anthropology*, 33(1): 47–65.

Grisaffi, T. (2014) 'Can You Get Rich from the Bolivian Cocaine Trade? Cocaine Paste Production in the Chapare', *Andean Information Network Policy Memos*. Andean Information Network.

Grisaffi, T. (forthcoming) 'Community Coca Control in Bolivia: A Humane Alternative to the Forced Eradication of Coca Crops', in Labate, B., Cavnar, C. and Rodrigues, T. (eds) *Drug Policies and the Politics of Drugs in the Americas*. Cham, Switzerland: Springer.

Grisaffi, T. and Ledebur, K. (2016) 'Citizenship or Repression? Coca, Eradication and Development in the Andes', *Stability: International Journal of Security and Development*, 5(1): Art. 3, 1–19.

Harris, O. (2000) *To Make the Earth Bear Fruit: Essays on Fertility, Work and Gender in Highland Bolivia*, London: Institute of Latin American Studies.

Harris, O. and Albo, X. (1976) *Monteras y Guardatojos: Campesinos y Mineros*

en el Norte de Potosi, La Paz: Centro de Investigación y Promoción del Campesinado.

Harten, S. (2011) *The Rise of Evo Morales and the MAS*, London: Zed Books.

Harvey, D. (2003) *The New Imperialism*, Oxford: Oxford University Press.

Hickel, J. (2012) 'Liberalism and the Politics of Occupy Wall Street', *Anthropology of this Century*, 4.

Kohl, B. (2006) 'Challenges to Neoliberal Hegemony in Bolivia', *Antipode*, 38(2): 304–326.

Kohl, B. and Farthing, L. (2006) *Impasse in Bolivia: Neoliberal Hegemony and Popular Resistance*, London: Zed Books.

La Patria (2001) 'El Narcotráfico (del Chapare) Quiere Fomentar el Terrorismo', *La Patria*, Oruro, 28 November.

Lazar, S. (2008) *El Alto, Rebel City: Self and Citizenship in Andean Bolivia*, Durham, NC and London: Duke University Press.

Ledebur, K. (2005) 'Bolivia: Clear Consequences', in Youngers, C. and Rosin, E. (eds) *Drugs and Democracy in Latin America: The Impact of U.S. Policy*, pp. 143–184. Boulder, CO and London: Lynne Rienner.

Lucero, J. (2008) *Struggles of Voice: The Politics of Indigenous Representation in the Andes*, Pittsburgh, PA: Pittsburgh University Press.

Orduna, V. and Guzman, G. (2001) 'Prohibido Cantar "Coca-Cero": Advertencias de un Zar', *Pulso*, La Paz, 2–8 November.

Perreault, T. (2006) 'From the Guerra Del Agua to the Guerra Del Gas: Resource Governance, Neoliberalism and Popular Protest in Bolivia', *Antipode*, 38(1): 150–172.

Postero, N. (2006) *Now We Are Citizens: Indigenous Politics in Post-multicultural Bolivia*, Stanford, CA: Stanford University Press.

Rivera, S. (1987) *Oppressed but not Defeated: Peasant Struggles among the Aymara and Quechua in Bolivia, 1900–1980*, Geneva: United Nations Research Institute for Social Development.

Vegas, L. (2002) 'Gobierno Tiene Agenda de Evo con Direcciones de las FARC y ELN', *El Deber*, Santa Cruz, 27 January.

Webber, J. (2011) *Red October: Left-Indigenous Struggles in Modern Bolivia*, Leiden: Brill.

Zegada, T., Torrez, Y. and Camara, G. (2008) *Movimientos Sociales en Tiempos de Poder: Articulaciones y Campos de Conflicto en el Gobierno del MAS*, La Paz: Centro Cuarto Intermedio, Plural.

3 | THE LABOUR UNION MOVEMENT AND 'ALTERNATIVE' CULTURE IN TUNISIA: THE LONG VIEW OF A CLOSE RELATIONSHIP

Mohamed-Salah Omri

Since 2011, Tunisia has witnessed a rare event in postcolonial societies, namely a social and political revolution that overthrew an authoritarian regime that had suppressed all aspects of dissent and attempted to co-opt unions as well as alternative cultural production in the country. This revolution itself and its aftermath have been significantly affected by the Tunisian labour movement, and in particular the Tunisian General Union of Labour, better known by its French acronym, UGTT.[1] The fit between the revolution and UGTT was almost natural since the main demands of the rising masses, namely jobs, national dignity and freedom, have been on the agenda of the union all along. UGTT has enjoyed continuity in history and presence across the country that parallel only the ruling party at its height under presidents Bourguiba and Ben Ali. With 150 offices across the country, an office in every governorate and district, and over 700,000 current members covering the public as well as private sectors, it constituted a credible alternative to this party's power and a locus of resistance to it, so much so that to be a unionist became a euphemism for being an opponent or an activist against the ruling party.

UGTT has been the outcome of Tunisian resistance and its incubator at the same time. For example, in 1984 it aligned itself with the rioting people during the bread revolt; in 2008, it was the main catalyst of the disobedience movement in the Mining Basin of Gafsa; and, come December 2010, UGTT, particularly its teachers' unions and local offices, became the headquarters of revolt against Ben Ali. The union was also very well represented in the remote hinterland where the revolution started. After January 2011, it emerged as the key mediator and power broker at the initial phase of the revolution, when all political players trusted and needed it. And it was within the union that the committee that regulated the transition to the elections of 23 October 2011 was formed. As Tunisia moved to a political, and even ideological phase, characterised by multiplicity of parties and polarisation of public opinion, UGTT led the Quartet – which was later rewarded with the 2015 Nobel Peace Prize – with the Tunisian Association of Human Rights, the Lawyers' Association and the UTICA (the Tunisian Union of Industry and Commerce) to set up national dialogue, which oversaw compromises in writing the constitution and national elections of a permanent government.

At the same time the revolution opened the gates to widespread radical and violent Islamist politics hitherto virtually unknown in the country. Identity politics, long seen as a thing of the past in Tunisia, saw a major resurgence, while the left-leaning UGTT found itself at odds with assertive and powerful Islamism that saw in unions an enemy and in alternative culture either a threat to its projected re-Islamisation of society or a deviation from the path it sought (Omri 2013). In this context, unions saw culture as a battleground they must enter and win.

This chapter takes the long view of a relationship it considers close and significant. It proceeds through tracing key moments of the relationship then zeroes in on alternative music in particular, motivated by the singularity and impact of this tradition in Tunisia since the 1970s. It then devotes some time to the post-revolution orientation of the union in this regard. The argument is that linkages between unionism and alternative culture have shaped the configuration of protest and contention in Tunisia, giving both the impact they have had. In turn, the seemingly unnatural relationship has affected unions as well as culture.

Research on Tunisia and the MENA region as a whole before 2011 has focussed on political actors, identity politics and socioeconomic factors. Michael Hudson (2012) suggests that such research worked with a 'conventional wisdom', which maintains that authoritarianism in the region is durable, democratisation is an inappropriate goal and is impossible to reach in the Arab world, populations are passive either due to rentier state policies or coercion, Arab nationalism is dead and the Middle East regional system is essentially stable. These assumptions, Hudson suggests, have led analysts and academics to focus on the system as such and on the state, with the consequence that 'the strength and durability of protest movements' were ignored

(2012: 27). This could be due to 'group-think, theoretical tunnel vision, ideological agendas, insufficient attention to the work of Arab intellectuals, or a lack of multidisciplinary approaches' (2012: 27). In addition, one could even speak of *de facto*, and often willing, academic and media collusion with authoritarian regimes in the region and with their supporters abroad. Pascal Boniface goes even further and talks about forgery in his book, *Les intellectuels faussaires: le triomphe médiatique des experts en mensonge*, which analyses the French scene (Boniface 2011). Local alternative subjectivities have been dismissed or overlooked as insignificant. Subjectivities with a labour or leftist cultural content have remained largely outside this lens. However, since 2011, material has become available online and in public spaces, and access to the archives and cultural actors themselves has been relaxed, providing researchers with the potential to generate deep revision of knowledge about the region and its dynamics, including the aesthetics of contention. This may explain why after an initial wavering among specialists, the complexity of Tunisia has been gradually emerging as the country moved from marginality to a prominent position in MENA studies and more globally.

Earlier on in the Tunisian revolution, I was struck by two narratives. The first one stressed the spontaneous nature of protests while the second painted it in exotic and benign colours with the label 'Jasmine revolution'. The second soon faded while the first proved to be more resilient, largely due to the lack of detailed knowledge of the society and its history, which characterises media reporting and a certain kind of political science in the West (Omri 2011). Attempts to contextualise the revolution within Tunisian history and society have largely come from Tunisian historians.[2] Among the most significant features, they single out the labour movement; a significant history of progressive, secular opposition in the political and cultural fields, social and political marginalisation of large parts of the country and a heavy-handed and corrupt police state. In my view, the labour movement, particularly the main trade union UGTT, cannot be ignored in any serious analysis of this contextualisation, and indeed in understanding Tunisia as a whole, at least since the 1940s (Omri 2012). Here, I present this thinking and research stressing the intersection between culture (understood in its strict sense of literature and the arts, particularly poetry and music) on the one hand, and unionism on the other. This may seem counterintuitive as trade unionism and cultural practice are not usually seen as natural bedfellows. I argue that the Tunisian case disproves that impression. I will proceed in three interrelated movements, which follow a dialectical historical trajectory, highlighting the mutual effect culture and unionism have had on each other, as well as the social and political contexts that brought about changes in the relationship. I call these movements *the cultural beginnings of unionism, the unionist bases of alternative culture* and *the citizenship turn in culture and unionism.*

The cultural beginnings of unionism

It is of crucial significance that the founding of unions took place within the context of French colonial rule and amidst resistance to it. In fact, the extended history of unionism in the country goes back to the 1920s and clusters around the founding of the General Federation of Tunisian Workers in 1924 at a time when social reform and cultural revival were topping the agenda. In the areas of reform, culture and labour movement, three names come to mind: Tahar al-Haddad (1899–1935), Mohamed Ali Hammi (1884–1928) and Abu al-Qasim al-Shabbi (1909–1935).[3] Radical reform was theorised by al-Haddad; action on the ground was led by al-Hammi while al-Shabbi poeticised the moment. He did this in conjunction with the prolific group of artists and writers, *jama'at tahta al-sur* (Tahta al-Sur Group) whose work continued throughout the 1930s and 40s. The Tunisian elite at the time was rather small. They knew each other well, debated each other's ideas and acted on them collectively. For example, al-Haddad was a founding member of the Federation of Tunisian Workers led by al-Hammi and its historian at the same time. In his book *Tunisian Workers and the Rise of the Union Movement,* published in 1927, al-Haddad chronicles the gestation of a movement through discussion and the hard groundwork of its founders. He notes how they became convinced of key principles: the need for independence from French unions, opening up to all workers regardless of religion or race, membership in the workers international movement (al-Haddad 1987: 103).

But most significantly, the group came to the conclusion that the country was not ready for revolution and what al-Haddad calls, 'class warfare'. He says: 'The idea which settled in minds as the basis for the workers federation was the idea of reform, and it is upon it that the foundations were laid out' (al-Haddad 1987: 115). The mission of unions was conceived primarily to educate workers about their rights and in literacy more generally. 'For there is a task which is greater and more delicate than [salary claims]: it consists in social work inside union institutions. . . . [We must] publish books and pamphlets to the public; and help educate the children of workers' (al-Haddad 1987: 116). The first union was therefore not a trade union as we know it: it was intended as a social and cultural reform organisation. The content of the reform was of course laid out by al-Haddad himself, by al-Hammi who gained international experience and education in Germany, by the rising rebellious poets and artists of the time, and a number of reformist ulama.[4] The idea of reform, with various degrees of radicalism, is in fact a continuation of the nineteenth-century *nahdha*, which swept across much of the Arab lands, and of which Tunisia was a major site, particularly in education, administration and culture (Hourani 1983). Al-Shabbi and his generation sought freedom in its widest sense, freedom of creativity and expression as well as liberation from French rule, while unions focused mainly on organising workers and defending their rights, or strengthening collective action and solidarity, and on education. This idea of radical social, political and cultural reform will prove to be a constant feature of protest throughout Tunisia's colonial and postcolonial history

In the 1940s and early 1950s, which witnessed the founding of UGTT and the peak of the nationalist movement, three names come to mind: Farhat Hashad (1914–1952), Mohamed Fadhel Ben Ashour (1908–1970) and Mahmoud al-Mas'adi (1911–2005). Ben Ashour was an important figure in the reform of education and religion, Hashad organised the labour movement and al-Mas'adi gave literary expression to the determination as well as the trepidations, which marked the moment. We would not be surprised to know they worked in synch. Ben Ashour, who was a prominent literary historian and critic, was also founding member of UGTT in 1946. He would also lead in the reform of the Personal Status Code a decade later. Hashad led the organising and mobilisation effort, and when he was assassinated on 5 December 1952, al-Mas'adi, who was by then the leading figure in the cultural sphere, replaced him (see Omri 2006). The latter would dedicate his seminal play, *al-Sudd* (The Dam) to Hashad's soul in 1955. In fact, critics see in the book's protagonist,

Ghaylan, a representation of the labour leader in his determination and vision. UGTT was a movement of social reform and of national liberation in addition to being a trade union. This was its mission from the start, and it would become consolidated over time and through close ties between Habib Bourguiba, the leading political figure of his time, and the political movement as a whole. The story of this link and the union's pivotal role is well known, but it would not be remembered by the post-independence state when UGTT wanted to reassert its political and social role, as I will explain below.

A review of UGTT congresses and major statements demonstrates that what we might call the 'societal project' of UGTT did not really change in any substantial way since its founding. These aims were articulated by Hashad on 16 May 1947:

> The workers' struggle to improve their material and moral conditions is then tightly linked to the higher interests of the country, because such improvement requires a social change which cannot be obtained as long as the nation is subjected to the colonial system. (Mansouri 2013: 81)

There are global resonances to this strategy, as he explains:

> If union movements in free nations fight big capitalism and the governments which support it, it is incumbent upon the workers of colonized nations to combat that system which is in reality the exploitation of an entire people for the benefit of foreign capitalism.

All UGTT congresses would stress the nationalist character of their organisation as well as its commitment to democracy and to social justice. The practice of its leadership occasionally changed but the union as such has toed this line pretty much throughout its existence. As a result, it stood with liberation movements in the Arab world, Africa and Latin America. An important cultural element was attached to this perspective and promoted by the union. It is often designated as *thaqafa multazima* (committed culture) or *thaqafa badila* (alternative culture). It offered a response to neoliberal entertainment and to official cultural production at the same time. It took the form of political poetry, music and other forms of cultural practice as tools for mobilisation and raising awareness among the general public, as I will outline in detail.

The unionist bases of alternative culture

Soon after Tunisia's independence, discontent with the rule of the state began to grow and repression ensued, political opposition groups and individuals were often subdued or co-opted. UGTT remained a zone of refuge, where political dissent was either diverted into labour activism or hibernated. In my view, oppositional cultural production was one of the areas that benefitted most from this social and physical space, which the Tunisians simply called *al-ittihad* (The Union). We would be hard pressed to find an alternative music band, which did not perform in or was sponsored by *al-ittihad*. Amateur cinema clubs were supported by UGTT and named their gold medal after Farhat Hashad; key dates in the local, Arab and global protest calendar have been regularly celebrated there. But some cultural work was less tied to occasions and calendars. An example is the Regional Union of Ben Arous, where literary, cinema and theatre clubs as well as music performances run on a regular basis from 2004.[5] The continuity of this cultural engagement can be revealed through the archives of the union, partial as these are.[6]

My research on the union's newspapers and magazines demonstrates that its engagement with the cultural field was continuous in time, wide in geographical reach and covered a variety of areas. It also becomes possible to detect the moments during which the union took the lead in literature and the arts as well as in philosophical and other intellectual areas. In the 1990s when the state repressed all dissent and spaces for free expression were severely reduced through censorship, closing down newspapers, banning books and tightening control over publishing, the union newspaper *al-Sha'ab* issued a regular cultural supplement, *manarat* (light posts), which soon gained credibility thanks to the seriousness of the contributions, the variety, and the richness of content. Throughout its long life (1990 to 2010), *manarat* attracted key actors in the intellectual and cultural scene. The supplement of June 2004, for example, includes articles on philosophy ('Frederick Nietzsche: From Philology to Philosophy') and world cultural history ('What Is Left of 1968?'), an essay on globalisation, studies on cultural heritage, Al-Tawhidi's epistle about the burning of his books and a report on the first conference of the unionist poets and the manifesto emerging from it. This is a significant event in and of itself, and marks institutional alignment between poets and the union.[7]

Such alignment between poets and unionists, in reality, predates this congress, and can be observed in times of crises and increased repression. Historically, the crisis following the so-called Bread Rebellion of January 1984 was one of the most serious tests to trade unionism in Tunisia since the death of Hashad. It also reveals the position of UGTT and the stakes in its survival for the society as a whole. For this reason, it allows us a productive view of a society in rebellion and how the labour movement engaged with it when protest culture was at its most vulnerable phase and repression at its height. The basic story was the attempt by the ruling party to install a parallel trade union under the pretext of 'rectifying the direction' of a UGTT whose leadership was judged to be openly hostile to the ruling party and government policies, and a nest for left-wing dissent. A group of state-sponsored unionists called *al-Shurafa'* (The Honourables), a title conferred on them by the PM at the time, Mohamed Mzali, took over the union by force.

Indeed, the ruling party had little presence in the union. There was a clear divide between state loyalists and the opposition. During the crisis, support for the UGTT came from all sides of the country's civil society, most prominently the university, lawyers and human rights activists. Repression was meted against everyone, filling up jails and forced military service camps. The poet Awlad Ahmad, who wrote a seminal poem on the Bread Rebellion of 1984, 'Hymn to the Six Days', captured this aura of the unionist and unionism at the time in the poem, 'The General Trade Union Manifesto', written during his brief spell in jail with unionists and students in 1985.

A trade unionist,
I confess.
Disciplined
And different.
The light of dawn is upon me
And this night is waning.

Enough!
It's enough!

I toured your prisons,
And now I must stand up and confess:
I am the recorded victory in your defeats.
I am the sea shells.
The creaking of the door is my clock,
The face of water my mirror.
And when my brothers take a stand,
'Honourables' and honour come tumbling down.[8]

But this confluence of alternative culture and unionism saw its fullest expression in music and singing where the relationship was close and enduring. At the root of it was the story of the Egyptian icon of protest music, Cheikh Imam Issa. Imam and his partner Ahmed Fuad Nigm are the deans of Arabic colloquial political and social protest poetry and music.[9] The genre itself and its practice have a longer history, of course, but two related features have remained constant throughout – or until Imam. These have been the local character of the lyrics and the music on the one hand, and the linkages with oral vernacular poetry, on the other. It draws on poetic forms in local dialects, usually raising issues of local interest. Today, Imam needs no introduction in Tunisia and his death is commemorated regularly, but the way he was introduced to the country and his wide effect on local alternative music is closely tied to UGTT and the Tunisian left.

Hechmi Ben Frej, an influential figure in the Tunisian civil society and cultural scene was at the centre of it all. In the 1970s, he was a young student at Paris 8, and a member of Movement Perspectives. 'What attracted me to Imam was this: here we have an Egyptian who is talking about the concerns of Egyptians for justice at the height of pan-Arab nationalism in song and poetry,' he told me in a personal interview in 2012.[10] 'His Egypt was that of the poor, the marginalised and the repressed. It was an Egypt that was different from the one beaming through Radio Cairo, the speeches of Nasser, and television and film screens'. At the time, Imam was banned from leaving his country and from giving public concerts. Ben Frej, the sound engineer and young activist, decided to go to Egypt to record him. He did so in private houses, and then released the first album of Imam in Paris in 1974 under the title-song, ''uyun al-kalam' (Fountains of Speech) with Le Chant du monde.[11] The album was noticed by Habib Belaid, presenter for Radio Tunis International, who became the first person to play it to Tunisian audiences in the summer of 1978, Ben Frej recounts.[12] In September 1984, Imam was invited to Tunisia by members of the Banking and Insurance Federation of UGTT and held concerts in several cities.[13] The Federation's president, Salah Zghidi, explained to me in a personal online interview:

> It was us, with our means and union structures who organised the 10 concerts, from A to Z, including two at Qobba (Dome) in Tunis, others in Bizerte, Sousse, Beja, Gabes, Sfax, Kairouane and Jendouba. 50,000 paying spectators attended, 5,000 in the first concert in Tunis and 4,000 in the second.[14]

Cheikh Imam was held at the airport under the pretext that he was 'a communist invited by another communist', Zghidi added. The union protested and he was allowed to enter the country and sing. But by the time he arrived, Imam's songs were the main staple of the Tunisian student movement in particular, made famous by emerging bands and individuals (Majmuat al-Bahth al-musiqi, Gabes Group for Musical Research, the singer Hedi Guella and several others). His fame was such that Imam, in a sense, came home. While in Tunisia, he sang the anthem of UGTT, written by the poet Adam Fethi, gave private concerts and collaborated with young artists and poets.[15] From as early as 1977 the prestigious Carthage International Festival was able to put on stage this alternative music – Hedi Guella, Hammadi Boulares, Ali Saidane, singing Cheikh Imam.

Several other bands and individuals became well-known figures in this alternative music, playing at UGTT local offices and at university campuses. One of these was awlad al-manajim (Sons of the Mines). The plight of workers figures prominently in this group's music, and none more so than the fate of miners in the region known as the mining basin, a space of high concentration of working-class and frequent labour and popular protests for decades – most recently in the 2008 rebellion which prepared the ground for the 2011 revolution. Gafsa and its neighbouring towns live off mining phosphates, are heavily unionised and famously militant. Awlad al-manajim was formed specifically from there and carries the name. It started in 1977 and has continued its mission and style uninterrupted since. 'Al-Damus' (The Mining Tunnel) is one of their landmark and signature songs.

The song is a lament recording a tragic accident one night in the mining town of Om Laarayes, and from there, recounts the plight of the region as a whole. The song addresses the mining pit:

> Long are the stories of our plights.
> Your wonders have surpassed The Thousand and One Nights.

Then it goes on to describe in an elegiac tone those who lost their lives in the mine, mourning the loss of effort of those who toil underground like rats to gain nothing but pain.

> You covered our homes in darkness
> And left our children fatherless.
> Oh, mine! You are the darkness of night.[16]

A citizenship turn in unionism and culture

The 2011 revolution brought about a reversal of the cultural field in the country and new challenges to unions, UGTT in particular. One of the key changes in the cultural landscape has been the end of restrictions on alternative and oppositional expression on the one hand, and an opening up of public space for hitherto banned expression on the other (e.g. see Hawkins 2014 for a discussion of images of revolution on the internet). Carthage summer festival, the most prestigious of the country's many festivals, had been the occasion to 'showcase a deliberate emphasis on the culture of exhibition and consumption, liberal but not critical'.[17] Things changed dramatically in 2011.

> The festival became the stage of the marginalised, the censored, and emerging talent. The opening show was given to Ridha Shmak, a leftist singer who presented 'Songs of Life', a show inspired by the poet Chebbi, while the closing was turned over to the poet Awlad Ahmed and his cast of poets from the 'Arab Spring'.[18]

The trend was consolidated by what might be called, a 'revolutionary conversion' by which hitherto repressive state institutions, exclusive public spaces, and an acquiescent public turned into ardent supporters and sponsors of revolutionary culture almost overnight. That situation faded within about two years, as we will see, but alternative music took centre stage, even becoming virtually compulsory in state-sponsored as well as private venues. Awlad al manajim, for example, with their distinctive miner's blue uniform (*dingri*), moved from union offices and university halls to performing in over 300 concerts in two years and featured on national television and an al-Jazeera documentary.[19] Ajras had 150 performances in 2011–2012. The same goes for al-bahth al-musiqi and individual singers.

On the side of unionism, UGTT gained more clout as a powerbroker and unavoidable national player. But it was challenged to surrender politics to the newly formed political parties and adjust to emerging plurality in unionism. At the same time, it also began to redefine its relationship to culture. UGTT set out a new agenda and opened up debate within its ranks regarding the cultural dimension of their work within the new context. Its Tabarka congress of 2011 paid attention to the kind of culture it supports. Its General Motion states:

> To emphasise the need to give culture the attention it deserves because it is a fundamental pillar of national sovereignty in a world characterised by a strong cultural and media invasion supported by colossal technological means. Such invasion aims to empower a standardised model, which limits human cultural diversity and prepares the ground for imposing the consumerist model which serves the interests of big powers and multinational companies. For this reason the congress stresses the need to hold on to our Arabic language and to deepen the sense of Islamic identity away from close-mindedness and fanaticism, and advocates openness to global human cultural heritage without falling into cheap entertainment.[20]

The implications of this general orientation have been worked out in a series of workshops and seminars, the third of which I attended as a participant observer on 8 April 2014 in the city of Sousse. It brought together UGTT branches in the governorates of Sousse, Kairaouan, Mahdia, Monastir, Sfax and Sidi Bouzid. It was convened by the UGTT section for training and education, under the heading: 'Cultural action is a fundamental pillar of union struggle', and was supported by the German foundation, Friedrich Ebert Stiftung. The aim was to rethink the cultural role of the union and the position of cultural activity within it, as Mohamed Mselmi, Member of the Executive Bureau in charge of Union Training and Workers' Education, explained in his framing introduction.[21] On the practical side, the project aims to launch a strategy specifically motivated by the post-2011 revolution, which includes regional festivals and regular cultural activities at UGTT offices. The colloquium was attended by over 20 participants; about 40 per cent of them were women, representing the six regional unions. The workshops were run by union members involved in the fields of literature, film, theatre and music. For debate was the question: What legitimates the subject, historically, in terms of remit and at that time in history? The other questions included: What type of culture should the union promote? How does it relate to wider cultural practices in the country?

Participants argued that UGTT was never restricted to traditional trade union activity; it has had a societal project, and culture was part of that. Historically, however, the practice was either a means of recruiting new members, occasional or haphazard. In addition, culture is seen with suspicion by some unionists and in several unions cultural activity declined since the 1980s. The issue of overtly political cultural production as a limitation was raised. After 2011, the rise of a 'new culture of violence' has given the UGTT, which has always been on the progressive side, the responsibility to fight it. 'This is not a need but an emergency', argued one participant. UGTT framed a revolution and now that the revolution has gone off course, it must step in to protect its path. A cultural project is the best way to do it. But what kind of culture must UGTT engage in or promote in the new context? Should it restrict itself to 'workers' culture', engage with mainstream trends or highlight regional and local practices? And what relationship should it have with other cultural institutions? Some participants called for an 'interactive' relationship with the other cultural institutions and spaces not a break with them, as was the case before 2011. One option was to develop a workers' culture, which touches popular sections of society and does not oppose other aspects of cultural activity. More opening up to the society at large was advocated. One proposal consisted in turning UGTT offices into open spaces for cultural activities, for example on weekends ('We need to save our children from *salafia* [Salafis]', said one participant).

Beyond the series of workshops, UGTT went on to implement some of these ideas. The festivals that took place under this strategy were guided by this vision: they included local cultural production and traditions as well as progressive music and colloquia. The third edition of UGTT festival held in Gabes, 3–5 September 2015 included cinema, music, a study day on green economy, a street festival, poetry recitals, as well as an evening of alternative music. During the opening, Mselmi stressed that UGTT has since moved its Tabarka congress to cultural action rather than a supporting role, particularly in the marginalised regions. 'The festival showcases and valorises the tangible and intangible cultural heritage of each region, and adopts new ways to move from consumer culture to a producer culture'.[22] Houcine Abbasi, UGTT secretary-general, on the other hand, says that the union was, and continues to be, a welcoming space for alternative culture of all types, hosting and defending the right to free expression and creation despite restrictions on UGTT itself. He recognised that intellectuals and artists have rushed to the union's defence whenever it came under attack, including on 4 December 2012 when its headquarters came under violent attacks by the so-called Leagues for the Protection of the Revolution. For Abbasi, the new strategy aims at avoiding the culture of occasion and instituting democratisation of the arts, particularly in the deprived and marginalised regions of the interior.

The new role assigned for cultural practice supported by the union is motivated by mobilisation against what it perceives as the twin dangers of consumerist culture and Islamic fundamentalist culture. In the course of this endeavour, redefining the meaning of alternative culture becomes important. The redefinition also opens up critical perspectives on the relationship between unionism and culture in the past. Often-asked questions included: Has cultural production been over-determined by politics? Has this limited its aesthetic range and ambition? Has it been marked out as specific, niche culture, minoritarian, with a limited audience? Has it lacked linkages with musical traditions as well as global radical trends, such as rap music? Implicit in the debate within UGTT reviewed above is a rethink and new orientations. A more explicit intervention comes from Adel Bouallegue, academic, and leader of the band Ajras, established first in 1999, and musician since the 1980s.[23] In a personal interview, he takes stock of three decades of this experience. 'I call this "alternative song", not "alternative music" since music is a wider field, as I learned from working with the group al-Hama'im al-Bidh (White Doves) for 30 years'. The distinction he makes goes to the heart of the relationship between aesthetics and politics.

> The focus on song has to do with the focus on the word, which is determined by politics. What interest politicians is singing, not necessarily music. In addition, there are cultural reasons for this, including the history of Arabic music and the focus on the word in Arab culture as a whole. The ruling power may have played a role in this since the word is easier to restrict, control, monitor.[24]

Bouallegue argues that UGTT believes workers needed a discourse, therefore it encouraged bands closer to its purposes (Awlad al manajim, al-Bahth al-Musiqi, Lazhar al-Dhawi). This is of course an overgeneralisation since musical research and innovation are noticeable in al-Bahth al-Musiqi and others, including keen attention to national forms, and the tradition of colloquial poetry.[25] UGTT may have gone more in the direction of social rights before 2011 by practising mobilisation by means of a particular type of music or singing. It has to think beyond that. Bouallegue agrees by distinguishing between social and natural rights: 'Social rights are limited to contention against institutions, whereas natural rights lead to revolution because they entail going beyond the institution itself'. The idea of training in citizenship and the practice of democracy, which have become part of UGTT discourse, are the outcome of the radical changes I have been discussing. Bouallegue explains: 'Democratising arts and aesthetics is key. We need to expand the field of interest and work to protect ourselves and think of the future. Alternative music should train people to be citizens'.[26] Absent from this discourse is a proper engagement with other forms of youth music in particular, which have had considerable appeal before and after 2011, with rap being the most popular form.[27] Bouallegue, despite his critical take on UGTT cultural orientation, remains sceptical about rap music, suggesting it has been wrongly presented as the alternative at the expense of an entire history that goes back to the 1960s.

Conclusion

For seemingly unnatural bedfellows, in Tunisia, unionism and culture have had in fact a long and evolving relationship. This has to do as much with the nature and social history of unionism as it does with the social and political roots of alternative culture. Focus on unions and UGTT in particular allows us to observe protest and resistance over a long period of time, along various sections of society and across the country. This is possible because UGTT has had the historical extent, geographical spread and social reach, equalled by no other body except the ruling party. As such it can be considered a parallel organisation to it, at all levels. By January 2011, UGTT was well entrenched in the social memory of protest in Tunisia, more so, I think, than any political party or political orientation, including Islamism. This lent it credibility and clout to act as catalyst and framing force for popular protest and for the articulation of demands for work, freedom and dignity.[28] Its offices across the country became focal points and operation rooms for protest activity. UGTT nurtured, willingly or under pressure from its rank and file, a parallel view of society and culture, which has made of it a privileged position from which to begin to understand wider social and cultural phenomena, including the nature of protest over a long period, and the political limitations of protest movements in Tunisia. In addition, the intersection of unionism and the culture of protest can be a productive frame for explaining the revolution and, I would argue, the transitional period – it is remarkable how no one locally was surprised to see UGTT emerge as the powerbroker when the politics of transition came to a deadlock.

The confluence between a largely secular and humanist education and an engrained labour activism have been, I claim, the main bases of a Tunisian formation, which allowed it to develop a culture of resistance to authoritarianism with a specific humanist and social justice content. An alignment of these two elements against Islamists has taken place during and since the 2011 revolution. With regard to culture, the culture of occasion, and the politicisation of all cultural activity has resulted in a particular aesthetic – under the term alternative (*badil*).

UGTT is now in the process of developing a new cultural strategy, based on a reading of the post-revolution situation and under pressure from a freed public space, which made alternative culture no longer an exclusive domain of UGTT and redefined the field itself. This culture as well as the union remain secularised at the moment and focused on freedom, citizenship and social justice. Both align themselves against the re-Islamisation of society, authoritarianism and resurgent neoliberal policies. For after the initial celebration of alternative music and culture, mentioned above, interest soon waned and well-entrenched players regained the ground they ceded. Bouallegue explains: 'There is a serious planning to control artistic taste in general'. He argues that in the first and second years of the revolution, there was an exploitation of alternative art/culture by taking on the revolutionary garb, as if to say: we, too, are revolutionaries and we gave you fora to perform (main venues, festivals and public media). In 2014 an orientation towards the spectacle (e.g. Yanni at Carthage festival) returned in force. By 2015 we had returned to the old days, to dominant music from giant entertainment companies such as Rotana and Lebanon, etc. There was also an attack in preparation by the private sector as the state was weakened. But the cultural field had evolved greatly, particularly in two areas. One is youth culture where rap, for example, is very popular, and where there has been a rise of what might be termed spiritual music. In addition, plurality of trade unionism is now a reality, albeit limited at the moment, while political parties compete for presence among youth and workers.

The poetics of contention in Tunisia, viewed in a dialectical relationship with unionism, questions the usual tendency to separate union protest and culture into distinct spheres of activity. Conversely, unionism viewed from the vantage point of alternative culture becomes an activity with a wider remit and aims even in its beginnings in the 1920s and during the height of the liberation movement in the 1940s and 1950s. Such a picture begins to probe the complexity of contention or what might be called the contentious field or situation in Tunisia during authoritarian rule and the transition period. Being more than an ordinary civil society association – in its history, social roles and political dimension – UGTT managed to serve its members, protect other dissidents against state repression and ensure that the democratic transition would lead to democracy, rather than a return of the old dictatorship or the emergence of a new one. In this, it meets a vigorous civil society, and a cultural field intent on standing against neoliberal policies and counterrevolutionary Islamist forces on the right.

Notes

1 See Omri, Mohamed Salah, *Confluency (tarafud) between Trade Unionism, Culture and Revolution in Tunisia*, Tunis: UGTT information and publishing section, 2016. An extended version of the present chapter constitutes part 2 of the book.

2 These local sources include: Abdeljalil Temimi's numerous works, most notably the *Observatory of the Tunisian Revolution* in three volumes (2011 and 2015); Hedi Timoumi's *The Deception of Soft Dictatorship in Tunisia: 23 Years of Ben Ali's Rule* (2012); Ahmed Jdey's 'Pour une histoire de la Tunisie du 14 Janvier 2011: la fin d'un dictateur et l'amorce de la construction démocratique', in *La Tunisie du XXIème siècle: quel pouvoir pour quels modèles de société. EurOrient*, no. 38 (2012). For the events themselves and chronologies, see, for example: Weslati (2012), which chronicles in detail 90 days (January 14–March 14, 2011), with background to the 2011 revolution.

3 Mohamed Ali Al-Hammi was self-educated, travelled extensively, including to Germany where he studied political economy. The details of the founding are recounted by Al-Hammi's companion, the reformer and womens' rights advocate, Tahar al-Haddad, in his seminal book *The Tunisian Workers and the Rise of Labour Unionism in Tunisia* (1927) (al-Haddad 1987) (in Arabic). Al-Shabbi is a Tunisian national poet, and one of the most loved poets of modern Arabic (see Omri 2010).

4 On the secular and religious intellectuals of the time, see Sraieb (1995) and Green (1980).

5 Archived by Ridha Ben Hlima in the documentary, *The Experience of the Regional Union of Ben Arous in the Cultural Field* (UGTT–DFSCO, 2013).

6 Research was conducted at al-Sha'b headquarters in Tunis in April 2014. Sami Tahri, Director, *al-Sha'b*

newspaper and spokesperson of the UGTT, expressed his fear that part of the archive may never be recovered because it was either lost during raids by the secret police or destroyed in the chaotic weeks after January 2011. Personal interview with Sami Tahri, on 17 April 2014 at *Al-Sha'ab* newspaper.

7 For a review of the conference and the manifesto resulting from it, see *Al-Sha'ab*, no. 763, 29 May 2004.

8 Tunis – Gourjani prison, November 1985. For more on the poet as an index of Tunisian protest culture, see Omri (2012).

9 'Sheikh Imam: A Profile from the Archives', www.jadaliyya.com/pages/index/18236/sheikh-imam_a-profile-from-the-archives.

10 Interview with Hechmi Ben Frej, Tunis, 13 June 2012.

11 See the telling album cover image: www.cdandlp.com/en/le-cheikh-imam/chante-negm/lp-gatefold/r117634622/.

12 The date was confirmed to me by Habib Belaid in an online communication on 11 October 2015.

13 For an album of photos of Imam's UGTT visit and concerts, see http://moultaka.net/cheikh-imam/content/concertstunisie/10.php.

14 Personal online interview with Salah Zghidi, 7 July 2015.

15 Adam Fathi wrote the lyrics of the union's anthem ('nashid al-Ittihad'), which was put to music by Salah Toumi, leader of awlad al-manajim. Fethi has also written 'ya waladi' (My Son!) for Cheikh Imam, a song which regained popularity since 2011. The full text of the anthem can be found in *al-Sha'b* of 28 June 2008. His collection, *ughniyat al-naqabi al-fasih* (The Song of the Eloquent Trade Unionist) was published by dar al-Taqaddum in Tunis in 1986.

16 Documentary on Gafsa and the literature of the mines, with video clips

of awlad al manajim etc.: www.aljazeera.
net/programs/pages/d6382053-787c-
4a22-856e-a9f6c9bcaea7.

17 The programme of the 2010
festival reads like the hall of fame of
Arab popular culture: Latifa Arfawi,
Sabir Riba'i, Majda al-Rumi, Samira
Said, Raghib Alama, Sabah Fakhri, Lotfi
Bouchnaq (Omri 2012: 142).

18 For the full programme of the
Carthage Festival 2011, see www.
festival-carthage.com.tn/. For the 2010
programme, see www.tunivisions.
net/programme-du-festivalde-carthage-
2010,367.html.

19 Interview with the founder of the
band Salah Toumi, *al-Shuruq* newspaper:
http://tinyurl.com/z277y8a.

20 *Documents: The 22nd Congress
Held in Tabarka 25–28 December 2011*
(UGTT section on media, communication
and publications, 2012), p. 53.

21 Personal recording of the
workshop, 8 April 2014.

22 *al Maghreb*, Saturday 5
September 2015, p. 18. The two previous
editions took place in Kef (3–5 November
2013) and Beja (4–6 September 2014).

23 See http://tinyurl.com/jhnjhh5
and 'Al-Hama'im al-bidh at 35' http://
tinyurl.com/z8y2n4t.

24 Personal Interview with the
author at Aykar, Tunis, 5 September 2015.

25 Amel Hamrouni, lead singer
and the best known female vocalist of
alternative musc in Tunisia explains:

The name [Gabes Group for Musical
Research] is important to us since we
endeavoured to create an aesthetic
of the song, which consists of a
new text at the levels of form and
content but one which is in synch
with people's aspirations. I take
images and forms from the local
music traditions. (Personal online
interview with Amel Hamrouni, 31
October 2015)

26 He locates the work of Ajras in
this horizon: 'Our project goes beyond
mobilisation and towards the right to
aesthetics and the arts'.

27 A landmark was the popularity
of a rap song, 'Houmani' (2013), with
over 20 million views. See also: 'Rap
in Tunisia: Art or Resistance?' www.
al-monitor.com/pulse/culture/2013/10/
tunisia-rap-art-resistance.html#.

28 It was remarkable how
international media, almost without
exception, spoke to unionists first, and
sometimes exclusively. Their speaking
skills were honed in the union work;
they knew the demands and were
willing to step forward to express
them.

References

al-Haddad, T. (1987) *The Tunisian Workers
and the Rise of Labour Unionism in
Tunisia* (1927), Tunis: Dar Bouslama
(in Arabic).
Boniface, P. (2011) *Les intellectuels
faussaires: le triomphe médiatique
des experts en mensonge*, Paris:
Jean-Claude Gawsewith.
Green, A. (1980) 'A Comparative
Historical Analysis of the Ulama
and the State in Egypt and Tunisia',
*Revue de l'occident musulman et de la
méditerrannée*, 29: 31–454.
Hawkins, S. (2014) 'Teargas, Flags and
the Harlem Shake: Images of and
for Revolution in Tunisia and the
Dialectics of the Local in the Global', in
Werbner, P., Webb, M. and Spellman-
Poots, K. (eds) *The Political Aesthetics
of Global Protest: The Arab Spring
and Beyond*, pp. 31–52. Edinburgh:
Edinburgh University Press.

Hourani, A. (1983) *Arabic Thought in the Liberal Age: 1879–1939*, Oxford: Oxford University Press.

Hudson, M. (2012) 'Awakening, Cataclysm, or Just a Series of Events? Reflections on the Current Wave of Protest in the Arab World', in Bsheer, Rosie and Ziad Abu Rish (eds) *The Dawn of the Arab Uprisings: End of an Order?*, pp. 26–27. London: Pluto. [His comments were first published on 16 May 2011.]

Jdey, A. (2012) 'Pour une histoire de la Tunisie du 14 Janvier 2011: la fin d'un dictateur et l'amorce de la construction démocratique', in *La Tunisie du XXIème siècle: quel pouvoir pour quels modèles de société. EurOrient*, no. 38.

Mansouri, S. (2013) *Risalat al-ittihad al-'am al-tunisi li al-shughl, 1964–1956* (The Mission of the Tunisian General Union of Labour, 1946–1956), Tunis: Dar Mohamed Ali.

Omri, M.S. (2006) *Nationalism, Islam and World Literature: Sites of Confluence in the Writings of Mahmud al-Mas'adi*, London and New York: Routledge.

Omri, M.S. (2010) 'Abu al-Qasim al-Shabbi', in Allen, Roger (ed.) *Essays in Arabic Literary Biography, 1850–1950*, pp. 292–303. Wiesbaden: Harrassowitz Verlag.

Omri, M.S. (2011) 'This Is not a Jasmine Revolution', Transnational Institute, 27 January 2011. www.tni.org/article/tunisia-revolution-dignity-and-freedom-can-not-be-colour-coded.

Omri, M.S. (2012) 'A Revolution of Dignity and Poetry', *boundary 2*, 39(1): 137–166.

Omri, M.S. (2013) 'The Perils of Identity Politics in Tunisia', *al-Jazeera English*, 27 January 2013. www.aljazeera.com/indepth/opinion/2013/01/2013127142856170386.html.

Omri, M.S. (2016) *Confluency (tarafud) between Trade Unionism, Culture and Revolution in Tunisia*, Tunis: UGTT information and publishing section.

Sraieb, N. (1995) *Le College Sadiki de Tunis (1875–1956): Enseignement et nationalisme*, Paris: Les editions de la Méditerrannée.

Temimi, A. (2011 and 2015) *Observatory of the Tunisian Revolution*, 3 vols, Tunis: FTERSI.

Timoumi, H. (2012) *The Deception of Soft Dictatorship in Tunisia: 23 Years of Ben Ali's Rule*, Tunis: Dar Mohamed Ali (in Arabic).

Weslati, S. (2012) *Democracie ou guerre civile*, Tunis: Nirvana.

PART TWO

IDENTITY AND PRECARITY

4 | MIGRANTS' STRUGGLES? RETHINKING CITIZENSHIP, ANTI-RACISM AND LABOUR PRECARITY THROUGH MIGRATION POLITICS IN ITALY

Irene Peano[1]

Within the latest wave of anti-austerity protests in Europe and beyond, the Italian case is often considered to be a sort of anomaly. The country has not experienced the same coherently organised and readily recognisable forms of opposition to the neoliberal onslaught that have characterised others, such as Spain or Greece.[2] At the same time, it has never lacked radical anti-capitalist politics, which developed in different forms. Indeed, for decades Italy has constituted, in some ways, a reference point for social movements outside its borders. Here, I wish to reflect on the presence within the heterogeneous constellation of struggles that has emerged in recent years of specific subjects, namely *migrants*, and on the importance of the *labour* dimension in their mobilisations. If not always self-evident or acknowledged, both aspects are central in understanding some of the most significant instances of struggle that have shaken Italian public opinion and the social-movement scene – all the more so following the current mediatised hype about a supposed 'migration crisis' across the EU, with Italy as one of the main locations in this spectacle.[3]

Of course, as other contributions to this volume also highlight, in order to fully understand such processes it is crucial to situate them within a wider historical framework, as well as to consider them as part of a transnational and postcolonial space on account of the very character of migration (cf. Cobbe and Grappi 2011: 89; Mellino 2013) – without discounting national-level specificities and the role of nation-states in disciplining mobility.[4] Since the late 1980s, social movements in Italy, as elsewhere across the globe, have been increasingly characterised by the participation of migrants of all ages, genders and origin, and by a growing sensibility towards migration-related demands. Such attention and presence are predictable, if hardly assured, given the surge in the number of immigrants from both within and outside the EU who for over three decades have settled in Italy more or less permanently, making it one of the countries in Europe with the highest number of migrants.[5] Yet, their participation in grassroots politics is not simply a mathematical addition to pre-existing platforms and organisations. As part of the wider impact it has on social forms and relations, migration has contributed to significantly – though by no means smoothly – shape and modify the modes and languages of militancy, different understandings of politics and thus the very nature of collective demands. This influence results not only from migrants' active participation in political struggle, but it is the outcome of several processes: migrants' mere, unsettling presence in the social context first; the forms of governance to which they are subjected from the very start of their migration experience (and even before), and through which they are shaped as subjects; and the repercussions such measures have on others. All such dynamics impinge upon the discourses, tactics and strategies of radical social-movement politics.

The range of subjects, organisations, groups and collectives involved in such mobilisations, like the scope of their claims, are particularly broad, with marked differences in terms of longevity and internal mutations. Furthermore, no linear historical evolution can be identified in their practices and demands. Yet, despite these differential and sometimes discontinuous intensities, migration and migrants have been one of the undisputed protagonists of social struggles since the end of the 1980s. Across these different strands and tendencies, a crucial but often unacknowledged and controversial category of analysis and mobilisation can be isolated – that of *labour*. Indeed, not only has migrants' presence within and outside social movements problematised taken-for-granted analyses of labour. It has also been one of the propelling forces for its reinsertion into the agenda of radical politics, which seemed to have set it aside precisely since the 1980s, with the neoliberal turn and its backlash against the workers' movement.

In order to analyse the role of migrants in contemporary social movements, scholars and activists differentiate struggles where migration, its regulation and exploitation are central concerns (also defined more properly as *migrants' struggles*) from those where migration and migrants as such exert a more indirect or less immediately discernible influence, and which are considered as *struggles of migration*.[6] Within the first category fall struggles concerned with *rights and citizenship* (against immigration and citizenship laws, among others), but also with *racism* more broadly (in its institutional and street-level manifestations alike) and, crucially, with *labour*. If labour struggles are not the purview of migrants alone, the *dispositifs* that regulate migrants' 'differential inclusion' within a polity (Mezzadra and Neilson 2013) are a form of control and exploitation of their labour. Immigration laws often bind the right to work and residency to a labour contract, thus encouraging migrant workers' docility *vis-à-vis* their employers through the threat of detention and deportation (cf. De Genova 2002) – or, perhaps more poignantly, simply of permit loss and thus of the loss of all rights.[7] Racialisation and racism also serve the same purpose, confining migrants to the lowest, most dangerous and worst paid, often informally run sectors of the labour market. In turn, this precludes forms of sociality and learning that could be empowering in terms of knowledge of the language, of one's surroundings and rights, and undermines the possibility for the construction of alliances with workers of other origins, be they citizens or not.

Against such fragmentation, one of the mobilisations that most explicitly connected the issue of labour to that of migration was the so-called 'migrants' strike', that took place for the first time on 1 March 2010 in several Italian cities. It saw the participation of Italian and migrant workers 'united by the awareness that institutionalised racism . . ., exclusionary policies, labour exploitation, rights violations are part of a unified repressive strategy which, starting from the weakest and most defenceless, aims to hit everyone and impose precarity as a living horizon'.[8] The strike was not meant so much as a unionist instrument for negotiation, but rather it was an attempt to re-compose different subjectivities by opposing immigration laws – which, whilst ostensibly affecting migrants, has repercussions on the labouring classes as a whole.

Thus, issues to do with rights and citizenship, with racism, and with labour and its exploitation are constitutively intertwined within social struggles involving migrants and migration. Immigration laws, which deny or qualify certain political, civil and social citizenship rights to differently classified subjects, are one of the principle tools for discrimination and for differential inclusion into the labour market. Yet, if the institutional dimension of racism, like the disciplining of mobility and labour subtending to immigration policies, highlight the porosity of categories of political struggle, forms of mobilisation in fact have often laid the emphasis on one or the other aspect, also creating conflicts and divisions among subjects that promoted different perspectives. In fact, in the very occasion of the mobilisations of 1 March 2010, the possibility and desirability of a 'migrants' strike' was questioned and gave rise to tensions and misunderstandings among those sectors of trade unions, anti-racist and radical organisations that either saw it as divisive of a supposedly unitary working class, because it addressed what were thought to be migrants' exclusive concerns, or paternalistically considered migrants as needy and powerless subjects in whose name the appropriate forms of mobilisation are represented by 'integration campaigns' (Cobbe and Grappi 2011). In line with this narrow perspective, anti-racism represents one of the primary motivations for the mobilisations of and for migrants. These began, according to the movement's own self-narration, in 1989, when immigration laws in Italy were still extremely patchy. Indeed, such mobilisations contributed to produce the systematisation of immigration laws, as we shall see.

However, migration can be viewed as potentially subversive not only when migrants mobilise self-consciously as such. As many commentators have argued (cf. Papastergiadis 2000), migrant movement destabilises all borders – symbolic, material, social, cultural, political, including those of social struggle and its codes – and it enforces rights even where these are denied. This perspective was put forth, among others, by the Frassanito Network that took shape after the 2003 No Border camp held in southern Apulia:

> Migration, as we see it, needs to be considered as a *social movement* and we need to take into account the *social protagonism of migration*. We need to look at the manifold ways in which migration movements and struggles confront and challenge the reality of domination and exploitation. We must look not only at exclusion from citizenship, but also at *practices of citizenship* that take place even under the condition of illegality. We must look at behaviours, desires, imagination and the individual and collective projects that criss-cross the movements of migration.[9]

Hence, migration struggles occur in shapes that may not always be recognisable according to traditional militant canons. At the same time, we can view struggles of migration (and thus the influence of migration on radical politics more broadly) as the product of the specificity of a migrant condition not only in terms of multiple border-crossings, but also since *the migrant condition carries with it a heightened form of precarity*, which exceeds the confines of the workplace and thus demands different kinds of resistance strategies. In the words of Raimondi and Ricciardi, 'migrant labour today is the condition that anticipates and shares the general conditions in which contemporary labour as a whole is provided. In this sense, it can be said that all contemporary labour is becoming migrant' (2004: 19, my translation). Here, 'migrant' indicates that quality of hypermobility that identifies contemporary forms of non-guaranteed labour, as well as the increasing criminalisation of sectors of the population that are deemed 'dangerous' or out of control (cf. Raimondi 2011). Indeed, migration in a sense prefigures a generalised state of precarity, where this identifies not only 'all possible shapes of unsure, not guaranteed, flexible exploitation: from illegalized, seasonal and temporary employment to homework, flex- and temp-work to subcontractors, freelancers or so-called self-employed persons', but 'also extends beyond the world of work to encompass other aspects of intersubjective life, including housing, debt, and the ability to build affective social relations'.[10] Of course, this feature of migrant labour intersects with what many commentators have dubbed the 'feminisation of labour', meaning both the progressive, mass involvement of women in the labour market and the monetary valorisation of capacities that are usually deemed 'feminine' (relational, communicational, affective/emotional/libidinal) in different forms of labour defined as 'immaterial'. Furthermore, as it becomes ever more precarious, labour acquires features (such as flexibility and the extension beyond the traditional boundaries of employment, towards the colonisation of life as a whole) that assimilate it to reproductive labour. In these processes, transnational migrant flows have played a decisive and progressively greater role, and they are themselves characterised by an ever more marked female component worldwide, which is often subjected to heavier forms of blackmail and exploitation.[11]

In such a scenario, 'labour' itself expands beyond the workplace and 'multiplies' (Mezzadra and Neilson 2013). But it also ceases to be the ground upon which the legitimacy of citizenship rights can be built, as used to be the case in welfare-state 'national' capitalism, when social rights of citizenship aimed at guaranteeing the enjoyment by all citizen-workers of civil and political rights on an equal footing (Marshall 1950; Raimondi and Ricciardi 2004; cf. Muehlebach 2012 and Manzano this volume, for slightly different takes that consider regimes of workfare and voluntary labour as the contemporary heirs to the welfare system). Indeed, migration signals a crisis of the labour-citizenship dyad (Raimondi 2011). Thus, struggles concerned with and influenced by migration have naturally taken on wide significance and have acquired novel, creative and diverse forms – from housing occupations to resistance and mobilisations against institutional and everyday racisms, as well as other forms of discrimination; through more properly conceived workers' struggles as struggles against precarity; but also in the myriad acts of defiance or flight that migrants perform and which might escape too narrowly conceived perspectives of political mobilisation – leading to original conceptions of rights, and of right itself.[12]

Given the splintering of labour forms and the widening of precarity anticipated by migration, one of the areas of struggle where the presence of migrants has exerted its influence most prominently is that of housing rights – with particular reference to the city of Rome, where such movements have a long history and where migrants currently play a very significant role, in terms of both numbers and organisational capacity. It was indeed in Rome that one of the very first examples of migrant-led housing occupations took place: in 1990, a group of over 2,000 people squatted the abandoned mill bakery of Pantanella, in the heart of the city. The migrants' occupation came after they had been evicted from several other informal settlements in the wake of the football world cup and the related city-council- and police-led 'sanitisation' campaign. Support from the newly founded United Asian Workers Association was instrumental in securing the success of the occupation. The spaces were organised autonomously by migrants, who installed a mosque, a market and a school in the squat, with the help of Catholic organisation Caritas and of other activists, until their eviction in January 1991.[13] Similarly, in September of the same year in which Pantanella was occupied, North African migrants squatted two buildings in Bologna and subsequently marched across the city in the thousands claiming the right to housing, following a racist attack on one of the makeshift reception centres situated in the working-class neighbourhood of Pilastro (Borghi 2007).[14]

Given this analytical and historical setting, the remainder of this chapter is dedicated to a genealogical re-tracing of some of the most significant episodes that have characterised migrants' struggles in Italy in the last three decades. Through the years, perspectives that consider migration as a central, broad analytical lens for contemporary social movements have coexisted with more narrowly conceived interventions where racism is reckoned in isolation from structural, juridical forms of discrimination, or, even where that is not the case, where discrimination against migrants is not put in relation to the generalisation of a state of precarity. The reflections presented in this chapter are the result of my direct involvement, as a researcher and as an activist, in some such struggles, particularly in those involving migrant agricultural labour, and of elaborations of others' narrations, analyses and experiences. The so-called 'green factory', which employs hundreds of thousands of migrant workers in Italy,[15] has been the stage for significant episodes of struggle and revolt. Indeed, it represents one of the original settings of migrants' struggles, and – also given the wide array of differently focused mobilisations that have been staged through the years, and the impossibility to account for all of them – it will therefore be through this lens that the genealogy of migrant struggles is traced.[16]

Beyond precarity and racism: struggles of migration and social unionism

According to the movement's own historiography, as it can be gathered from oral and written sources, on- and offline, the first recorded anti-racist demonstration in Italy took place in Rome in October 1989, gathering over 200,000 people. The march followed the murder of South African asylum seeker and casual farm worker Jerry Essan Masslo, in August that year, and the wave of emotional and sympathetic reactions to this event. The previous year, Masslo, an anti-apartheid activist, had been denied asylum, which at the time was granted only to citizens of the Eastern bloc. For the second consecutive summer he had found accommodation in an abandoned house with no facilities near the town of Villa Literno, in the Campania region. There, together with other migrants, he toiled for a meagre salary picking tomatoes, and lived in the conditions of extreme precarity that still characterise casual farm labour across the country.

Episodes of overtly violent racism and intimidation (including murder) against these 'foreign bodies' had been recorded in the area since 1986. In addition, local administrations refused to provide any form of assistance to seasonal workers in the wake of the strong opposition from some sectors of the citizenry and political class.[17] This scenario had led migrant agricultural workers in the area to found the first embryo of self-organised unionism, 'Coordinamento delle comunità africane della zona domiziana' (Organisation of African Communities in the Domitian Area), with the support of local activists. They demanded, among other things, the application of the 1986 amnesty for undocumented migrants, as well as housing and healthcare. At the time, casual farm labourers were for the most part undocumented and always worked without a labour contract and social insurance, for well below the minimum wage. The movement was supported by CGIL (Confederazione Generale Italiana del Lavoro), Italy's main union, who organised a three-day anti-racist event in July 1989, and subsequently established information and support centres for migrants in the area, as well as an organisation of migrant workers.

On 24 August, the cycle of racism-inflected violence in the Domitian area culminated in an ambush, during which Masslo and others refused to surrender their money to a commando of hooded and armed men. As a result of his resistance, Jerry Masslo was shot dead and others were wounded. His dual identity – that of an asylum seeker who had been denied legal status, and of a precarious worker without rights – is emblematic of the condition of migrant labour. As an asylum-seeking migrant and a militant anti-racist, Masslo's extreme gesture of resistance also became the symbol of struggles to come.

At the same time, his condition of migrant-labourer, like that of many others in similar situations, was forced into a mould of analysis that considered migrants' predicament as exceptional, rather than recognising it as the vanguard for a generalised precarisation process. Such exceptionality was in turn constrained within another supposed anomaly, that of southern Italy, represented as a place where archaic conditions of backwardness persisted in the present and proliferated through equally anomalous mafia-related violence.[18] In the aftermath of Masslo's death, mobilisations thus prefigured a rift within migrants' struggles that endures into the present. The October anti-racist demonstration was preceded by a much-less publicised and memorialised event: a strike of some 300 (mostly undocumented) African farm labourers against the exploitation they were subjected to by gangmasters and Camorra[19]-affiliated bosses and landowners, in Villa Literno and the surrounding countryside. The appeal that migrant workers launched to fellow Italian workers read thus:

> Our condition as undocumented migrants [*clandestini*] allows dishonest employers and organised crime to use us to endanger the rights that you, Italian workers, were able to conquer ever since the [anti-fascist] Resistance. . . . We, clandestine immigrants, are therefore not willing to be instrumental in eroding your rights. For these reasons we strike today. We ask you to support us in this struggle. We ask this to each and every one of you, to your unions and mass organisations, aware that Italian workers have a great tradition of democratic struggle and solidarity. United we win! (cited in Di Luzio 2006: 80, my translation)

The platform of the strike, organised with the support of CGIL, encompassed a broad set of demands, which included a generalised amnesty for all undocumented migrants and opposition to the government's proposals to implement a quota-system immigration law, the possibility of family reunion, housing, healthcare, education, administrative voting rights, the enlargement of asylum rights to citizens of countries beyond the Soviet bloc, and economic investments for migrants. To some extent, this broad focus could qualify this first migrants' strike as a 'political' and 'social' strike, prefiguring the March 2010 event recalled earlier. The width (and ambiguity) of the claims also derived from the fact that migration governance was still undefined. Looking back at those demands, such initial breadth also signals a regression of stances on immigration on the part of unions and of other sectors of the movement. On the other hand, generic and paternalistic 'anti-racist' attitudes (dealt with as issues of 'integration') already characterised the union's first engagements with the issue, as in the case of the event organised in Villa Literno before Masslo's murder.

Unlike what would happen in years to come, on the occasion of the strike the importance of an alliance between migrant and Italian workers was recognised also by the union and the communist party (then on the verge of dissolution), whose national and local-level representatives took part in the mobilisations of September 1989. However, such acknowledgement remained a mere formality, and migrant workers' appeals largely fell on deaf ears. Subsequent battles for the preservation of certain fundamental workers' rights, such as the 2002 three-million-strong demonstration against the abolition of a clause preventing termination without cause, saw the participation of large numbers of migrant workers. Yet, the same cannot be said of Italian workers in demonstrations for the abolition of immigration laws, and especially of the clause binding work permits to labour contracts (*contratto di soggiorno*, cf. Raimondi and Ricciardi 2004; Ricciardi 2011). At the same time, party and union leaders' indifference towards the migrant condition is also the result of their bureaucratisation – very cynically, one could point out that migrants do not vote.

Furthermore, this lack of initiative towards political composition on the part of unions is inserted in a larger process of progressive *managerialisation* of the unions themselves, that began in the 1970s within broader processes of neoliberal restructuring and found its culmination with the politics of austerity that followed the financial crisis.[20] Large, confederate unions have been reduced to mere service providers, and play an active role in the fragmentation of the labour force as well as in the transformation of the welfare system (cf. De Nicola and Quattrocchi 2014). Indeed, even their (rare but successful) attempts at large-scale mobilisations in recent years betray a non-conflictual understanding of the relationship between labour and capital, which is thought to be solvable through compromise, and a general indifference to the process of precarisation that affects the entire social horizon.

Masslo's death and the reactions it had provoked stirred media attention and public outcry on the issue of migration and of exploitation, and – together with the occupation of Pantanella that was previously mentioned – paved the way to the Italian government's widening of the right to asylum. However, these events also spurred the first systematic attempt to regulate migration, with the Martelli law of 1990, which included a generalised amnesty (the third of a series of eight in Italian history to date). At the time, ample sectors of politics and civil society, including the Communist Party, other parts of the left, but also Catholic figures and organisations, all opposed the Schengen agreements and their insistence on immigration quotas – only to support them a few years later, in 1998, when a centre-left coalition approved the first organic immigration bill with the connivance of CGIL and other major leftist organisations. The law instituted administrative detention and the possibility of forced repatriation for undocumented migrants, and paved the way to subsequent, even more restrictive measures. Such a U-turn also determined the demise of the anti-racist network (Rete antirazzista) that since 1995 had gathered together wide portions of the left and many among the myriad anti-racist organisations scattered across the country. That network had elaborated incisive reflections and an articulate platform of demands on immigration issues that continue to be relevant today, ranging from voting rights to the transfer of jurisdiction from police to local authorities in matters of residency, and a new citizenship law.[21]

Likewise, on the labour front – and specifically as far as agricultural labour is concerned – little, if anything, changed after the murder of Masslo. Also as a consequence of increasingly restrictive immigration rules and of the globalisation/liberalisation of the agricultural economy, conditions worsened for farm labourers, as for workers in most other sectors. Heightened precarity, austerity measures and the growing spectre of racism – on whose instrumental instigation many political movements have founded their success – produced effects of fragmentation, which traditional trade unions and political parties have been unable and unwilling to counter. Migrants' increasing presence within the rank and file of the major unions (and their progressive, if limited, access to leadership roles) has not translated into a rethinking of the forms and contents of labour struggles. Since that first double mobilisation that followed Masslo's death, the cleavage between anti-racist campaigns (often predicated on a humanitarian, ethically based paradigm) on the one hand, and (dwindling) labour struggles, on the other, has continued to cut through many forms of protest and resistance and, even more so, through the way they have often been represented in both mainstream and radical circles.

Indeed, the response of 'traditional' unions and the institutional left to the conditions of extreme precarity that characterise migrant agricultural labour highlight their paternalistic stance concerning migration in general. Ever since the summer of 1989, they have actively promoted a model of intervention based on the notion of '*accoglienza*' (roughly translatable as 'sheltering' or 'reception') that adopts a humanitarian stance, favouring the institution of emergency labour camps.[22] Migrants are generally not treated as workers entitled to housing and transport facilities as per collective agreements, but as foreign bodies and lives to be managed according to special measures that symbolically confine them to a domain of 'bare life'.[23] This precludes their access to citizenship rights, whilst promoting their differential inclusion through *dispositifs* that manage and pace their mobility and enforce their isolation, thus playing into the current system of economic governance.

Since those first instances in 1989, significant episodes of struggle have seen migrant farm labourers mobilise across the last three decades, and particularly in the last ten years – starting from the riots that took place in Rosarno (Calabria) and Castel Volturno (Campania) between 2008 and 2014. In Rosarno, a small town whose economy revolves around the cultivation of citrus and thus the employment of migrant labour, African workers revolted twice, in 2008 and 2010, to protest against racist aggressions and unbearable living and working conditions. In Castel Volturno, possibly the Italian town with the highest percentage of migrants, a peculiar form of struggle was also organised in 2010, dubbed the '*kalifoo ground*' strike, after the African workers' expression that indicates the roundabouts where they usually wait for employers to hire them for the day. On that occasion, workers bore banners saying 'Today I will not work for less than 50 euros' (cf. Caruso 2015). In 2011, a self-organised strike that lasted for over two weeks saw around 400 African farm workers demand better working conditions in Nardò, Apulia (cf. Brigate di Solidarietà Attiva *et al.* 2012). Following the second revolt in Rosarno, that echoed greatly across the country and worldwide, several of those who had taken part in the events were deported to Rome by the Ministry of Interior, and left to their own devices, whilst many others were detained and/or deported to their countries of origin. There, together with activists, many of whom were members of the squat that had hosted the migrants, they initiated an assembly process that led to further mobilisations, after which all the migrants obtained permits of stay on the basis of the conditions of severe exploitation they experienced when working in Rosarno as citrus pickers. This represented an important victory, particularly as it entailed the state's recognition of exploitation as valid ground for the acquisition of legal status.

Such episodes, and especially the revolt in Rosarno, the subsequent period of self-organised struggle, and the strike in Nardò, led several individuals and groups of activists to embark on a project aimed at supporting the mobilisations and claims of migrant farm workers across different agro-industrial areas of Italy. Since 2012, this network of activists and workers has progressively grown. From activities such as language classes, legal support, bike repair workshops, a pirate radio, that took place in the shantytowns, camps and other dwellings where workers live, we have come to organise a series of demonstrations and obtain the regularisation of some of the workers, denouncing police authorities and local institutions for their arbitrary and restrictive application of immigration laws. Furthermore, through such forms of engagement migrants and activists could uncover the economic interests underlying the management of migrant bodies and lives through camps of various kinds in different agro-industrial districts, and seek alliances at various levels along the food commodity chain. At the same time, through years of activity in the field together with workers, the members of the network have gathered significant knowledge and experience both on immigration laws and their application, and on the organisation and regulation of agricultural labour and agro-industrial chains, which constitute the precondition for any form of struggle.[24]

Calls to humanity and its frontiers

In all these instances, it was never through unions or parties, but despite them, that migrant workers were able to self-organise and mobilise. Despite the role of the institutional left and its union in consolidating a generalised regime of precarity, and their insistence on an obsolete paradigm of citizenship rights together with the parallel neglect of migration-related issues, the significant episodes of revolt and mobilisation that have occurred in the agricultural sector point to a different conception of the notion of strike and of unionism, and to an unsuppressable demand for freedom and equality. For ever since that first strike back in 1989, and through the numerous subsequent episodes of struggle that have occurred in the Italian green factory as elsewhere, the claims of migrant workers and of some of their allies moved towards two directions: first, they simultaneously addressed the productive and reproductive components of existence, anticipating what has recently been dubbed a 'social strike'.[25] Second, their struggle for substantive rights manifested as a peremptory claim to recognition as human, which at the same time implies the redefinition of what humanity is about.

Those acts of dissent highlighted how precarity, to which migrants working in agriculture are perhaps most exposed, shatters the confines between labour and life, making of sociality the very terrain of struggle. Indeed, those activists that supported the 2011 Nardò strike, and that had been engaged in forms of solidarity and mutualism with workers since 2010, identified these practices as acting in the sphere of *social reproduction*, through cooperation and self-organisation (against conflict-by-proxy cultures). At the same time, struggles and forms of solidarity in the reproductive domain were understood to foster direct conflict in the sphere of production (Nigro 2012, citing Ferraris). Even episodes of spontaneous revolt, such as occurred in Rosarno in 2008 and 2010, acquired the character of a *strike* in participants' own understanding and in their dynamics. They were moments of refusal of work in the strict sense of the term, but at the same time they represented a forceful rejection of social invisibility, physical vulnerability and marginality, the claiming of a desire and a right to proper housing, to a social and an affective life – in short, to what migrants *themselves* called *humanity* and pitted against their treatment as 'animals'. More than labour, civil, social or political rights, it is in the language of human-ness (and against a de-humanising humanitarianism that projects migrants as needy, vulnerable and passive) that many migrants frame their demands.

This realisation leads us to the second thread underlying such acts of protest: the reclaiming of the *right to have rights* (Arendt 1958: 296), which several scholars have identified with the right to belong to humanity, to a common world of equals that must be perennially reinstated through a politics of dissidence (Balibar 2000, 2014; Butler 2004). In Rosarno, as in Castel Volturno or in Genoa (where one of the first spontaneous riots erupted in the summer of 1993 against racist attacks), and across the many detention centres scattered throughout Italy – that is, in all those instances in which revolt followed a life threat against a migrant or their bodily confinement and hence *de facto* deprivation of life – the claim for recognition of a common humanity through the exercise of forceful dissent was made through the acknowledgement of vulnerability as structuring each and every subject, regardless of their citizenship, skin colour, origin and background. By threatening citizens and attacking their property, by sewing their lips, going on hunger strike, burning the scanty furniture in their cells, migrants reminded their opponents – guards, police, citizens – of their common humanity. The result was at least the temporary cessation of physical attacks against them (in Rosarno, Castel Volturno or Genoa) and the closure of some detention facilities.

Judith Butler (2004, ch. 2, *passim*) has defined the unrecognised vulnerability of certain categories of humans in terms of 'precariousness', which, unlike its cognate term, precarity, designates that fundamental characteristic of bodies as socially constituted, exposed and attached to others. For Butler, recognising such vulnerability and mourning the injury that may result from it is precisely a step towards 'an insurrection at the level of ontology' (2004: 33) that would return 'the Other' to the sign of the human from which it is excluded. Yet, in the cases considered here this was obtained not through a 'peaceful' act of mourning performed by the dominant group, by public opinion or by civil society, as Butler implies, but through acts of physical threat enacted by those Others in response to repeated attacks. Indeed, it might be argued that the only real means for excluded groups to have their humanity restored or affirmed is precisely to enact their political subjectivation: they cannot be made into passive recipients of a dominant subject's act of concession. Furthermore, beyond the plane of violence and the recognition it allowed, in all cases cited above riots gave rise to longer-term political projects, in the forms of associations, collectives and assemblies that gathered citizens and migrants, and led to forms of social struggle in the broad sense of the term, through practices of mutualism, solidarity and conflict. These acts, thus, are not simply about recognition, but rather they represent forms of active re-appropriation, indeed of enlargement and re-definition of the very meaning of humanity.

In conclusion, by briefly overviewing the struggles of migrants and migration in the last three decades, with a special focus on the plight of those who populate agro-industrial districts, we can appreciate their creative force *vis-à-vis* radical social struggles more generally. Not only did migrants' (and migration) struggles bring the issue of labour back within the militant picture, from where it had progressively disappeared, defeated by processes of large-scale restructuring and backlash against workers' hard-won conquests, against which traditional leftist organisations mainly showed impotence. They also highlighted how labour itself needed to be rethought as a category of critique and resistance, prefiguring forms of social struggle that were later to be generalised to the whole field of precarious work and life. Furthermore, rather than reclaiming an obsolete set of citizenship rights, by calling to humanity, those struggles point to the need of overcoming such a framework. Whether the domain of the human proves a sufficiently powerful weapon in the struggle for social justice remains to be seen, but migrants' mobilisations have certainly played a crucial role in keeping that struggle alive.

Notes

1 I would like to thank all those who contributed to bring forth and support the struggles, of which a very partial account is given here, and to subsequently gather the knowledge that went into writing this piece. I am grateful to Sian Lazar, Sandro Mezzadra and Veronica Padoan for reading and commenting on an earlier draft, and to Dario Fontana for bibliographic suggestions. To Sandro Mezzadra I owe thanks also for providing crucial information and guidance on the subject of this piece.

2 For an analysis of Italian specificities in relation to the Occupy and anti-austerity movements, see Zamponi, L. 2014. 'Pre-Occupied and Dis-Occupied: Italian Movements and the Challenges of Anti-Austerity Protests', as part of *Dis-Occupi Researchers Studying Europe's Exploding Social Movements*. Available online at http://councilforeuropeanstudies.org/critcom/enough-dispatches-from-researchers-studying-europes-exploding-social-movements-3/, accessed 25 September 2015.

3 I am using the term 'spectacle' in the sense in which De Genova (2002, 2013) has used Debord's famous notion to analyse how border enforcement is staged, masking the fact of migrants' inclusion as exploited labour force. For a specifically situated analysis of these mechanisms in the Italian context, with particular reference to the island of Lampedusa, see Cuttitta (2012). For a critical appraisal of the discourse on migration and crisis, see De Genova and Tazzioli (eds) 'Europe / Crisis: New Keywords of "the Crisis" in and of "Europe"' (forthcoming in *Europe at a Crossroads, Near Futures online*, January 2016, Zone Books); and cf. also interventions on the *Focaal Journal* blog: http://www.focaalblog.com/tag/refugee-crisis/, accessed 12 January 2016.

4 A key entry point into Europe, given its geographical position within the Schengen area, Italy also features a large informal economy and a certain 'tolerance' towards the presence of undocumented migrants. It is also a country where immigration began in large

numbers much later than in northern Europe – only in the 1980s and in the absence of a clear juridical framework regulating it – with a long history of emigration and of internal migration. Furthermore, soon after its unification in the late nineteenth century Italy set out to become a colonial power, whose historical span partly overlapped with fascist rule and its implementation of racial laws. The elaboration of the impact and legacy of these processes (together with that of experiences of emigration and of racism against southerners, and against Italian migrants in general) remains controversial and keeps haunting the present. On the other hand, Italy also bred a fertile ground for labour and student movements in the 1960s and 1970s, genealogically related to anti-fascist resistance, whose influence on radical social-movement politics persists until the present day.

5 Between 1989 and 2013, roughly the two ends of the historical spectrum considered here, the migrant population in Italy has risen from approximately 1 million to 5.9 million individuals, growing from 0.9 per cent to about 8.2 per cent of the total population. These figures, that seek to account for undocumented presences as well (which would currently amount to around 300 to 500 thousand), are of course approximate, but nonetheless they give a sense of the scope of this demographic shift (cf. Centro Studi e Ricerche IDOS 2015 and G. Papavero 2015, 'Sbarchi, richiedenti asilo e presenze irregolari', available online at www.ismu.org/wp-content/uploads/2015/03/Report-1-G.-Papavero-16.02.pdf, accessed 12 January 2016).

6 Cf. Mezzadra, S. 2014. 'L'Italia e vent'anni di fenomeno migratorio', talk delivered as part of a series of seminars titled *Autoformazione – Rivoluzione!*, organised by Network Antagonista Piacentino, 21 December. Available online at www.youtube.com/watch?v=-Ncow9iTU-Y, accessed 14 January 2015.

7 Indeed, many migrants in Italy are not aware of the existence of detention centres, which were partly dismantled as a consequence of the revolts that erupted inside them. Generally, a permit is regarded as desirable not only, or not so much, to avoid deportation (which in Italy affects relatively low numbers of undocumented migrants if compared to other European countries: in 2014, they were 15,726, around half of those undocumented migrants intercepted by authorities, according to official estimates, cf. Centro Studi e Ricerche IDOS 2015) but for the possibilities it affords in terms of labour, housing and, more generally, of access to services.

8 http://primomarzo2010.blogspot.it/2009/10/chi-siamo.html, my translation. The strike was inspired in part by the 2006 May-Day migrants' strike in the US, and related to similar initiatives in other European countries.

9 www.fluechtlingsrat-hamburg.de/content/TheFrassanit%20Network_Mai06.pdf, accessed 20 January 2015, emphasis in the original.

10 Neilson and Rossiter 2005, http://five.fibreculturejournal.org/fcj-022-from-precarity-to-precariousness-and-back-again-labour-life-and-unstable-networks/.

11 Ibid.

12 To be sure, current forms of social mobilisation on this terrain are not devoid of internal conflicts either. If in some sectors of the Italian social-movement scene contemporary struggles are explicitly referred to as 'meticce' (mixed, *mestiza*), on account of their power of composition across racial-national divisions (and thus seeking to overcome any distinction between 'migrants' and 'locals'), others critique such outlook for its flattening of the very real cleavages (of class, race, gender, citizenship status) among different

components of the movement, and of the consequent need to contrast them in their specificities and conflicts (cf. www. connessioniprecarie.org/2013/11/18/lapoteosi-del-meticciato/, accessed 12 January 2016). Furthermore, issues of representation and paternalism keep resurfacing in many instances.

13 See www.youtube.com/watch?v=aR62UXhhyRU, accessed 19 January 2015 (where the issue of racism clearly comes to the fore, with images of the eviction showing a North African migrant shouting all his rage and frustration against 'racists'), and the 1993 novel *Pantanella: Canto lungo la strada*, written Tunisian author Moshen Melliti.

14 See also http://ricerca.repubblica.it/repubblica/archivio/repubblica/1990/09/21/molotov-contro-neri.html, accessed 19 January 2015.

15 According to the national institute for social insurance (INPS), in 2013 around 400,000 foreign-born agricultural workers were employed in Italy (cf. Centro Studi e Ricerche IDOS 2015). However, given the high degree of irregularity in this sector, figures have to be taken cautiously and generally considered as underestimated by at least 25 per cent (cf. ISFOL 2012).

16 For reasons of space, here I cannot account for the very significant and often successful cycle of struggles in the logistics sector, which since 2008 has seen mainly immigrant workers mobilise to see an improvement of their working conditions, but also articulate their struggle to broader social movements. For a collection of accounts by some of the protagonists of these struggles in Bologna, see Massarelli (2014).

17 For a detailed account of Jerry Essan Masslo's story and subsequent developments after his death, cf. Di Luzio (2006).

18 Elsewhere, I have elaborated on the 'normal exceptionality' of such conditions and their relations to contemporary forms of governance (cf. Peano 2016). On the contrary, exceptionalist analyses of the condition of migrant agricultural labour and of southern Italian agriculture more generally persist into the present (see, for example, the synthesis of a report published in Centro Studi e Ricerche IDOS 2015).

19 The term Camorra is commonly employed to designate the organised cartels that originated in the region of Naples and currently manage well-established, illicit business networks across the globe.

20 However, a mediating tendency was arguably latent in the bureaucratic structure of the union since its foundations (cf. Balestrini and Moroni 1986).

21 The experience of the anti-racist network has been partly reconstructed in an article by Moreno Biagioni, titled 'Un'esperienza significativa: La ricostruzione dell'esperienza, oggi dimenticata della Rete Nazionale Antirazzista' that appeared in 2007 in the journal *Guerra e Pace*, available at: https://sergiobontempelli.wordpress.com/2008/03/31/dieci-anni-fa-la-rete-nazionale-antirazzista-di-moreno-biagioni/, accessed 21 January 2015. For the anti-racist network's platform of demands, see also www.tightrope.it/galleria/pellilli/Antirz31.htm.

22 Instances are numerous and have kept multiplying through the years. For a (sympathetic) account of the institution of such camps in the region of Villa Literno and in Apulia, following the murder of Jerry Masslo, see Di Luzio (2006). For a systematic, critical account of more recent instances of such emergency-based humanitarian policies, and of struggles against them, see Peano (2016).

23 Giorgio Agamben's (1998) notion of bare life – the biological life of those who are included in the political

community by way of their exclusion, reduced to merely biological beings – has been subjected to thorough scrutiny and critique (which I partly address in another piece). Whilst not totally in agreement with his take on sovereignty, I nonetheless think that it constitutes useful imagery to represent a subjectivity deprived of (social, political, civil) citizenship rights.

24 See campagneinlotta.org, and articles published in other fora: Rete Campagne in Lotta, 'Dai campi di raccolta all'EXPO: Contro la filiera dei padroni del cibo', www.zeroviolenza. it/editoriali/item/72130-dai-campi-di-raccolta-allexpo-contro-la-filiera-dei-padroni-del-cibo; Rete Campagne in Lotta 2015, 'Filiera e autorganizzazione', in Potito, M., Borghesi, R., Casna, S. and Lapini, M., *Genuino clandestino: Viaggio tra le agri-culture resistenti ai tempi delle grandi opera*, Florence: Terra Nuova Edizioni; Rete Campagne in Lotta 2014. 'Rosarno, tre anni dopo: Dentro e oltre lo stato d'eccezione permanente', *Lo straniero* 158/159; Collettivo RicercAzione, 'Migrant Workers' Struggles, Their Composition and Facilitation in Italy, http://collettivoricercazione. noblogs.org/post/2013/11/27/ migrant-workers-struggles-their-composition-and-facilitation-in-italy/; Collettivo RicercAzione, 'Ricerca per la composizione, oltre il precariato e l'isolamento', http://collettivoricercazione. noblogs.org/post/2013/11/27/ricerca-per-la-composizione-oltre-il-precariato-e-lisolamento/; Collettivo RicercAzione, 'Collective Militant Research: Building on the Experience of a Volunteer Camp with Migrant Workers in Southern Italy', http://collettivoricercazione.noblogs. org/post/2013/01/30/collective-militant-rcollective-militant-research-building-on-the-experience-of-a-volunteer-camp-with-migrant-workers-in-southern-italy/; Attiviste e attivisti del campo 'Io ci sto', 2012, 'Radio Ghetto', *Gli Asini*, 3(11): 96–102.

25 Cf. http://scioperosociale. it/ (the first self-consciously named 'social strike' was proclaimed in Italy in November 2014; for accounts of 'social unionism', cf. De Nicola and Quattrocchi 2014; Moody 1997).

References

Agamben, G. (1998) *Homo sacer: Sovereign Power and Bare Life*, Stanford, CA: Stanford University Press.

Arendt, H. (1958) *The Origins of Ttotalitarianism*, Cleveland, OH: Meridian Books.

Balestrini, N. and Moroni, P. (2003). *L'orda d'oro: 1968–1977*, Milan: Feltrinelli.

Balibar, E. (2000) 'What We Owe to the Sans Papiers', in Guenther, L. and Heesters, H. (eds) *Social Insecurity*, pp. 42–43. Toronto: Anansi.

Balibar, E. (2014) *Equaliberty: Political Essays*, Durham, NC: Duke University Press.

Borghi, P. (2007) 'Immigrazione e partecipazione sociopolitica nei contesti locali: Dalla "voice" alla rappresentanza', in Grandi, F. and Tanzi, E. (eds) *La città meticcia: riflessioni teoriche e analisi di alcuni casi europei per il governo locale delle migrazioni*, pp. 83–101. Milan: Franco Angeli.

Brigate di Solidarietà Attiva *et al.* (2012) *Sulla pelle viva. Nardò: la lotta autorganizzata dei braccianti immigrati*, Rome: DeriveApprodi.

Butler, J. (2004) *Precarious Life: The Powers of Mourning and Violence*, London and New York: Verso Books.

Caruso, F. (2015) *La politica dei subalterni: Organizzazione e lotte del bracciantato migrante nel Sud Europa*, Rome: DeriveApprodi.

Centro Studi e Ricerche IDOS (2015) *Dossier statistico immigrazione 2015*, Rome: Centro Studi e Ricerche IDOS/ Immigrazione Dossier Statistico.

Cobbe, L. and Grappi, G. (2011) 'Primo marzo, percorsi di uno sciopero inatteso', in Mometti, F. and Ricciardi, M. (eds) *La normale eccezione. Lotte migranti in Italia: La gru di Brescia, lo sciopero del primo marzo, la tendopoli di Manduria*, pp. 55–90. Rome: Edizioni Alegre.

Cuttitta, P. (2012) *Lo spettacolo del confine: Lampedusa tra produzione e messa in scena della frontiera*, Milan: Mimesis.

De Genova, N. (2002) 'Migrant "Illegality" and Deportability in Everyday Life', *Annual Review of Anthropology*, 31: 419–447.

De Genova, N. (2013) 'Spectacles of Migrant "Illegality": The Scene of Exclusion, the Obscene of Inclusion', *Ethnic and Racial Studies*, 36(7): 1180–1198.

De Nicola, A. and Quattrocchi, B. (2014) 'La torsione neoliberale del sindacato tradizionale e l'immaginazione del "sindacalismo sociale": appunti per una discussione', www.euronomade. info/?p=2482, accessed 21 January 2015.

Di Luzio, G. (2006) *A un passo dal sogno: Gli avvenimenti che hanno cambiato la storia dell'immigrazione in Italia*, Nardò: BESA Editrice.

ISFOL (2012) *Dimensioni e caratteristiche del lavoro sommerso/irregolare in agricoltura*, http://isfoloa.isfol. it/bitstream/123456789/120/1/ Iadevaia_Mainardi_ Lavoro%20sommerso.pdf, accessed 10 January 2015.

Marshall, T. (1950) *Citizenship and Social Class, and Other Essays*, Cambridge: Cambridge University Press.

Massarelli, F. (2014) *Scarichiamo i padroni: Lo sciopero dei facchini a Bologna*, Milan: Agenzia X.

Mellino, M. (2013) 'Migrazioni, razza e cittadinanze postcoloniali', in Mezzadra, S. and Ricciardi, M. (eds) *Movimenti indisciplinati: Migrazioni, migranti e discipline scientifiche*, pp. 166–191. Verona: Ombre Corte.

Melliti, M. (1993) *Pantanella: Canto lungo la strada*, Rome: Edizioni Lavoro.

Mezzadra, S. and Neilson, B. (2013) *Border as Method, or, the Multiplication of Labour*, Durham, NC: Duke University Press.

Moody, K. (1997) 'Towards an International Social-Movement Unionism', *New Left Review*, 1(225): 52–72.

Muehlebach, A. (2012) *The Moral Neoliberal: Welfare and Citizenship in Contemporary Italy*, Chicago, IL: University of Chicago Press.

Nigro, G. (2012) 'Lavori in corso: Pratiche e idee per la liberazione del lavoro migrante', in Brigate di Solidarietà Attiva *et al. Sulla pelle viva. Nardò: la lotta autorganizzata dei braccianti immigrati*, pp. 76–100. Rome: DeriveApprodi.

Papastergiadis, N. (2000) *The Turbulence of Migration: Globalisation, Deterritorialisation, Hybridity*, Oxford: Blackwell.

Peano, I. (2016) 'Emergenc(i)es in the Fields: Affective Composition and Counter-camps against the Exploitation of Migrant Farm Labour in Italy', in Alexandrakis, O. (ed.) *Impulse to Act: A New Anthropology of Resistance and Social Justice*, pp. 63–88. Bloomington, IN: Indiana University Press.

Raimondi, F. (2011) 'Migranti e sindacato: Tra sciopero e cittadinanza', *Outis!*, 1: 183–203.

Raimondi, F. and M. Ricciardi (2004) 'Introduzione', in Raimondi, F. and Ricciardi, M. (eds) *Lavoro migrante: Esperienza e prospettiva*, pp. 5–21. Rome: DeriveApprodi.

5 | THE SPANISH CRISIS: FROM COMPLACENCY TO UNREST, FROM UNREST TO MOBILISATION

Salvador Martí i Puig and Marco Aparicio Wilhelmi

Translated by Patrick O'Hare

Spain underwent profound change between the death of General Franco in 1975 and the beginning of the twenty-first century. For three decades, Spain appeared in the international arena as an example of successful transition towards – and consolidation of – democracy and economic development. From the 1980s until the 2007 crisis, the economy modernised, whilst at the same time receiving huge sums of money from the European Union Cohesion Fund. At a political level, the state consolidated a set of institutions appropriate for a liberal representative democracy and undertook a process of territorial decentralisation, while citizens generally supported democratisation.

Yet following the financial crisis of 2008, the Spanish economy collapsed. Unemployment increased exponentially, the building industry disintegrated, business and personal loans contracted and inequality rapidly increased.

Two relevant phenomena emerged in the face of this debacle. The first was the immediate promulgation by the government of laws that restricted rights and instigated neoliberal policies that affected the most vulnerable; the second was the weakness of Spanish society's response during the first years of the crisis.

With a few exceptions, it was not until 2011 that social discontent was made manifest in an event that acted as a watershed moment for a new cycle of social and political mobilisation. We are referring here to the episode that began on 15 May (henceforth known as 15M), involving a huge citizens' protest in Madrid and then across the country, against the political class, the economic situation and the functioning of a democracy now regarded as neither young nor particularly successful.

The event took people by surprise with the publicity it generated and the support it received from the population. Statistics from the Centre for Sociological Research (CIS) indicate that 15M was keenly followed by a majority of citizens, with over 70 per cent viewing it positively (CIS 2011). There was, following 15M, a sudden outburst of social mobilisation against budget cuts, and an accelerated discrediting of the ruling political system and its main actors, especially the mainstream parties – the Partido Popular (Popular Party, PP), the Partido Socialista Obrero Español (Spanish Socialist Workers Party, PSOE), Izquierda Unida (Unified Left) and the Catalan nationalists of the centre-right Convergencia i Unió (Convergence and Union, CiU) – and the two main trade union federations: the socialist Union General de Trabajadores (General Union of Workers, UGT) and the communist Comisiones Obreras (Workers Commissions, CCOO).

How can we interpret this episode? The task certainly isn't easy. Nevertheless, we shall attempt an interpretation in the following pages. In the first instance, we shall refer to the situation of young people in Spain: their expectations and attitudes during the last decade. Second, we will highlight the already existing protest movements and how these converged in the protests of the *indignados* on 15M. We will also analyse the demands of the 15M movement, as well as its organisation, structure and repertoire of collective action. Third, we will attempt to draw out the consequences and impact of 15M on the elections that took place several days later (on 22 May 2011) and on the cycle of protests and social conflict that began at the end of 2011 and lasted until 2014. Finally, the text concludes by referring to how, during this 'short' period (2007–2015), Spanish citizens appear to have reconfigured their political preferences, losing faith in traditional parties and beginning to support new formations that demand a regeneration of the political system that was first born at the end of the 1970s upon the death of Franco.

Young people in the country of the *nouveaux riches*: from NEETs to futureless youth

The expansion and growth experienced by the Spanish economy for three decades generated a certain – albeit precarious – social cohesion, as well as a general feeling that Spain was comfortably seated aboard the train of first world development.

And yet not everything was in order. Aside from the money the political class frittered away on events like sporting championships, and unnecessary and sometimes sumptuous infrastructure projects, there were two elements that represented a painful Achilles' heel in the Spanish economy: burgeoning personal debt and an unemployment level double the European average. Unemployment particularly affected the young, who were frequently stigmatised with different and often contradictory epithets, such as hedonists, lazy and consumers – at the same time as representing the most educated generation in the history of the country.

What was beyond doubt was that the economy showed little capacity to absorb these young people into the labour market, and it offered them few incentives to improve their abilities and skills. We should also mention here the precarity of many jobs whose conditions were possible only due to the existence of the large reserve army of an immigrant workforce, both legal and clandestine. Many young people were not prepared to work for low wages and did not move from their native cities where they could benefit from the comforts of the family home. The phenomenon, which became known as the NEETs (young people Neither in Employment, Education or Training), was based on youngsters' tendency to ignore the 'striving' discourse preached by authorities and parents, which denied them space to develop themselves, responsibilities to assume and, very often, examples to follow.

In this context, a particularly incisive and iconoclastic singer-songwriter called Albert Pla composed a song called 'Sunburn' in which he highlighted the attitude held by a section of young people for whom society was unattractive. The song lyrics read:

Sat senselessly/ in the porch facing the sun/ we're nobodies and have nothing/ just the sun and the porch/ without obligations, ambitions or interests/ without anything to do/ nor anything to win or lose/ we're just fine here . . . without qualifications or jobs/ we're like lizards/ neither cowardly nor brave/ nor revolutionary/ we're mute and a little deaf/ and although we know/ who the guilty ones are/ we shut our mouths/ and give thanks because we are here/ caring about nothing/ sunning ourselves.

Without going into the declamatory aspects of the song, it isn't true that the majority of young people were apathetic and 'cared about nothing'. What can be affirmed, however, is that they did not care about conventional politics. Surveys of young people offer a clear picture: abstentions in elections reached 60 per cent; activism in trade unions and political parties was amongst the lowest in Europe; and trust in politicians, the government, parliament and the justice system was almost null (Vallés 2010).

Why did politics enjoy such a bad reputation among the young? Fundamentally, there were three reasons. First, the disappearance of the aura of commitment and heroism surrounding the activity of politics during the late Franco era and the transition. Second, the persistence of a long-term political culture that distrusted political actors and institutions and encouraged passivity, despite calling itself democratic. Finally, an institutional architecture and electoral system that favoured bipartisan politics and safeguarded party organisations, generating a political class distanced from its members and electorate and tying public bodies to political parties, creating a sensation of political clientelism and abuse of power (Colomer 2008). It was not only parties and institutions that had a bad reputation but the two mainstream trade unions as well, perceived as organisations reluctant to confront economic and institutional power due to their enjoyment of corporate privilege; protective of those already in the labour market; and unable to voice the demands of unemployed or precariously-employed youth.

The 'unexpected' crisis and the emergence of unrest

The year 2007 saw the appearance in Spain of a previously taboo word: crisis. The alarm was raised shortly after, and the 'Spanish miracle' collapsed like a house of cards. The economy shuddered to a halt, budget and wage cuts loomed, and unemployment reached 21 per cent, with youth unemployment at over 43 per cent, according to OECD figures. In this context a young woman explained to the political authorities present at an academic forum in Madrid that Spanish graduates had three options after obtaining their degree: to leave by land, sea or air.

The Spanish case was not, however, an isolated one. Iceland, Ireland, Greece and Portugal had previously experienced the rigor of fiscal management during financial crises and had taken to the streets. In Portugal, on 12 March 2011, 300,000 young people demonstrated in Lisbon under the banner of the 'troubled generation' to denounce their unhappiness with the measures taken in response to the crisis and complain that they had been made to pay for it. In Greece, from the first structural adjustment measure implemented in 2008, harsh clashes periodically broke out between demonstrators and police. Despite the different context, it is also important to point out that the 'Arab Spring' also had a notable symbolic impact on various activist collectives. The protests against autocratic regimes organised by the 'Rai-Rap generation' in Tunisia and Egypt, who were educated on Facebook and led by young 'hacktivist' leaders, galvanised activists on the opposite shores of the Mediterranean.

These events encouraged and invigorated various activist collectives already present in Spanish cities, collectives that, though small, were relevant and active long before 15M. Among them it is important to highlight the *V por Vivienda* (H for Housing) movement and the *Plataforma de Afectados por la Hipoteca* (Platform for those Affected by Mortgages, PAH), who fight for a right to dignified housing; the Youth Without a Future collective, which rose up against precarity and the commercialisation of education; the protests in Catalonia against austerity policies in health and education introduced by the autonomous Catalan government (under the slogan, *Prouretallades* – Enough Cuts!); and the *No los Votes* (Don't Vote for Them) and Real Democracy Now movements, which proclaimed their rejection of the traditional parties.

The official response to the crisis

Since the financial crisis exploded in Spain in 2008, the management of it by representatives of the national government – firstly the PSOE and then PP – involved a severe restriction of rights. The set of legislative reforms carried out from then until the present has indiscriminately affected a plethora of rights.

Different reforms, starting with labour, education and sanitary reforms, were approved in Spain through the law-decree formula. That is a norm with the weight of a law but which is approved by the government as an 'extraordinary and urgently needed measure', allowing it – at least in the first instance – to avoid parliamentary debate. From 30 December 2011, the date on which the first law-decree was approved by the recently appointed government, until 2013, almost four law-decrees were approved per month, reaching a total of 19. They all substantially restricted a good number of constitutionally recognised rights. The reforms have demonstrated in a very practical way the fragility of all existing rights in Spain.

The restriction of the substance of rights began in January 2012, by way of a labour reform that, amongst other things, reduced compensation for unlawful dismissal, broadened the scope of lawful dismissal, removed red tape from the regulation of employment, allowed private agencies to act as recruitment agents, prioritised business contracts over collective bargaining agreements and even allowed businesses in difficulties not to comply with collective bargaining agreements.

This intense restriction in the scope of workplace rights was immediately accompanied by reforms that affected the right to education and public health. With regard to health, the universal nature of access to the public health system was broken by introducing – once again through a law-decree – 'insurance' and tying it more tightly to labour market participation (and other conditions). The reform also excluded undocumented migrants from access to free healthcare, with the exception of emergencies and the treatment of children and pregnant women. In the field of education, the reforms undertaken from 2012 onwards placed Spain amongst the countries that have most curtailed education funding, leading to a reduction in teaching staff and the clear precarisation of labour conditions, through pay freezes, the suppression of overtime, increase in teaching hours, the effective elimination of support for special needs, larger class sizes and an aging teaching staff. See Compton in this volume for a discussion of similar processes in the UK and Mexico.

Measures restricting economic and social rights have not gone unaccompanied. We might also mention the reform of the penal code in which the scope of public order offences was expanded, with clear consequences for the right to assemble and protest, as well as for freedom of expression.

Without doubt, it is the Law of Citizen Security – passed in 2015 and nicknamed 'the gagging law' – that has most curtailed the exercise of rights linked to protest. The new law legalises the so-called 'hot handovers', that is to say, the rejection of immigrants (or potential asylum seekers) at the border with Morocco without due process; and it increases the maximum fine to 30,000 euros for 'disturbing citizen security' in unplanned protests, serious street disorder or the obstruction of authorities in the exercise of their administrative or judicial duties, a measure thought up to target actions taken against evictions, promoted by PAH. The same sanction applies to cases of civil disobedience, and refusing to disband meetings or demonstrations or to identify oneself.

The reforms have also meant an erosion of many other interdependent rights that have been restricted in the current climate: the right to dignified housing is still measured by the ability to access the market through rents, which remain high, or through mortgage loans, which, following the crisis, have been reduced to an almost anecdotal level. The Spanish Youth Council estimates that in the case of rent, under-thirties are having to spend an average of 47.4 per cent of their salaries to be able to access a home, with the figure rising to over 70 per cent in some regions.

The impact of the financial crisis has also meant that many mortgage holders who have lost their jobs have also been evicted from their homes after foreclosure. This has occurred in the context of mortgage legislation that allows banks to repossess homes while also continuing as creditors of existing debts. This debt is the result of subtracting *current* house prices from loans, prices much lower than those originally paid. As a result, another right has been affected: the property rights of thousands of people who took out investments under fraudulent circumstances, such as preferential rates and other financial products launched by the banks in search of liquidity.

It is thus clear to see that the authorities' crisis management has been centred on a wholesale restriction of rights. This link is especially clear in the case of rights that were traditionally weak in Spain, such as social, economic and cultural rights. But it is even clearer in the case of weak subjects. Such is the situation of immigrants, whose rights are in a permanent state of constitutional precarity. It should nevertheless be pointed out that the constitutional weakness of immigrants is not a product of the crisis but rather has been coterminous with the construction of the entire social and economic model that entered into crisis in 2007. Faced with such a situation, instead of helping to challenge this state of juridical precarity, the response has rather gone in the opposite direction, that of deepening social and juridical inequality, especially with regard to undocumented immigrants and asylum seekers.

The 15M movement and the *indignados*

In this context of crisis and attacks on rights, something took place on 15 May 2011 that caught people's attention. On this day, the Real Democracy Now collective organised a demonstration in the city centre, which was met with repression on the part of authorities. This was nothing new in Madrid. However, the reaction of many citizens was to join the protest, gathering within a few hours in the epicentre of the city: the Plaza del Sol. This mobilisation was the start of one of the most important demonstrations in Spain's recent history: the 15M of the *indignados*. Scholars attempting to find out why people rebel have asked why *at a given moment* people shout, protest and take on power. There is no easy answer. However, in seeking a response to the question of why Spanish citizens mobilised massively on the last two weeks of May of 2011 (not before or after), it is helpful to turn to the social movement theorist Sidney Tarrow.

Tarrow (1997) argues that the 'when' to a large degree explains the 'why' and the 'how'. This refers to the conjuncture that facilitates the emergence of movements: it is this conjuncture that theorists refer to as the 'structure of political opportunity' (henceforth SPO). SPO refers to the consistent, though not necessarily formal or permanent, dimensions of the political environment that foment or discourage collective action. In this way, the SPO concept emphasises the resources outside the group that reduce the costs of collective action, highlight allies and reveal the vulnerable points of authorities. Following this line of argument, it could be argued that 15M occurred because elections were to take place three days later on 22 May 2011 – elections to choose the local authorities throughout Spain and autonomous authorities in 13 out of 17 Autonomous Communities.

What was the relation between the imminent elections and the dynamics of the 15M mobilisations? They possibly inhibited the authorities from using security forces to break up the demonstrations, leading citizens to conclude that taking to the streets to express their unhappiness and frustration in public space was possible, gratifying and not particularly risky. This assertion does not mean that 15M was the fruit of 22M but it is possible that without 22M, 15M would not have been what it was. Furthermore, the camps in Madrid, Barcelona, Seville and other cities continued over the weekend on which elections took place, despite their prohibition by the Electoral Court. The police let it be known that they would not intervene unless provoked. Given the media coverage of the movement, a violent eviction from the plazas would undoubtedly have taken its toll on Spain's image abroad, especially since the country was once again dependent on the tourist season about to begin. The image of Spain abroad was at stake and the authorities knew it. So too did the demonstrators.

But there's more. 15M had a strong ability to attract sympathy and support, as well as boasting an excellent organisational and communicative capacity. And to top it all, it was able to get a large and heterogeneous group of people behind particular grievances and demands. In this sense it is important to point out that the large expressive demonstration that emerged was centred more on denunciation than proposition and it was within such a logic that the demonstrators referred to themselves as *indignados*.[1]

It isn't easy to synthesise the number of grievances raised by the *indignados* but following Taibo (2011) we can point to three important expressive axes: the rejection of establishment parties and unions because of their corporatist and clientelist nature as well as their estrangement from the citizenry and their concerns; a critique of how markets and financial institutions dictate government policy; and the rejection of labour precarisation and job losses in the name of competition, as well as the practice of moving production overseas to increase profits.

On the basis of participative research carried out with the 15M movement in the university city of Salamanca, it was possible to develop an idea of the objectives of the movement and the motivations of its members. Questioned on the three most important motivations for participation in demonstrations, the following answers emerged: anger with banks, corruption, the electoral system and the media. With regard to the 'objectives', the following appeared, listed in order of importance: the fight against corruption, electoral reform, limiting the power of the financial markets, transformation of the democracy, media pluralisation, labour market reform, reform of the education system and the defence of the welfare state (Calvo *et al.* 2011: 15).

The slogans shouted and scrawled by the 15M demonstrators also expressed these demands, albeit with a heavy tinge of irony and humour. Postill describes these kinds of communications as embodying 'jocose emotivity' (2014: 351). Slogans included:

There's not enough bread for all the sausages (translator's note
– a play on words, chorizo meaning both sausage and thief in
Spanish).
They call it democracy and it isn't.
They don't represent us.
I think, therefore I'm a nuisance.
There's enough money, just too many thieves.
If you don't let us dream, we won't let you sleep.
France and Greece fight, Spain wins at football.
Politicians and bankers, go get a conscience.
Concentrated on robbing you (in reference to a PP campaign
slogan – 'Concentrated on You').
I think of Iceland.
Yes We Camp.

With regard to its communicative and organisational capacities,
15M was a 2.0 movement. Like the mobilisations of the Arab Spring,
the collective action of the *indignados* spread like wildfire across the
internet, first from the movement's websites and then from the
Twitter accounts of different camps (like @*acampadasol* in Madrid
and @*acampadacatalunya* in Barcelona) – you could even follow
some debates held in Plaza del Sol in real time, broadcast over a
webcam.

In this sense we might also note that the majority of participants
in 15M were young people of university age and graduates who used
virtual networks – we might call them 'digital natives'. Data from a
multiple choice survey carried out with demonstrators in the city of
Salamanca (Martí i Puig 2011: 8) leaves no room for doubt: 65.3 per
cent of those surveyed found out about the demonstrations through
Facebook/Tuenti, 34.7 per cent through a friend, 17.8 per cent
by email, 17.7 per cent through a website, 13.9 per cent through
the media, 11.9 per cent through an organisation and 9.9 per cent
through Twitter.

It was precisely this successful capacity to communicate what was
happening in real time to a generation of digital natives that created
a snowball effect, with the movement replicating itself in almost all
the provincial capitals, as well as other large cities. It was then that
the movement experienced a change of scale as it went from being a
protest in Madrid to a movement spread across the country.

The occupation of squares: anything new?

The most striking aspects of the protest were its longevity, its ability to spread and its resilience in occupying public space. Beyond the camps' longevity – in the case of Madrid and Barcelona they continued throughout June and July[2] – the movement had three stand-out characteristics: the nature of the call to protest, its organisational logic and the repertoire of its collective action.

With regard to the first, we should note the importance of new technologies in the process of organising and bringing about the protest, beyond the mediation of activists. This aspect, so naturalised at the current time, is not a minor one. The call to protest 'without mediation' is new and reflects a style of mobilisation specific to new generations for whom virtual connectivity replaces the micro-networks of trust that had prevailed in the activist world (Diani 2009). Previously, it was these communities that, in particular circumstances and based around certain slogans, got people active and impelled them onto the streets to protest. For this reason, theories of social movements until recently looked to the associative networks active in daily urban life. Once activated, these networks created a geometry of concentric spaces that structured the movement: in the centre, the 'hard core', beside it, a group of activists and surrounding it a group of sympathisers (Ibarra *et al.* 2004). The hard core activists had a clear political trajectory in associative, neighbourhood and oppositional movements that, despite their long histories, were not given much media attention in the years of the economic boom.

Thus in order to predict the emergence of a protest, it was until recently imperative to know whether an associational density existed in a given area. 15M, however, showed us that the activation of activists can take place without any (or little) mediation since the network made up of face-to-face interaction and trust between activists and sympathisers could be replaced by calls to protest emanating from digital social networks. This new feature made the 15M demonstrations not only unexpected but also instantaneous, surprising and geographically extensive: they started in Madrid but very quickly spread as far as London, Paris, Managua, Mexico City and Buenos Aires.

The scale of the protests did not mean that they had the same characteristics in every city. The demonstrations were more or less robust and had differing demands depending on the nature of the social networks in each locality. Yet unlike in previous demonstrations, participation in protests went beyond existing social networks to include young and old people without previous activist experience. This phenomenon undoubtedly granted the movement freshness, novelty and spontaneity but it also weakened cohesion and thus lessened the threat posed to authorities.

As for the organisational logic of the movement, it was assembly based (common to the tradition of neighbourhood organisations), leader-less and had a decentralising ethic, where each city's movement was sovereign in the establishment of priorities, demands and manifestos. In this way, the movement was effectively a confederation of local movements based around concrete demands, such as the fight against property speculation, precarity, or the privatisation of services; that is to say, movements that shared fundamental demands but had different sensibilities. With respect to the assembly-focused organisational structure, this was based around a series of open forums that took place in the plazas and which were structured around different commissions and working groups, on legal matters, communication, action, information and so on. Within such a framework, the movement's visible faces were working-group spokespersons.

The groups with lasting impact were those focused on fighting against budget cuts in health, education and social policy, against the precarisation of labour and against the privatisation of services. Thus a pluralistic, assembly-based process was born in the occupied squares of 15M. Smaller trade unions (such as the anarchist and autonomist Confederación General de Trabajadores) and members of mainstream trade unions (such as CCOO) were present in these assemblies on a personal basis. But although the trade unions did at one point attempt to lead the movement, they were unsuccessful, since the protests were always more citizen-based than corporatist. There was, in other words, a dynamic of sector-specific protest that attempted to include all affected parties, regardless of political party or trade union affiliation. For this reason, new protest symbols were created based around a system of colours: white for health, green for education, yellow for justice, orange for social services, red for unemployment and so on.

Finally, with regard to the repertoire of collective action, the methods that stood out most were the occupation of public space and the use of non-violent forms of direct action (Postill 2014).[3] In this regard we are in agreement with Albert O. Hirschman (1992) when, against Rational Choice theory, he argues that collective action is attractive not only because of the excitement and risk involved but also due to its expressive potential.

The impact of 15M: elections and demonstrations

One of the most complex tasks in social science is to measure impact and thus the task of working out the impact of the 15M movement is a difficult one. All things considered, it is to a certain degree possible to imagine that what happened in the days after 15 May influenced the elections of Sunday 22 May 2011. Nevertheless it is obvious that the impact of the movement transcended election day. We believe that 15M brought about two main consequences: the abstention of left voters in the election of 22 May and the activation of demonstrations for social rights organised through broad and plural platforms.

As for the results of 22M, we can observe a rise in the 'protest vote' in the 48 per cent increase in spoiled ballots and the 37 per cent increase in abstention compared with 2007. At the same time, if the local results are inspected in more detail, we can see that in municipalities with more than 75,000 inhabitants – places where the movement was strongest – the protest vote (abstention, blank votes and spoiled ballots) was more intense (Jiménez Sánchez 2011). On the other hand, we should also note the resilience and increase in the conservative vote for the PP, in spite of the discourse of 15M being directed against the establishment parties. Finally, it is necessary to point out that the governing party, PSOE, suffered the loss of a million and a half votes, equivalent to 19.13 per cent of their vote in 2007.

It is not easy to establish a causal relation between the PSOE's loss of votes and the 15M protests but one can deduce the existence of a protest vote by progressive citizens against a government that carried out harsh adjustment policies, many of them dictated by the EU, and which had proved incapable of stemming the massive job losses of the previous three years. In this way, the Spanish social democrats suffered the same fate that had befallen their Portuguese equivalent months earlier. Undoubtedly, as often happens, the voters most attuned to questions of equity, justice and transparency were those who most quickly deserted at the ballot box a political formation that called itself centre-left but implemented structural adjustment policies.

The other consequence of 15M was the increase in intensity of demonstrations against privatisation policies and cuts implemented by central and autonomous regional governments, the latter being responsible for the implementation of a large part of welfare policy.

Towards the end of 2011, different spaces of protest were energised to support groups threatened by cuts. The most important in this regard is the movement linked to the defence of the right to housing. Unlike other social rights, the right to housing has never been even minimally guaranteed by the Spanish system. As is well known, the marketisation of housing was one of the motors of Spanish development of the last decades, leading to a highly speculative economic model. Faced with such a situation, different initiatives had already been launched prior to 15M, such as the aforementioned PAH.

Together with the defence of the right to housing and the campaign against the eviction of those who could not meet their mortgage payments or pay their rents, other plural platforms set up to defend the public realm were invigorated and consolidated in the aftermath of 15M. Thus were born movements (known as *Mareas* – Tides) set up to combat policies that eroded social services and cut rights, education, public health, unemployment benefit, etc. These mobilisations reflected citizens' central concerns and demonstrated the increasing divorce between citizens and the government.

Of the different 'tides', the White (Health) and Green (Education) Tides have been the most active, generating the most important socioeconomic-based mobilisation of the last decades – particularly in Madrid, although it has spread to other parts of the country.

It is worth pausing briefly to explain some of the dynamics of the 'Tides'. Firstly, it is important to mention the fact that despite their clear sector-specific demands (in education, health, housing, social services), they appear as a broad challenge to neoliberal policies. The Tides thus go beyond demanding an end to cuts and demand structural political and economic change.

This element of transcending sector-specific demands can be shown in the way that the Tides, together with other activist spaces, have converged in 'dignity marches' that, from different points and at different times, have brought thousands and thousands of people to the streets of Madrid to participate in huge protests repudiating cuts and austerity. If the trade unions, even large ones, participated in these demonstrations, they did not lead or organise them.

One of the most important Tides is that set up to defend public education: the so-called Green Tide. In this case, there has been ample reason to protest. One reason has been the approval of the Law for the Improvement of Quality in Education. This is a normative and ideological reform with aspects that structurally transform the education system by de-capitalising it and introducing social stratification. In the face of the reform, three days of strikes were declared (on 22–24 October 2013) in which students, teachers and parents from primary up to university level participated. With a turnout of 80 per cent including private schools, the strikes culminated in big demonstrations in the country's largest cities.

For its part, the White Tide (in defence of public health) organised protests against decisions by the authorities to impose important financial cuts that translated into a reduction in public health care cover, an increase in waiting lists, the sacking of health professionals, the co-payment of medicine and the privatisation of certain services. An important moment in the birth of this movement was on 31 October 2012, when the PP government in the Madrid City Council announced a plan to privatise 6 hospitals and 27 health centres. The measure also included the scrapping of 26 categories of non-medical professionals from hospitals. Another relevant measure was the decision to convert the La Princesa Hospital to a geriatric hospital, something that sparked a spontaneous reaction in the hospital grounds the very day it was announced. Thousands of residents, hospital workers and 15M participants gathered in the entrance to La Princesa over the following days, in a personal capacity but with the support of the main health care trade unions. Lock-ins began in many hospitals, including those targeted by the Plan. From 31 October then, one could already glimpse a 'self-organized, spontaneous movement that emerged from the people and shared the dynamics of 15M', explains Jesús Jaén Urueña, hospital worker in La Princesa and participant in the White Tide (Cortavitarte 2014).

As for the repertoire of actions, it should also be mentioned that alongside more conventional strikes, demonstrations and marches, the Tides also included more playful and fun methods. For example, the decentralised assemblies of the Green Tide organised flash mobs and marathons, as well as promotional videos and human chains. In a similar vein, the White Tide also combined diverse types of actions. The different platforms, collectives, medical associations and trade unions did not base their struggle on a single response either but also carried out cultural events (Gil de Biedma 2013). These new and carnivalesque forms of less traditional collective action are an outcome of the transmission of methods of struggle between social movements (Auyero 2004).

Since the demands raised by the Tides were those traditionally articulated by the trade union movement, one of the questions we must ask is to what extent the 15M movement and the Tides have occupied spaces of struggle normally occupied by the mainstream trade unions, the Workers Commissions (CCOO) and the General Workers Union (UGT). Yet, from the first teachers' assemblies to the closing of hospitals, and despite their best efforts, the traditional trade unions could not lead or control the direction of the protests, even if grassroots members participated in them (Cortavitarte 2014).

Since workers make up their largest component, the Tides are certainly inscribed in a class conflict, but they are not limited to the workplace, something that allows for the participation of other collectives – such as service users – in the struggle. More importantly, they also inspired the creation of a democratic and participative community, based around the management of a public service and which has been proactive in the search for solutions and alternatives. It is no exaggeration to argue that 15M inspired new repertoires of action and new ways of doing politics on this new terrain, including a reformulation of the role and practices of trade unions. The latter were still to a large degree anchored in the consensus of the transition to democracy and a corporative and semi-public organisational structure that accommodated itself to the powers that be. In the context of the Spanish crisis, and 40 years since their legalisation, the mainstream trade unions (although not their grassroots members) were seen by society as actors implicated in maintaining the status quo. This is because the trade unions had not been active in denouncing the precarity of many emergent productive sectors, but had been recruiting in the public sector, where workers have greater protection and trade union leaders have developed clientelistic practices.

Before concluding this summary, it is necessary to mention another space where rights have been restricted and which has consequently seen much mobilisation in recent years, even if it is a phenomenon whose links with 15M are much less direct. We are talking about the campaign for the 'right to decide', understood as the collective right of the Catalan people to be consulted in a referendum on the political future of Catalonia and its relation with Spain. This took place on 9 November 2014, with the result rejected by the national government and deemed illegal by the Constitutional Court (Martí i Puig and Vilaregut 2015).

Post script: a new regime?

Finally, by way of a post script, it is necessary to point out that during 2011–2015 it seems that, according to opinion polls and the results of some 2015 elections, Spanish citizens have reconfigured their political preferences. They have lost faith in the traditional parties, especially the PP and PSOE, and begun to support new formations that demand a regeneration of the political system born at the end of the 1970s. This phenomenon is undoubtedly linked to the fact that these two parties have been in government in Spain since 1982 until the current day and especially to the fact that they have jointly managed the crisis that blew up during Jose Luis Rodriguez Zapatero's (PSOE) government and continued into that of Mariano Rajoy (PP).

The rejection of traditional parties and politicians is linked to citizens' opinions about the issues that concern them most. According to information from the CIS, since 2007, Spanish citizens have been mostly concerned by unemployment but also by corruption and the conduct of politicians and their parties. Unemployment was perceived as the most important concern of 35 per cent of the population in 2007, and 81 per cent by the end of 2014. In the same period, the population believed corruption to be Spain's second biggest problem and 'politicians and political parties' the third biggest, over and above 'economic problems' (Revilla *et al.* 2015).

In this climate of discontent and mistrust of the political class, new political formations appeared to take advantage of the European parliamentary elections of the 26 May 2014. It is no accident that the new parties should focus on the European elections since, of all the elections in Spain, these offer the smaller parties the best chance of obtaining seats due to a mechanical element – 54 seats are distributed according to the D'Hondt method of proportional representation – and a psychological one: citizens take advantage of this election to exercise a protest vote, because they perceive it as less important.

Among the new parties could be found some on the far right, such as Vox, and others inspired by the demands of 15M, like the X Party, RED – Democratic Citizens Renewal and Podemos.[4] Of these, the arrival of Podemos onto the political scene stands out.

Podemos was created in January 2014 by a group of political science professors at Madrid's Complutense University who actively participated in 15M and who decided to launch a new party in response to the demands of the movement and people's lack of trust in institutions and the existing political parties. This party, led by a professor known for his interventions in televised debates, elaborated a discourse based on a critique of 'old politics', the gulf separating economic and political elites (whom they call 'castes') and ordinary people, and the need to oppose austerity policies promoted by the European Union and applied unquestioningly by Spanish governments.

In this political context, polls following the European elections of 2014 indicated that the almost perfectly two-party system, which has been in place from the 1980s until 2014, has started to break down. According to surveys undertaken by the CIS since 2013, the total of intended votes for the two mainstream parties (the PP and PSOE) did not reach 50 per cent, down from a more usual height of over 70 per cent, while Podemos has risen on the left and Ciudadanos on the right, especially in 2015.

The appearance of new political actors and the flagging of the two traditional parties continued throughout 2015, what might be described as a 'super electoral year' given that elections took place in Andalusia on 22 March, in all the municipalities and 13 Autonomous Communities on 24 May, in Catalonia on 27 September and throughout Spain on 20 December to choose deputies, senators and the national government.

Of all these electoral events, the May municipal elections – the same type of elections that initiated the 15M protests in 2011 – and the recent national elections interest us most. To a certain degree it is possible to say that between the local elections of 2011 and those of 2015 there has been a political cycle of mobilisation, protest, reconfiguration of actors, emergence of parties and political proposals. This emphasis on the local is of vital importance because it was in the large and medium sized Spanish cities that the *indignado* movement took shape and, four years later, it was also where citizen platforms inspired by the demands of 15M took power. These political platforms were the fruit of a confluence between social movements, independents and Podemos and they put themselves forward with a clear message against policies of austerity.

The clearest demonstration of this new political cycle was, on the one hand, the victory of left-wing candidates in the most important local governments, a result of the convergence of movements linked to 15M and figures opposed to the neoliberal measures implemented following the 2008 crisis: Madrid and Barcelona are the examples best known overseas, but similar coalitions won in Badalona, Zaragoza, Valencia, Cadiz, La Coruña, Ferrol and Santiago de Compostela. And on the other hand, bi-party politics disappeared with the results of the general elections of 20 December 2015. The vote for the two hegemonic parties (PP and PSOE) together reached 50.73 per cent of the votes cast (winning 123 and 90 Congress seats, respectively). Podemos and its allies erupted onto the scene with 20.66 per cent of the vote and 69 seats; and Ciudadanos won 13.93 per cent and 40 seats. In addition to these, Catalán and Basque nationalist parties as well as other minor formations obtained 10.71 per cent of the vote and 28 seats. These results created a distribution of seats in the Chamber of Deputies that for the first time in the history of democracy required pacting between more than two formations, unless the PP and PSOE managed a 'great coalition' between themselves. This despite the fact that the PSOE's electoral law had favoured the PP. But beyond the electoral results and possibilities for governing coalitions, we should signal that politics in Spain today has very little to do with pre-15M politics. For that reason, with each election it is more and more common to hear talk of 'regime change' in Spain.

Notes

1 In calling themselves *los indignados*, 'the indignant ones', protesters borrowed and adapted the title of a Stéphan Hessel pamphlet published a few months earlier in France that, against all expectations (and to the surprise of the author himself) became a bestseller.

2 In the case of Madrid, the Plaza de Sol was cleared definitively on 3 August due to the imminent visit of the Pope for the Catholic World Youth Day celebrations.

3 Thus it is important to point out that collective action has four essential functions: (1) to communicate and transmit demands, (2) to generate solidarity and identity amongst its members, (3) to convince its members that they are stronger than they actually are, (4) to challenge its adversaries through the creation of uncertainty.

4 The four parties fared differently in the European elections. Podemos was the biggest surprise, obtaining 7.98 per cent of the vote and five seats. Vox obtained 1.56 per cent, RED 0.65 per cent and X Party 0.64 per cent.

References

Auyero, Javier (2004) '¿Por qué grita esta gente? Los medios y los significados de la protesta popular en la Argentina de hoy', *América Latina Hoy*, 36: 161–185.

Calvo Borobia, K., Gómez-Pastrana, T. and Mena, L. (2011) 'Movimiento 15M: ¿quiénes son y qué reivindican?', *Zoom Político*, 2011(4): 4–17. Madrid: Laboratorio de Alternativas.

Centro de Investigaciones Sociológicas (CIS) 2011 'Barómetro de octubre', *Estudio*, 2914. Madrid: CIS.

Colomer, Josep M. (2008) 'Spain and Portugal: Rule by Party Leadership', in Colomer, Josep M. (ed.) *Comparative Eurpean Politics*, pp. 174–206. New York: Routledge.

Cortavitarte, Emili (2014) 'El movimiento obrero en 2014: los brotes no tan verdes y la dignidad de las Marchas', in Ibarra, Pedro and Curells, Marta, *Anuario de Movimientos Sociales 2014*, Barcelona: Icaria-Fundación Betiko. http://fundacionbetiko.org/wp-content/uploads/2015/03/Movimiento-Obrero-2014.pdf.

Diani, Mario (2009) 'The Structural Bases of Protest Events: Multiple Memberships and Networks in the February 15th 2003 Anti-war Demonstrations', *ActaSociologica*, 52(1): 63–83.

Gil de Biedma, Carla (2013) 'El movimiento social de las Mareas: la reapropiación ciudadana de lo público Cuando sube la marea', in Ibarra, Pedro and Curells, Marta, *Anuario de Movimientos Sociales 2013*, Barcelona: Icaria-Fundación Betiko.

Hirschman, Albert O. (1992) *Retóricas de la intransigencia*, Mexico: Fondo de Cultura Económica.

Ibarra, Pedro, Martí i Puig, Salvador and Gomà, Ricard (2004) *Creadores de democracia radical*, Barcelona: Icaria editorial.

Jiménez Sánchez, Manuel (2011) '¿Influyó el 15M en las elecciones municipales?', *Zoom Político*, 2011(4): 18–28. Madrid: Laboratorio de Alternativas.

Martí i Puig, Salvador (2011) 'Pienso, luego estorbo. España: Crisis e indignación', *Nueva Sociedad*, 236: 5–15.

Martí i Puig, Salvador and Vilaregut, Ricard (2015) 'Política de la contienda en Cataluña y la batalla de los significados: El Derecho a Decidir', unpublished.

Postill, John (2014) 'Spain's Indignados and the Mediated Aesthetics of Non-violence', in Werbner, P., Webb, M. and Spellman-Poots, K. (eds) *The Political Aesthetics of Global Protest: The Arab Spring and Beyond*, pp. 341–367. Edinburgh: Edinburgh University Press.

Revilla, Marisa, Garrido, Anabel, Martínez, Ignacio, Molina, Carlos, More, Herico and Rodríguez, Karen (2015) 'Unexpected Consequences of Protest Actions: Ideological and

Electoral Reconfiguration in Spain (2010–2014)', paper presented in ESA Research Network 25, Social Movements, Mid-Term Conference.

Taibo, Carlos (2011) *Nada será como antes. Sobre el 15M*, Madrid: Ediciones de la Catarata.

Tarrow, Sidney (1997) *El poder en movimiento. Los movimientos sociales, la acción colectiva y la polítca*, Madrid: Alianza Editorial.

Vallés, Josep M. (2010) *Ciencia Política. Una introducción*, Barcelona: Editorial Ariel.

6 | WHAT ARE THE POSSIBLE STRATEGIES FOR THE EMERGENCE OF A DEMOCRATIC AND REVOLUTIONARY LABOUR MOVEMENT IN LEBANON?

Walid Daou

Translated by Yassmin Ahmed

To the soul of Bassem Chit (1979–2014)

The labour and trade union movement in Lebanon has witnessed a slow transformation since the civil war, adopting economic and sectoral methods of activism and refraining from making political demands or even criticising the ruling regime. Over time this has led to the weakening and fragmentation of the movement and its organisational structure, and declining class and union consciousness, in the face of the adoption of a widespread sectarian and clientelistic discourse among members of the working class.

This chapter sheds light on the factors that have led to the depoliticisation of trade union activism. Specifically, it focuses on the sectarianism, racism and gender discrimination employed against many Lebanese and foreign male and female labour groups due to trade union bureaucracy. It also investigates the problematic relationship between the grassroots labour struggle and the bureaucratic balance at the top of the trade union hierarchy. The chapter discusses the impact of this relationship on the forms and structure of trade union struggle and labour, the construction of class consciousness, the possibility of the expansion of the labour movement and its ability to recruit new male and female members.

In light of the revolutionary transformations in the region over the last five years, the chapter then asks what strategies might revive the labour movement and trade union activism, not only to achieve direct labour rights but also to build a democratic and revolutionary trade union structure capable of confronting both the reality of the class-based ruling regime in all its different aspects and the hegemonic sectarianism, racism and sexism that dominate the working class. What could empower Lebanese and foreign workers (the latter constituting approximately 30 per cent of the workforce in Lebanon) to unite in a labour movement that poses a serious threat to the regime and the bourgeois ruling class?

The labour movement in Lebanon

The labour and trade union movement that has emerged in Lebanon, particularly in the years following the civil war (1975–1990), has been characterised by increasing economic, sectoral and group demands. Yet the large majority of trade unions ceased to make political demands for regime reform, suggesting that most trade unions are inclined to compromise or strike deals with the regime to protect it from grassroots worker pressure. This has weakened the trade unions' bureaucratic leadership and internal democracy, and both unions' and workers' rights have become gifts granted by political leaders, for which they are expected to be grateful.

Furthermore, trade unions became fragmented, their organisational structures have been weakened, and their desire to confront the regime receded. In addition, sectarian and clientelistic language is now common among members of the working class, and the majority of Lebanon's trade unions are in one way or another affiliated to one of the ruling sectarian parties.[1] The stagnation and weakness of the trade unions contrasts to their historically contentious nature prior to the civil war. There are several reasons for this transformation, not least because the civil war seriously affected the trade union movement, as the militia[2] attacked it to prevent any possibility of the rise of a labour protest movement, which had begun to radicalise. However, the trade unions maintained a reasonable ability to confront such attacks, especially in the late 1980s, in particular by organising livelihood-based, anti-hunger and anti-killing protests. For example, on 15 October 1987 demonstrations of this type broke out all over Lebanon, and demonstrators from East and West Beirut assembled in an impressive show in front of the National Museum of Beirut. On 5 November the trade unions called for a general strike, which was suspended on 9 November following mass demonstrations in East and West Beirut (Salibi 1999).

The complicated relationship between unions and the state has a long history. For example, in 1945 workers at the Wool Mill led Lebanon's longest strike demanding the licensing of their union, increased salaries and family compensation. Despite the fact that the General Confederation of Lebanese Workers (see below) announced solidarity with the strike, it did not participate in it, claiming that 'the country is going through an independence struggle and foreign armies were forced to flee' (Al-Buwary 1986: 229) and the Communist Party also adopted this stance (Cliff 2001). *Sawt al-Shaab* (Voice of the People), the Lebanese Communist Party (LCP) newspaper, wrote on 15 July 1944 after a strike led by workers at a soap factory in Tripoli: 'We hope the employers respond to the workers' demands. The demands are not huge, and the government will intervene to solve the problem between employers and employees in a just manner'. What concerned the communist political parties at the time was to domesticate class struggle for two main reasons: (1) the priority of collaboration with the nation's bourgeoisie, and (2) the importance of the workers obeying the nation's capitalist class and not affecting its interests and possibilities for expansion. Furthermore, Syria's *Al-Itihad* newspaper, also belonging to the LCP, called both parties, the employers and the employees, to make sacrifices and collaborate with one another in the struggle for the sake of freedom and independence.

The tendency of trade unions to assume a bourgeois class position can be attributed to a continuation of specific thinking in the trade union mechanism, which is bound by the geographical boundaries imposed by the colonial powers after the First World War. Trade unions have obeyed the rules imposed by the ruling regime; at first they adopted the principle of 'ask and demand', then of 'negotiate and demand' and then of 'beg and beg'. We should bear in mind that the contemporary regime, the parliamentary assembly and the bourgeois class have never been kind to the working class, so it is not clear why the trade unions have been kind to them. This regime does not respond to demands unless pressure is brought to bear on them, in which case it resorts to the use of the armed forces – and the civil war is still at the forefront of its citizens' minds – internal security forces, or the domestication of trade unions.

The weakening of the trade union movement

One factor that led to the weakening of the trade union movement is that the Lebanese regime – a product of an American–Saudi–Syrian agreement – gave executive and legislative authority to the militia. Hence the militia's duties moved from the street to political authority, having as their objective the weakening of trade unions, and crushing of workers' mobilisation. This paved the way for the adoption of neoliberal policies. The Ministry of Labour, dominated by ministers affiliated to the Syrian regime, has issued a series of declarations over the years licensing dozens of trade unions that do not represent labour groups. The Executive Council includes two appointed members, one member for each trade union, regardless of the size of trade union. The Ministry of Labour's decrees aimed to change the power dynamics within the General Confederation of Lebanese Workers (GCLW).

The GCLW was established in 1958, and included non-leftist trade unions. It represented workers of the private sector because the Lebanese Labour Law excludes workers of the public sector. The years that followed the GCLW's establishment witnessed tension between the Confederation and unlicensed trade unions with a leftist orientation. In 1966–1967, the Minister of Labour licensed leftist trade unions, following trade union-led political pressure on the government. Then, a general assembly was established to coordinate between the Confederation and the trade unions with leftist orientations. On 3 May 1970, leftist trade unions joined the GCLW.

The GCLW participates in the work of three assemblies (the state, employers and workers) through: the Committee for Monitoring Prices, the Social and Economic Commission and the National Fund for Social Security. However, following the civil war, the Minister of Labour licensed a number of trade unions that are not representative of workers and instead work hand in glove with sectarian political parties. This weakened the GCLW, in addition to its bias toward the employers and the governing authority.

In addition, the Ministry of Labour systematically and forcefully intervened in union politics, arresting trade union leaders, imposing curfews to prevent workers from protesting and manipulating election results, especially in the 1990s. Meanwhile, the absence of a democratic organisational structure within the GCLW increased authoritarian interference in internal affairs.

Furthermore, workers' unionisation fell below 7 per cent, especially in trade unions that are affiliated to the GCLW (Salibi 1999); more recently, Toufic Gaspard (2005) indicates that unions represent less than 4 per cent of the total number of workers. In addition Lebanon's Labour Law (1946), which regulates the work of trade unions, prohibits a wide range of workers from forming or joining a union, such as domestic workers, workers in institutions that only employ family members under the administration of the father, mother or guardian, and day workers in the Lebanese public services. Moreover, in the context of small and dispersed industrial and economic institutions, the family-based and sectarian structure in Lebanon has contributed to 'strengthening familial and sectarian bonds at the expense of professional and economic relationships' (Salibi 1999), as 68 per cent of industrial institutions employ fewer than five workers.[3]

The trade unions in Lebanon, especially after the civil war, adopted an economic and demand-based discourse and avoided political discourse in their agendas, based on the argument that adopting a political discourse would lead to internal political divisions. They also agreed on a minimum number of common demands, which were often reduced to one, for instance on the minimum wage. This trajectory of avoiding political confrontation with the regime allowed sectarian parties to fill the political void and led to widespread sectarian and sectoral mobilisation within the trade union body. Left-leaning trade unions did not confront the subjection of the GCLW to the regime and preferred to ally with trade unions belonging to the ruling parties, with the aim of achieving reform through GCLW's elections. The trade unions continued to adopt this orientation over the years, until they withdrew from the GCLW in 2014 after the transformation of the latter to a body void of content.

In contrast to this bleak image, a wave of labour movement emerged within the private sector to organise into trade unions or labour committees. These moves, however, remained fragmented and were not sufficiently organised to play an efficient role on a wide scale. For example, in 2010 workers at the Future Gas Cylinders factory organised themselves to continue working despite a factory lock-out (Dagher 2010). Their mobilisation provided an example of grassroots labour activism for other trade unions, despite the lack of trade union solidarity and lack of media reporting on the matter. Furthermore, in 2011, a group of male and female workers at Spinneys rose up against the violation of their right to organise and the deprivation of a scheduled wage rise as per the minimum wage. In spite of such restrictions, physical assaults and the firing of a number of labour organisers, the Spinneys workers were able to form their own union. However, the clientelistic relations between the company's director and the workers led to a drop in the new union's membership; in addition, the company recruited workers to stand against their peers.

Trade union mobilisation in the public sector: successes and challenges

Before the Lebanese civil war, male and female public sector teachers' discourse was characterised by their aim of changing and improving pedagogical curricula and increasing wages. However, this radical stance receded in the period following the civil war, when the teachers' mobilisation focused instead on livelihood needs.

More recently, the Lebanese Teachers' Coalition, a non-unionised cultural network, has managed to confront the authorities through protesting against the state's adoption of neoliberal policies. These policies mainly focused on downsizing the number of workers in the public sector, privatising a number of public institutions and sectors and reducing ministry budgets, negatively affecting the quality of public services. The coalition mobilised through the Union Coordination Committee (UCC), an unlicensed and a non-elected coordinating coalition. It includes secondary education teachers, primary education teachers, technical school teachers, public sector employees and teachers in private schools. It meets every time issues of wage, salaries and promotions are raised. Public and private education employers make decisions in consultation with the UCC, while decisions at the UCC are based on the general assemblies. The groups undertake periodic elections for their administrative committees, although these elections have not escaped political and sectarian consideration. Nonetheless, the UCC is more representative for labour bases than the GCLW. The mobilisation contributed to imposing an amendment to the minimum wage for 2008 and confronted the authorities in a long strike, which paralysed most of the general directorates and public schools for more than a month in 2014 with a demand for higher salaries.

However, the UCC was hesitant about assuming a combative role on many occasions and endorsed pro-regime positions as a result of political interference at the leaders' level: its administrative body had been formed as a result of political alliances imposed from above. Moreover, the UCC did not complete its proposed collection of a million signatures on a petition that aimed to exert pressure on the authorities to approve a wage rise and promotions; and neither did it provide an explanation for this failure. Further, in 2013 the UCC called its grassroots base to a general strike that included boycotting setting, invigilating and marking examinations. Yet, despite the fact that there was a near-consensus about the call to strike among the general assemblies, the authorities succeeded in stopping the strike by manipulating the UCC's leaders and promising to respond to their demands; a promise that was never fulfilled.

The UCC's withdrawal from confronting the authorities was not subject to a general assembly vote, and many of those at the grassroots were not satisfied with their action. They considered that the UCC leaders' alliance with the authorities violated the simple rules of democratic trade unions. So, although the UCC had represented the potential for an alternative trade union movement – in contrast to the GCLW – they proved in fact not to be so different. The issue did not end here. In fact when the government had trouble forming new ministerial cabinets as a result of conflict among the authorities, the UCC issued several statements calling for the formation of a new government despite knowing quite well its position *vis-à-vis* the UCC demands. At the time, the UCC could have mobilised greater support from vulnerable groups against this authority instead of calling for a new government. The government, along with the Parliamentary Assembly, continued to offer false promises to the UCC. This, in turn, led to the termination of strikes and weakened labour mobilisation, contributing to the transfer of the initiative from the UCC to political leaders who are expert at political ploys and populism in a competitive political environment.

In this context we can also shed light on one retreat by the UCC during a conference organised by UNESCO in March 2013. The conference hosted different governing authorities, which publicly supported the UCC's demands at a time when the government had suspended the UCC's authorisation in both government and parliament. This led to frustration at the grassroots, with workers preferring to withdraw from the conference because they could not tolerate listening to the hypocrisy of the political forces' representatives. One unionist took a stand on the platform and publicly attacked the political authorities (al-Haj 2013). However, a unionist leader stopped him and apologised to the politicians present, saying 'Your solidarity is our right and we want you on our side. Our demands should be answered by you, not the moon'.[4]

The UCC thus replayed the collapse of the GCLW and did not become a trade union capable of confronting the dominant and destructive organisation of the state. Public sector workers and teachers paid a heavy price when the leadership of the UCC allowed their mobilisation to lose momentum and the authorities took the initiative; and they came to believe that there was no real alternative to a choice between bad and worse sections of the regime. The political parties quickly closed the case, through their control of the electoral lists that made up the UCC, without reaching an agreement on a pay scale or salaries.

No democratic trade union bloc appeared within the UCC or outside of it during the mobilisation. The argument here was, without a doubt, that of maintaining unity, and when trade union elections took place the communists and the independents were ejected from the lists. In the meantime, the other candidates considered the elections to be an exercise in allocation of seats according to a (sectarian) quota, thus reflecting the fact that they themselves had entered the bazaar of negotiations and the quota system during the elections.

Unions and Arab and foreign workers

Generally speaking, unions suffer from a nationalist orientation that makes them hostile toward Arab and foreign labour groups such as Palestinian – and now Syrian – workers. Several trade unions claim that foreign workers are in competition with Lebanese citizens for employment opportunities. Consequently the UCC and reformist leftist political parties failed to talk to and organise foreign workers, in a similar way to the case of the Italian migrant workers discussed by Peano in this volume.

For example, a study by trade unions and workers in north Lebanon titled 'Unemployment in Lebanon: Reality and Solution' looked at the impact of the Syrian revolution on Lebanon in terms of competition between Syrian and Lebanese workers for employment opportunities.[5] The study failed to discuss what many consider to be the main reason behind the employment of Syrian workers in Lebanon, namely that they are not entitled to social protection and earn lower wages, thus helping business owners to accumulate profits.

At a time when Syrian workers are facing official racism, because Lebanon does not recognise them as refugees, they have no access to education or health care in the country. Furthermore, they are prohibited from practising their political rights,[6] subject to curfews in some towns and villages and exposed to criticism on television programmes. The UCC missed an opportunity to take an alternative stance toward Syrian refugees, since the same set of powers that deprives Lebanese workers of their socioeconomic rights in the north and fires them from commercial institutions is profiting from exploiting the miserable conditions of Syrian refugees in Lebanon.

In this context a group of non-governmental organisations has organised a series of activities for four years running, one of which is a demonstration in celebration of Labour Day with participation from domestic workers and supporters of foreign workers' rights. The head of the International Federation for Domestic Workers told the newspaper *Al-Manshour* (Abdo 2014): 'Nobody is able to liberate male and female workers but the workers themselves'. She added: 'The struggle is a very long one; we have a long road in front of us because the authorities will not compromise an economic resource and propagate false ideas to defend their criminal policies'. The trade unions did not share this position or attend the demonstration, although the leftist National Union for Workers in Lebanon tried to form a union for domestic workers, an initiative that is still in the early stages. They established an office for domestic workers with a hotline where they can air their grievances (Kerbage 2013). Despite the fact that this was a good initiative, activists argue that the National Union should have made more effort to forge bonds between Lebanese and foreign workers, for example by calling Lebanese workers to participate in the foreign workers' demonstration, which was only attended by the National Union's president.

At the beginning of 2015, a decision was published by the General Public Security Directorate imposing almost impossible conditions for entry permits on Syrian and Palestinian refugees fleeing from Syria to Lebanon.[7] Despite this, not a single union took up the issue by issuing a statement condemning this racist decision, demonstrating their faithfulness to the dominant patterns of chauvinistic thought, just as it showed their continued commitment to the rules of the game as determined by the political forces and the security agencies. A number of associations did issue a light-weight statement protesting the decision, but this was not followed up with practical steps to contest it effectively.[8]

Trade unions and the traditional left could have confronted the regime's racism by demanding socioeconomic security in coalition with national and foreign labour. By strengthening the bonds between different working-class groups, they could have increased the pressure exerted by the working class and deepened the crisis of the bourgeois regime. Instead, these unions and the Lebanese left adopted national and chauvinistic policies by taking a racist stand against Arab and foreign labour.

Trade unions and women

The participation of women in the trade union movement is low, particularly at the leadership level. This is obvious in the case of the Teachers' Union, where the majority of the members are women and the majority of the leaders are men (72 per cent of teachers in public education and 75 per cent in public and private education are women).[9]

In March 2008, feminist organisations, using the slogan 'stop violence and exploitation', led a struggle against the authorities, calling for the issuance of a law protecting women against domestic violence. However, the UCC and the rest of the trade unions neither supported nor participated in the campaign. While trade unions claim to represent the working class in Lebanon and to defend their interests, arguably they marginalise half of society. It would have been possible for the union to expand its base, exercise pressure on the government and provide a space for the intersection and interconnection of class and gender activism, but it did not do this at all. The 8 March demonstration of 2014 organised by Kafa is a good example. At the time, the Parliamentary Assembly had suspended the issuance of the law protecting women from domestic violence. None of the Lebanese trade unions issued statements supporting the demonstration, despite the fact that it was held at a time when crimes against women were on the rise. One could question why the trade unions suppress social movements and support the regime; it is as if they support the dominance of a regime that deprives their members of their rights and demands. The feminist activists invited some trade unionists to lobby for and participate in their demonstration, but they refused to participate, and some even attacked the women who invited them.[10]

Another example is from 25 January 2015 when, as a result of efforts by the National Federation of Workers Unions, some domestic workers and a number of associations, the union of women domestic workers was founded, the first of its kind in the Middle East.[11] At the time, the Ministry of Labour refused to register the union, and the Minister of Labour Sejaan Azzi launched a racist and sexist campaign against the newly-formed union and the organisations supporting it.[12] In this context, it is necessary to support the formation of any union that defends the interests of its members, particularly if they are among the most marginalised and exploited groups in the country. This means broadening support from the Federation, particularly through future mobilisations backing the women's domestic workers' union.

The groups supporting the formation of the union did nothing more than issue a statement once again, which they sent to the Lebanese Ministry of Justice, singling out the requirement by the General Public Security Directorate for employers to make a legal record of a commitment that no sexual relations exist between the domestic worker and any person on Lebanese territory, and in the case of such relations taking place (whether inside or outside marriage), the worker would be expelled from Lebanon.[13]

Again, this lukewarm support or even outright opposition is not without historical precedent. In 1945, women and men of the Regie Company led a strike during which the martyr Warda Boutros was shot dead by security forces.[14] After the incident the strikers' demands were further radicalised. However, according to Malik Abisaab (2004), despite the fact that the women were neither organised in unions nor members of political parties, they were exposed to patriarchal practices by GCLW and leftists. The latter were intolerant of women's participation in their organisations. The strike showed that the women challenged all forms of authority and broke through the traditional boundary between the public and the private.

Bernadette Daou (2014) comments that traditional leftist parties exercised hegemony in women's organising within or around them and imposed their agendas in a way that particularly neglected feminist issues. This is one example of women's experience of the communist labour organisation of the 1970s. Furthermore, some female leaders were fired from the organisation because of their feminist backgrounds. These leaders were trying to revolutionise leftist thought and the struggle against the societal superstructure by encouraging women to prioritise their demands as women in the trade union struggle. Despite the fact that women earned their membership of the organisation on the basis of their significant participation in the workers' struggle they were fired on the basis of adopting bourgeois Western thinking that was alien to how the male members see Eastern society, and because the recruitment of new members could be threatened if the women open up taboo subjects in society.

Social mobilisation will not be achieved if it does not include vulnerable categories in this exploitative regime. The ways in which trade unions exclude and marginalise women signals their support for the current capitalist and patriarchal regime, weakening the trade unions' demands.

Where do we go from here?

Despite the regime's attempts to weaken the trade unions through political intervention and by exercising different kinds of pressure, labour mobilisation in Lebanon has been on the rise for the past few years. This indicates the radicalisation of the class struggle in Lebanon in the face of the bourgeoisie's support for statist neoliberal policies aiming to get rid of what remains of public welfare services.

In the context of a radicalised class struggle, grassroots activists argue that trade unions should support justice, secularism and the fight against racism, in addition to social justice. Support should not be restricted to carrying banners but should include calls for the adoption of strategic programmes. Furthermore, unions' internal elections should be democratic and should not discriminate on the basis of gender, nationality or religion. This should be reflected in the tactics of any trade union mobilisation. Confronting the regime does not require the adoption of ideologies led by the state apparatus, the media, the education system or the political propaganda of hegemonic parties. It requires the production of an ideology counter to that of this regime and its ideological machine. Otherwise its mobilisation will become a tool used by the regime to reproduce hegemony, exclusion and exploitation.

There is no doubt that trade unions organise labour on the basis of capitalist law, and work to increase pay and improve working terms and conditions. Their achievements in this regard are mostly reactions to the sit-ins, strikes and negotiations that they have led to enhance or protect earned rights in the capitalist regime. Of course, any success against the regime by labour groups is an achievement of the working class, even if it is only partial. However, such success should not be seen as the goal in its own right because it illustrates that trade unions are reliant upon the existence of an exploitative class, which in turn has furthered their exploitation and bureaucratisation. Furthermore, it is not possible for the capitalist class to reform. There should be objective circumstances leading to its collapse. Achieving partial success should be seen as an experience of solidarity, benefiting from lessons learned, and a step towards the fall of the exploitative regime.

The history of the labour and trade union movement is full of struggle and clearly highlights the basic elements of class conflict in Lebanon. However, in confronting the regime, in addition to the problem of union bureaucracy and leaders' quest for fame, any trade union mobilisation should learn from previous experience, their own mistakes, and those of the leftist political parties. In the context of the rising revolutionary momentum in the region and widespread global mobilisation, the basic question is whether the Lebanese trade union and labour movement is joining this movement. The answer is no. After five years of revolution the movement has been limited, despite the continuing mobilisation of union networks, particularly in the public sector. One common argument is that the movement fears the return of a civil war. This fear is legitimate, as the Lebanese government has managed to spread fear of revolution in the name of limiting sectarian tension in the country. Active trade unions like the UCC played a role in this with their organisation of mass mobilisation to decrease sectarian tension. However, its discourse and mobilisation did not go far enough to shake the exploitative sectarian regime, and nor did it aim to transform labour groups into unions or to provide an alternative to the GCLW.

Conservatism is dominant among the trade union bureaucracy, manifest in 'socioeconomic differentiation . . . based on the role of trade union bureaucracy in balancing power between employers and employees' (Daou 2014). Leftist revolutionaries should encourage and support any trade union or labour mobilisation financially, particularly supporting grassroots democratic workers and amplifying their voices in the face of the bureaucratic ploys of trade union leaders and the ruling regime. They should also strengthen the horizontal bonds between male and female workers of different nationalities and sects with the aim of achieving equality, secularism and social justice and of fighting racism. The vast majority of bureaucratic trade union leaders are elderly and coming to the end of their tenure. The revolutionaries' mission today is to: (1) play active roles in the bases with the aim of radicalising consciousness and achieving democracy and the politicisation of the unions and (2) break down the schism between economic and political demands that has been built by domesticated and bureaucratised trade unions.

In conclusion, we should return to Lenin's words:

And now some among us began to cry out: Let us go into the marsh! And when we begin to shame them, they retort: What backward people you are! Are you not ashamed to deny us the liberty to invite you to take a better road! Oh, yes, gentlemen! You are free not only to invite us, but to go yourselves wherever you will, even into the marsh. In fact, we think that the marsh is your proper place, and we are prepared to render you every assistance to get there. Only let go of our hands, don't clutch at us and don't besmirch the grand word freedom, for we too are 'free' to go where we please, free to fight not only against the marsh, but also against those who are turning towards the marsh.[15]

Notes

1 Sectarianism is a specific political relationship historically defined by class struggle within the conditions of the colonial social structure in Lebanon. It appeared under the Ottoman Empire as a result of the official *tanzimat* reforms and was reinforced with the European colonisation of the region, which supported specific communities and sects. It later evolved into an

integral part of the Lebanese political system, based on sectarian quotas of ministerial, parliamentary and administrative positions. A sectarian system of personal status also came in to place. Dominant media outlets, confessional schools, and people in power play a prominent role in sectarian incitement.

2 The militias were armed groups connected to political parties that existed prior to or emerged during the civil war (1975–1990) and transformed afterwards into political parties in their own right. Essential cadres in these militias were able to access the parliament and government after the Taef agreement and the amendment of the Lebanese constitution. They enjoy considerable power and influence within the economic system and the structure of corruption controlling the Lebanese administration, beside their role in the informal sector. Part of these militias still retains their weapons. Several armed clashes fuelled by sectarianism broke out among these militias after the civil war.

3 Central Centre for Statistics, 2004.

4 www.facebook.com/video/video. php?v=464498153616775.

5 The Lebanese Observatory for Labour Rights, 21 June 2006. The General Federation for Lebanese workers in the North.

6 The statement of the Minister of Internal Affairs Nihad al-Mashnuq, 'On the non-Organization of Syrian Refugees in the Lebanon', 22 May 2014.

7 www.al-akhbar.com/sites/default/ files/pdfs/20150103/doc20150103.pdf.

8 Moufakira Qanounia, Bayan Bich'an Alloujou' Alsouri Ila Loubnan, 30 Jan 2015, http://legal-agenda.com/ article.php?id=2570.

9 Statistics of the Centre for Education and Development Research for the Academic Calendar, 2011–2012.

10 Interview with a feminist activist who prefers to remain anonymous.

11 Eva El Choufi, Enaqaba Eljadidia 'Qadima': Wizaret Elamal Touwajih Amilat Elmanazil, 26 Jan 2015, http:// www.al-akhbar.com/node/224619.

12 Mounazimat Kafa Ounf Wa Istlghlal, *Man Youhaseb Wazir Elamal?*, 8 May 2015, http://tinyurl.com/ jm23vw8.

13 http://tinyurl.com/zdawvrz.

14 http://regie-web.rltt.com. lb/regie/Regie%20Overview.

15 Lenin quotes at www.marxist. org.

References

Abdo, T. (2014) 'The Trajectory of Domestic Workers: May 1st Is Our Day Too', *al-Manshour* website, 5 May.

Abisaab, H.M (2004) '"Unruly" Factory Women in Lebanon: Contesting French Colonialism and the National State, 1940–1946', *Journal of Women's History*, 16(3): 55–82.

Al-Buwary, E. (1986) *Tarikh al-haraqa al-Umaliyya wa al-Niqabiya fi Lubnan (1908–1946)* (The History of Labour and Trade Union in Lebanon, 1908–1946), Beirut: Dar al-Faraby.

al-Haj, F. (2013) 'Politicians "Kill" Their Bases: The Fate of Striking in General Assemblies', *al-Akhbar*, 8 March.

Cliff, T. (2001). *International Struggle and the Marxist Tradition*, Selected Works vol. 1, London: Bookmarks.

Dagher, K. (2010). 'Akkar, the Recurrent Resurgence for Class Struggle', *Al-Akhbar*, 18 August.

Daou, B. (2014), 'Les féminismes au Liban: un dynamisme de positionnement par rapport au patriarcat et

un renouvellement au sein du
'"Printemps Arabe"', Master's thesis,
Université Saint Joseph, Beirut.

Gaspard, T. (2005) *Iktisad Lubnan
al-Siyyasi 1948–2002 fi hudud al-
liberaliya al-iqtisadiyya* (The Political
Economy of Lebanon 1948–2002
in the Context of Economic
Liberalization), Beirut: Dar al-Nahar.

Kerbage, C. (2013) 'Domestic Workers
Confront . . . for a Trade Union',
Assafir, 2 February 2013.

Salibi, G. (1999) *Fi el Ittihad Kowa*, First
Edition, Beirut: Dar Mukhtarat.

7 | 'TO STRUGGLE IS ALSO TO TEACH': HOW CAN TEACHERS AND TEACHING UNIONS FURTHER THE GLOBAL FIGHT FOR ANOTHER WORLD?

Mary Compton

> I have no 'me' anymore and, for the children I love to teach, this is devastating. I will not do this for life, I simply cannot.

This *cri de cœur* from a UK teacher in response to a survey on workload from her union could have been made by a teacher in almost any country in the world (NUT 2014a). Teaching and teachers are in the eye of a global storm that is not only assaulting their pay, conditions and tenure but also their very identity as teachers and as human beings. Yet I will argue in this chapter that, partly because of this, they are in a key position to take a leading role in the global fight for economic and social justice.

We are living through a period characterised and dominated by neoliberalism as an organising paradigm, which shapes the nature, form and scope of the government of our political and economic organisation in almost every country in the world (Harvey 2005; Peck 2010). Neoliberalism is an ideology which holds that human's wellbeing is best advanced by liberating entrepreneurial individuals within a framework of strong property rights, free markets and free trade (Harvey 2005). In this chapter I argue that there is a global project to 'reform' education in line with this paradigm. Such 'reform' takes the shape of the weakening and, ultimately, the destruction of public education and its replacement with a form of privatised training for the majority of children, generating both corporate profits and a quiescent work force. I argue that this project not only sets out to destroy public education but that in the process it is also destroying teachers' sense of identity. This is one of the main issues that teaching unions have to address.

Institutions at the heart of the 'reform' project are consciously targeting and setting out to neuter, or, at worst, dismantle, teaching unions, since they see them as one of the biggest obstacles in their path. I will argue that they are right to see teaching unions as central to resistance to their project but only insofar as teachers are able to transform their unions and develop new forms of collective action. In particular teachers need to go beyond traditional trade union action and form coalitions with local communities and others in struggle. If they are to do this, they must also democratise their unions, as well as developing an alternative vision of education, which will be part of the struggle for a more just world. Teaching unions must also recognise the global nature both of the 'reform' project and of the resistance to it, and, in recognising this, develop strategies for global solidarity.

In the course of the chapter I will look at developments in teachers' movements globally and shall focus particularly on the situations in Mexico and in England.

The global project

Over the course of the last decade corporations have woken up to the potential for a multi-trillion dollar 'industry' in public education. One of the main actors in this field is Pearson, whose revenue from education in 2012 was $7.3 billion (Pearson 2013). But public education is not only a source of profits for capital. Its main 'products' are the workers who will continue to generate the surplus value to keep the profits flowing. So through their increasing control of education, corporations can also attempt to steer the kind of education that is being given to children, in order to produce the kind of flexible and quiescent workforce that they need.

The race to capture the global education 'market' can be described as a project, the architecture of which is becoming increasingly familiar to teachers in most parts of the world. Its first pillar is the privatisation of public schooling, either directly or through public–private partnerships (Robertson and Verger 2012). Corporations are able to mop up profits from the creation of so called low-fee private schools in the Global South and the increasing introduction of publicly subsidised for-profit schools in the North. A particularly egregious example of the former is the so-called 'School in a Box' for-profit franchise in Kenya, supported by Pearson, which charges parents for a child to be schooled in a corrugated iron shed by untrained school leavers using pre-scripted lessons (Compton 2014).

Its second pillar is an attack on public spending, involving deep cuts to education budgets. The results of this attack are seen in the so-called austerity policies across Europe as well as in the Global South where International Monetary Fund (IMF) conditionalities demand that indebted governments reduce public spending. As a result of this, not only is public education run down, thus increasing the space for private schools, but corporations can increase their profits still further since they are liable for less taxation (Harvey 2005).

The other main pillars of the project are constructed from managerial methods such as performance-related pay, scripted curricula and league tables. In order to institute these methods, there have to be standardised materials, both books and, more importantly, IT products for high-stakes testing, marking and data collection. They are not only one of the main sources of profit for corporations but also enable them to control the curriculum and how it is taught (Ball 2012).

This project is generally described as education 'reform'. Indeed it has got its own acronym: the Global Education Reform Movement (GERM) (Sahlberg 2012). While it directly profits corporations, it is framed in social justice rhetoric and is generally mediated both by putatively benign international organisations like the World Bank and UNESCO as well as corporate not-for-profit foundations like the Gates Foundation and corporate sponsored NGOs such as Pratham in India. The pretext for the project is that, as the World Bank puts it, 'educating children – particularly girls – has the greatest impact on eliminating poverty' (World Bank 2012).

While education is framed by reformers in social justice terms, included in this framing is the notion that the prime function of education is the creation of 'human capital' (Vally and Spreen 2014). The formula is straightforward: high quality education produces high quality human capital that in turn allows 'developing' nations to compete in the global marketplace. By competing and succeeding in this competition, economic growth is enhanced and nations and their populations are lifted out of poverty. The problem with this logic is that increased growth does not necessarily lead to decreased poverty. Indeed some of the fastest growing economies on earth, such as India and Nigeria, also have some of the highest proportions of their populations living in poverty and, in the case of Nigeria, the largest number of out of school children. Yet this skewed logic is frequently repeated in World Bank education policy documents (Bruns 2014).

Teaching unions

For the advocates of the GERM project, teaching unions represent the greatest 'institutional block to reform' (Corral 1999, quoted in Compton and Weiner 2008: 114). In a recent book published by the World Bank on the state of education in Latin America and the Caribbean, the author, having identified teachers themselves as the 'binding constraint on the region's progress towards world class education systems' (Bruns 2014: 50), says that the 'deepest challenge in raising teacher quality is not fiscal or technical, but political, because teachers' unions in every country in Latin America are large and politically active stakeholders' (Bruns 2014: 3). Having identified teachers and their unions as the problem, the author then goes on to lay out different strategies for defeating them. Three key tactics are identified throughout the book: joining together with civil society and businesses against teaching unions and encouraging a media narrative about the inadequacy of public education, conciliation and an attempt to co-opt unions into the project and outright confrontation.

The main development to be avoided, is the 'political juggernaut of teachers' unions and parent and civil society stakeholders united in opposition' (Bruns 2014: 296). The most common tactic of the advocates of reform to achieve this is to mount a sustained media attack on public education and in particular teachers and their unions (Ball 1990). This is partly made possible by starving public education of funds, thus enhancing the perception that public education and the people who work in it are of low quality. Moreover instruments like national league tables of schools, the naming and shaming of 'low achieving' schools, and the OECD's PISA league table of countries' education systems, all add to the perception that public schooling is failing, and enable reformers to make common cause with dissatisfied parents and businesses. When you add to this the framing discussed above, which casts education as the route out of poverty, dissatisfaction is understandable, particularly among low-income parents at a time of mass unemployment.

If, despite these tactics, advocates of the project are unable to get parents and other stakeholders on side, then the second tactic is to co-opt unions themselves into the project. In this they have had some success. Rather than asking why corporate elites are deciding education policy, union leaderships more often appear to be scrambling to get themselves a seat at the table. The global teaching union federation, Education International (EI), takes one small seat at any number of elite tables, such as the Universal Global Metrics Taskforce, which is co-chaired by Michael Barber, chief education adviser to Pearson (and himself originally a prominent officer of the UK NUT). Betraying a general failure to deconstruct the social justice rhetoric of the project, to understand its underlying ideology and to question the structural issues behind education inequality, union leaders are able to feel comfortable collaborating with it, rather than resisting it and advocating for alternatives.

It is frequently the case, however, that teaching unions are forced into resistance. The cuts in education funding result in cuts to teachers' pay, which is invariably the biggest item in education budgets, as well as attacks on pensions. Another major feature of these cuts, particularly in the Global South, is the employment of teachers on temporary contracts, which allows governments to get better value for money in the World Bank's terms since contract teachers are paid a fraction of what a regularly employed teacher would earn (Bruns *et al.* 2011) The lack of tenure is also useful as a disciplinary tool. All of these attacks on teachers' living standards as well as often grossly inadequate conditions of service (in the Global South classes of over 100 are commonplace, as are schools with no sanitary facilities) naturally result in a great deal of traditional and not so traditional trade union action, from strikes, to mass protests and even to hunger strikes and self-immolation. A week does not go by without a strike by teachers somewhere in the world (Teachersolidarity 2015).

In this sense then, the advocates of the reform project are right to see teaching unions as a 'block to reform'. By the very fact that their core business is supposed to be the defence of members' interests, they are forced into confrontation with states, local governments and other employers. On their own, however, these economic struggles rarely meet with much success. This is in part because teachers are now facing a globalised project. In Southern Europe and the so-called indebted countries of the Global South, cuts determined by international financial institutions mean that teachers frequently remain unpaid for months, or allowances are not paid, and governments, under pressure from the IMF, assert that they do not have the money to pay up. In the UK and US on the other hand, the problem is not so much direct external power from financial institutions as the assimilation of the GERM project into national policy. This takes the form of the break-up of the public education service into ever smaller units such as free schools or academies in the UK, or charters in the US, so that it becomes more and more difficult for teaching unions to fight for pay and conditions on a national scale (Carter *et al.* 2010).

So ultimately the only way to defend public education and the teaching profession is to overturn the global reform project itself. In order to do this, teaching unions must form precisely the kinds of alliances with communities most feared by the advocates of the project. By the nature of their work, teachers often live in and are respected members of their communities and their economic, social and personal interests are more or less bound up with these communities. This is nicely summarised in a slogan adopted by struggling teachers across the world: 'Teachers' working conditions are children's learning conditions' (Olson-Jones 2014). The very things that threaten teachers – low pay, oversized classes, lack of tenure, lack of teaching materials, deprofessionalisation, bad infrastructure – are also an assault on children, their parents and communities. The atomisation of communities and the teaching profession into competing individuals through the imposition of school 'choice' and managerial accountability frameworks are as much an attack on them as they are on teachers.

If such alliances are to be formed however, teachers also need to democratise their unions and develop a new vision for education. They also need to develop a global perspective and global solidarity. Such changes to teaching unions, which in many cases would require radical transformation, could be framed as a turn towards social movement unionism. Indeed there is already a literature from critical educators along these lines (Weiner 2012; Peterson 2015). To explore these issues in more detail I shall now look at teaching unions in Mexico and England.

Teaching unions in Mexico

The struggle against neoliberal education reform is at the heart of the political turmoil in Mexico. Unsurprisingly, all four elements necessary for the involvement of teaching unions in the struggle for social justice are far advanced in the Mexican teachers' movement.

The fight for union democracy has been particularly sharp in the rank and file of the Mexican teachers' union, SNTE. SNTE, with 1.6 million members, is the largest teaching union in Latin America. However, its recent history has been marked by corruption. Its most extreme manifestation is its now jailed leader, Elba Esther Gordillo, who was the darling of successive neo-liberal governments, so much so that she was declared SNTE president for life by the government in 2008. As a result of her role she enriched herself, spending millions on houses in California and Mexico, and gave large gifts to compliant local leaders bought from members' subscriptions. When the ruling elite changed tactics from co-opting the teachers union to all-out confrontation, it was this corruption that provided the pretext for Peña Nieto to arrest her.

But the SNTE did much more damage than corruption. While it was still in favour with successive governments, it took responsibility for forcing the so-called Alliance for Quality Education (ACE) 'reform' on teachers. This measure was actively promoted both by the World Bank and by corporate education lobbying groups, in particular the powerful Mexicanos Primeros. The chairperson of Mexicanos Primeros is Claudio Gonzáles Guajardo, co-founder of the Televisa television network in Mexico. He has since been appointed by Nieto as the head of his Education Transition Team (Bocking 2015). The ACE reform promotes standardised teaching based on globalised curricula, insists on Spanish and English as the medium of instruction (even though the government recognises 68 indigenous languages) and brings in standardised testing, performance related pay and an end to teacher tenure, as well as vouchers and increasing privatisation of schools. There has also been an increasing role for business in schools, with secondary schools teaching a curriculum dictated by local factories, where part of the week involves young people working for free, for example, in one school in the state of Puebla, they make police uniforms (Rincones *et al.* 2008). Crucially it aims to phase out the so-called Escuelas Normales – teacher education colleges that train predominantly low income and rural young people to become teachers, which have become centres of resistance to the reform project – and replaces these schools with private colleges. The degree to which the Escuelas Normales are seen to be a threat to ruling elites was arguably highlighted in September 2014, when 43 student teachers at the Ayotzinapa Escuela Normal were abducted by police. Since the event, the bones of one student have been identified, but the rest have disappeared without trace. While as yet no-one has been brought to justice for this outrage, it is widely believed that the state is at very least complicit and that it was precisely the revolutionary nature of the education at the colleges that made the young people a target (Goldman 2015).

While Gordillo and the official leadership of SNTE were the main cheerleaders and enforcers of the ACE, it has been vigorously contested by teachers in many parts of Mexico. A crucial part of this contestation has therefore been the fight for democracy within the union, so that it can represent the interests of its members and develop policy with them rather than serving a corrupt national and local leadership. Here a teacher from Morelos describes one action during a protracted struggle in 2008:

> The very moment teachers started the movement, they decided to take possession of the building of the Sección XIX of the S.N.T.E., the state run teacher union, ejecting the puppet union leaders who conversed only with the government and cared little for the teachers' opinions. New leaders were democratically elected and the government is now trying to fire them from their teaching positions in retribution. (Teachersolidarity 2008)

This fight for democracy was crucial to the survival of the anti-reform movement. The SNTE leadership in league with state forces attempted to stamp out dissent violently, organising the disappearances and arrests of some of the teachers and, on at least one occasion, ordering the assassination of an opposition leader. Moreover, the blatant corruption within the union enabled the press both locally and globally to frame the teachers' struggle as motivated by a self-interested desire to maintain corrupt privileges. This was a gift to the strategists of reform, reinforcing their tactic of trying to get the general population on side by attacking public education, teachers and teaching unions.

If such a framing was to be contested, it was vital to join with local communities not only in fighting for democratic education but against all the other structural issues that keep people in poverty and threaten their fragile way of life. In ways reminiscent of the actions described in this volume by Manzano in Argentina, the teachers framed their struggle as being against the neoliberal and pro-rich policies of successive governments: the struggle for control of education was seen as part of a much wider fight over public spaces and goods. The most celebrated example of this was the six-month struggle in Oaxaca in 2006, where what started as a teachers' strike for education resources, union democracy and labour rights became the impetus for a mass social movement for indigenous rights and against corruption and the dispossession practised on communities by corporations, in collusion with the neoliberal state (Favela 2010). Far from confining themselves to traditional forms of struggle – for example, school strikes for justified but sectoral economic demands, which temporarily inconvenience communities and risk alienating them – teachers occupied public squares for months on end in Oaxaca, all the while discussing their struggle with local communities. In this occupation, they interacted with and were supported by local populations. Here a participating teacher describes a similar occupation in the province of Morelos in 2008:

> During the strike, teachers started a sit in (plantón) in
> Cuernavaca's main square, the Plaza de Armas in front of
> the Government Palace. Teachers erected tents, for their
> headquarters, where they stood on guard, ate everyday, slept on
> the cold floors, sang and expressed their creativity on posters,
> leaflets and became closer with their compañeros in struggle,
> their second family. (Teachersolidarity 2008)

Similar actions continue up to the present, for example in Guerrero in 2013, tens of thousands came on to the streets, campaigning both against the ACE education reforms and against proposed new mining projects, the privatisation of the state oil company PEMEX and an increase in sales tax (Paterson 2013).

The fight for democratic and critical education has also been central to the struggle against education 'reform' in Mexico. Latin America has a distinguished history in this respect, not least through the legacy of Brazil's Paulo Freire. Freire saw education as a dialogue between the teacher and student in which both learned to understand their oppression in order to be able to transform themselves and the world, and, in the process, become more fully human (Freire 1970). This 'practice of freedom' informed the struggle for democratic education in Mexico. This contrasts with what Freire characterised as the 'banking' method of education, which sees students as empty vessels to be filled with knowledge by their teachers. This kind of education is promoted by education reformers today who, as Freire put it about elite education 'reformers' in the past, 'use their humanitarianism to preserve a profitable situation. Thus they react almost instinctively to any experiment which stimulates the critical faculties' (Freire 1970: 55).

Many parents in Mexico were prepared to support the teachers' struggle, not least because they were campaigning for an end to school fees and to improve the conditions in schools. However, it was important for teachers not only to acknowledge the shortcomings of education as it existed but to propose a different kind of education to the one being promoted by ACE, which indigenous groups in particular saw as culturally elitist, devaluing or ignoring their language and traditions and promoting a US-dominated view of the world, teaching and knowledge.

Teachers' leaders in Oaxaca have created their own strategy for improvement: the Plan for the Transformation of Education in Oaxaca (PTEO). While accepting that some knowledge is universal, the PTEO holds that the cultural context is important and therefore education projects should be decided by the school collective, teachers, students, parents and the local community, rather than elites. As one of the leaders of the PTEO project put it, a teacher has to 'see the cultural richness in these communities, in the people who live there' (Bacon 2013).

The plan also holds that evaluation of teachers should be done through interaction with colleagues and parents. Teachers and students keep portfolios that would then be looked at and analysed by teachers and families. Instead of focusing on competition, school communities would concentrate on collaboration. Above all, both teacher-training and school education would focus on the development of critical thinking. And so a teacher, according to the same PTEO leader, should not only have roots in the community but be 'a source of social change'. The combination of fighting for free and properly funded public education whilst also creating a project for a different kind of education was able to garner huge support from local communities.

International solidarity has also been central to the teachers' struggle in Mexico. There are two reasons for this. The first is the need for the world to know the degree of oppression with which social protest, including the protests of teachers, is met. There have been frequent calls for the international union movement to lobby governments, publicise and support teachers who have been disappeared, arrested or murdered. This has been very important in raising awareness of the Ayotzinapa 43 mentioned above, for example.

Apart from asking for global solidarity to support teachers who are being oppressed in their country, however, dissident Mexican teachers have always taken the lead in understanding that the neoliberal education reform project is global and therefore needs a global response. Shortly after the violent eviction of the occupation of Zócalo Square in Mexico City in 2013, the teachers organised a global solidarity conference. In its call for participants it said:

> At the Meeting the discussion will be about the 'educational' reforms to shed labor rights, override the intervention of unions, undermine free public education, close schools, lay off teachers, and exclude students, not only in Mexico but throughout the world. At the same time we will all look out to reach agreements about the actions to develop internationally a Campaign of Defense of Public Education and the labor rights of workers in education. (Teachersolidarity 2013)

Truly, the democratic teachers of Mexico bear out the popular slogan of teachers' struggles in Latin America: 'la maestra luchando también está enseñando', which I have used as the title of this chapter.

Teaching unions in England[1]

I shall now look at teacher unions in England through the lens of the four components of struggle described above: union democracy, alliances with communities, development of an alternative vision and global solidarity. I shall be concentrating on my own union, the National Union of Teachers (NUT) since I know it from the inside. It is the largest teaching union in Great Britain, if by a fairly small margin.

Under successive governments, England has been subject to the full assault of neoliberal education 'reform'. Like Reagan in the US, Thatcher was an early adopter of the neoliberal project. The so-called Great Education Reform Act of 1987 introduced a raft of 'reform' measures, such as privatisation, local management of schools, opting out of schools from local authorities, school choice, standardised testing and a national curriculum (Simon 1988). This was continued by successive governments (including a putatively Labour government), with the introduction of performance-related pay and the further break-up of the state education service through the semi-privatised academies programme. All these developments have been contested both in national campaigns like test boycotts and in local campaigns against specific forms of privatisation like academies and opting out.

With the election of a new left leadership in the NUT in 2006, a more determined and consistent national campaign was instigated. In order to make this happen, a decision was taken that, unlike the old leadership, which excluded members of other caucuses from positions of power, this one would be more representative of different political currents and therefore arguably more democratic, at least at leadership level. However, if the union is going to be genuinely democratic, it will need to build its base and find ways to involve teachers at the school level in national decision-making. While there are already structures in place that are meant to allow that to happen – for example, local branches send delegates to the annual conference where they vote on matters of national policy – the vast majority of members are not involved in those processes because branch meetings are poorly attended. This is partly because of the extreme workload of teachers – according to a government survey, primary teachers work on average 60 hours a week and their secondary colleagues only a little less, resulting in endemic levels of tiredness, demoralisation and stress (Department for Education 2014). It is also due to the power of neoliberal ideology, which devalues collective action and encourages individuals, including teachers, to see themselves as solely responsible for their own fate.

For the first time since 1986, the NUT has engaged in a series of national one-day strikes against government plans to worsen pension arrangements, freeze pay, increase workload and devolve more pay decisions to schools. While the strikes achieved the symbolic success of contributing to the sacking of a particularly unpopular and long-standing education minister in 2014, their effect on the substantive issues of pay and pensions have been small. A government proposal to completely deregulate teachers' terms of employment was overturned during the strike campaign, in itself a significant achievement, but a more piecemeal trend towards this remains something that constantly confronts the union. And the threats facing public education have only increased since the crisis hit in 2008, followed by the election of the coalition government in 2010, and even more so with the election of a Conservative government in 2015. The education reform pro-gramme has been ramped up, with forced conversion to academies as well as the introduction of government-funded free schools. And though the government is not under the direct control of the IMF, it is following the same economic policies of deficit reduction through cuts in public spending. As a result, the NUT has also joined forces with people working in other public sector jobs, meaning that the aims of strikes and demonstrations have been broadened beyond the immediate interests of teachers. However, there is little chance of success until the union is part of an even broader fight for economic and social justice, which means becoming increasingly involved with the general struggles of local communities.

On a small scale, particularly in fights against privatisation, the union has worked closely with local communities. A good example is the struggle against the planned demolition of Sullivan Primary School in London. The local council wanted to replace it with a Church of England free school for boys. A local activist described the campaign:

> The local NUT union group worked closely with the school community to challenge the proposals. Massive lobbies of the Town Hall were backed up with lobbies of the Mayor of London and the Prime Minister, with social media campaigns, fun runs, a day of prayer in the local mosque, leafleting and press and media campaigns. From one tiny corner of the London Borough of Hammersmith & Fulham this became a borough wide

campaign. Part of this was down to the union's mobilisation of support from other local schools who opened their playgrounds after school to allow campaigners to meet more and more parents. (Teachersolidarity 2014)

Partly as a result of the campaign, the local administration was thrown out at the next elections in 2014, and the plans were shelved. While not always so successful, such campaigns have been common in many parts of the country and have served to unite teaching unions with their local communities.

The NUT nationally has also tried to involve the local community in its campaigns. Its Stand Up for Education campaign has seen members in shopping centres and high streets across the country, gathering support from local people. However there are many spaces where the NUT has yet to forge alliances. In particular, there has been no significant engagement with the fluctuating rise in activism amongst both university and school students since 2010, which has also been reflected in rebellions of other young people, in particular in the riots of 2011. The possibility for solidarity and joint working over issues like the abolition of the Education Maintenance Allowance (a grant for low-income young people accessing sixth form and further education) were never really explored. Yet this was an area, the access to education for all, that is central to the campaigning aims of the NUT. Moreover there is a growing army of precarious young workers in schools. Thousands of graduates are working for agencies as teaching assistants, often on zero-hours contracts. At present, such workers are not eligible to join the NUT, since it is only open to qualified teachers. Yet, if they were eligible and could be persuaded to join, the possibilities for new forms of organisation, for democratic challenge, as well as new energy for the struggle, of the kinds described by Anagnostopolous and Evangelinidis in Greece in this volume, seem to me to be enormous.

In England there is not yet anything like the broad movement for economic and social justice that we have seen in Mexico. This is despite the fact that many millions of people in the country are seeing their services cut, their jobs disappear, are on zero hours contracts, live in poverty with their children and are, in short, victims of a situation where the rich are getting richer while they are suffering. If the NUT is to contribute to the building of such a movement, it will have to address the structural issues that are the cause of this increasing injustice and inequality. This brings me to the third strand of transformation that the NUT needs to address: the development of a new vision of education, based on an understanding of the underlying ideology of education 'reform' and of the economic relations that lead to inequality and poverty. The union has set up a Year of the Curriculum project with the laudable aim of bringing discussion and determination of the curriculum down to school level. However, its literature for the campaign does not question the underlying ideology of education reform. Indeed it accepts the concept of the highly prescriptive national curriculum, suggests that the role of the teacher is to create a 'product' who is 'equipped for life', implies that one of the main aims of education is to 'achieve high wages in the global economy', and places no emphasis on the need to develop democratic and critical education (NUT 2014b). Nor does it suggest involving local communities in the development of a curriculum that reflects the world in which they live.

Many teachers are feeling that their identity as teachers is being threatened by the ways in which they are made to work. Overwhelmingly these ways reflect a neoliberal view of society in which each person is in competition with everyone else in a 'race to the top' and is her own small enterprise (Mirowski 2013). In particular the managerial methods of accountability tend to strip away teachers' sense of themselves as teachers. The introduction of performance-related pay for example, and the tying of pay to students' results in standardised tests, disrupts both the relationship between teacher and teacher and that between teacher and student. If there is a limited pot of money and only some members of the school staff will be rewarded, then why should a teacher collaborate with her colleagues? If a student's test results determine his teacher's pay, then the teacher is no longer solely interested in his achievements for their own sake, she could be said to have a financial stake in his doing well. In this framework, the rate of pay becomes a measure of a teacher's worth and if the performance-related pay does not come her way, not only is she financially disadvantaged, she likely also feels she is a failure as a teacher. Large volumes of union casework involving teacher stress and feelings of worthlessness attest to this.

Not only does this reconstruction of teaching as a competitive, rather than a collaborative endeavour strike at teachers' identity, but the imposition by a small global elite of a group of knowledges that are officially sanctioned and a teaching methodology that is acceptable, strips away the individual creativity and interests of teachers as well as their cultural and linguistic references, substituting them with corporate instructions and globalised norms.

While teachers on their own cannot undo the ideological work of neoliberalism, they are in a position to challenge it, just as they are doing in Mexico, and their unions should be at the heart of this work, not least because younger teachers have been trained in a pedagogy that is permeated by the ideology of GERM. The union's accumulated knowledge and research capabilities should enable it to begin to set out the vision for a new kind of education that contributes to the building of a more just world. This in turn could lead to new forms of struggle. For example, early years teachers might feel that administering standardised tests to four-year-olds would be something that was completely at odds with their professional training and beliefs. One response to this would be to boycott such tests, an action in which the union has engaged in the past. Another strategy might be that teachers go on strike, but instead of sending the children home, occupy the schools for the strike and teach using methodologies that they are helping to develop with the union, in which they believe, thus giving them back their agency as teachers. For example, early years teachers could spend the day engaging in play activities, older children could be encouraged to talk about their communities and to question the injustices they face, linking their experiences to those of other communities all over the world. And parents could be invited in to take part as well.

Occupying schools would throw up all sorts of legal problems, as indeed would occupying squares, or local government offices as activists have done not only in Mexico but in many other parts of Latin America and in the Middle East, as illustrated throughout this volume. At present, UK teaching unions are constrained by some of the most illiberal anti-union laws in the world, and these laws are set to become even more punitive. But with increasing attacks on public services the union movement as a whole will need to revisit the ways in which those services and those rights were won in the first place. As was shown so graphically in the London student protests in 2010, or in the poll tax riots in 1990, it is only when people go beyond the law that protests catch the attention of the media, and, in the case of the poll tax riots, manage to reverse policy. It is possible that the severity of the attacks on union organisation coming from the Conservative administration will force a rupture in union bureaucracies, which could be both an extreme danger and an opportunity. In several chapters in this volume, new forms of struggle are described in which traditional labour unions are either sidelined, in the case of Greece, or display outright hostility, as in the migrant struggles in Italy, described by Irene Peano. As I have described above, teachers' work is uniquely embedded in and valued by communities. Most of those in struggle – the youth, migrants, the disabled, the unemployed – have an investment in schools and education of one sort or another. In Mexico as I have described and as Manzano described in Argentina, teachers' unions have to a certain extent been able to transform themselves and become part of a wider struggle. We in the NUT have a lot to learn from teaching unions and education activists in the rest of the world.

This brings me on to the fourth strand of a successful transformation of unions: global solidarity. The NUT is beginning to work its way towards that. It has used tactics practised by unions in other parts of the world. For instance, The Stand Up for Education campaign was partly inspired by the Chicago Teachers Union strike in 2012, when teachers mobilised massive protests all over the city against the anti public school policies of the Rahm administration. The NUT also organised a conference of education activists from across the Global North and South, to compare struggles and learn from each other. It is featuring Global Education Reform or 'GERM' in all its campaigning in an effort to make members aware of the global dimensions of the assault that they are undergoing. However, real global solidarity amongst teachers is still in its infancy. International work must move beyond a deadening charitable attitude, must cease to be taken in by the social justice framing used by education 'reformers', and instead promote real solidarity – by sharing experiences, by learning from unions in other countries, by publicising and supporting teachers' struggles globally and where possible co-ordinating campaigns and action.

Conclusion

Teachers are at the sharp end of an onslaught from corporate interests in the shape of a global education 'reform' project. This project has as its main components privatisation, cuts and managerial accountability measures. I have argued that this not only is destroying public education globally but is an assault on teachers' identity as teachers.

For the advocates of the project, teaching unions are one of the main obstacles in their path. For this reason they advocate neutralising or destroying unions by either uniting civil society and business against them, co-opting them into the project or through outright confrontation. Teaching unions globally have been subject to all of these tactics and sometimes succumb to them.

However, teachers are also in the forefront of resistance in many parts of the world. But because traditional trade union struggle in education is facing a powerful global project, it is necessary for teachers to transform their unions. I have argued that four elements are necessary to do this – democratisation, building alliances with communities, developing a new vision of education that contributes to the struggle for a more just world, and global solidarity.

In Mexico, teachers have galvanised a movement to transform the whole of that society. In England, things are not so far advanced because there is as yet no broad movement campaigning for social justice. If the NUT is to be part of building such a movement it will have to question the underlying structural issues that lead to the educational injustice that it is attempting to address, as well as transforming itself in the ways set out above.

Speaking on the Mexican situation, a recent commentator said:

> While each struggle has its own particularities, all are bound together by a common thread . . . Inevitably, as in Mexico today, the education issue quickly exposes a host of inequalities and injustices . . . . And in one important sense, like the factories of the 20th century, the classroom is ground zero for class struggle in the 21st century. (Paterson 2013)

While we have still got a long way to go in England, if we move in the directions I have suggested and learn from and work with our colleagues in the rest of the world, our classrooms too can become central to the struggle for economic and social justice.

Note

1 The UK education system is devolved to its four constituent countries, England, Scotland, Northern Ireland and Wales. The NUT organises and recruits in England and Wales only. For these reasons, although many of the points made refer to the whole of the UK, and others to England and Wales, others are exclusive to England. For that reason I refer to England throughout rather than the UK.

References

Bacon, D. (2013) 'US Style School Reform Goes South'. www.thenation. com/article/173308/us-style-school-reform-goes-south?page=full#, accessed January 2015.

Ball, S. (1990) *Politics and Policy Making in Education: Explorations in Policy Sociology*, London: Routledge.

Ball, S. (2012) *Global Education Inc: New Policy Networks and the Neo-liberal Imaginary*, Oxford: Routledge.

Bocking, P. (2015) 'Why Do Governments Adopt Neoliberal Education Policies?', *Alternate Routes: A Journal of Critical Social Research*, 26: 74–100.

Bruns, B. (2014) 'Great Teachers: How to Raise Student Learning in Latin America and the Caribbean'. www. worldbank.org/content/dam/ Worldbank/document/LAC/ Great_Teachers-How_to_Raise_ Student_Learning-Barbara-Bruns-Advance%20Edition.pdf, accessed 21 January 2015.

Bruns, B., Filmer, D. and Patrinos, H.A. (2011) 'Making Schools Work'. http://siteresources.worldbank.org/ EDUCATION/Resources/278200-1298568319076/makingschoolswork. pdf, accessed 21 January 2015.

Carter, B., Stevenson, H. and Passy, R. (2010) *Industrial Relations in Education*, New York: Routledge.

Compton, M. (2014) 'Companies Profit from Flat-pack Schools', *Red Pepper*, October. www.redpepper.org.uk/ education/, accessed 15 July 2015.

Compton, M. and Weiner, L. (2008) *The Global Assault on Teaching, Teachers and Their Unions: Stories for Resistance*, New York: Palgrave Macmillan.

Department for Education (2014) *Teachers' Workload Diary Survey 2013*. www.gov.uk/government/ uploads/system/uploads/ attachment_data/file/285941/DFE-RR316.pdf, accessed 15 July 2015.

Favela, A. (2010) 'Lasting Lessons from Oaxaca: Teachers as Luchadores Sociales: An Inside Account of the Historic 2006 Oaxacan Teachers' Movement and Why It Is Still Relevant Today', *Radical Teacher*, 88 (Summer): 63–72.

Freire, P. (1970) *Pedagogy of the Oppressed*, London: Penguin Books.

Goldman, F. (2015) 'Crisis in Mexico: Who Is Really Responsible for the Missing 43?' www.newyorker.com/ news/news-desk/crisis-mexico-really-responsible-missing-forty-three, accessed 15 July 2015.

Harvey, D. (2005) *A Brief History of Neoliberalism*, Oxford: Oxford University Press.

Mirowski, P. (2013) *Never Let a Serious Crisis Go to Waste*, London: Verso.

NUT (2014a) *Teachers and Workload*. www.teachers.org.uk/files/teachers-and-workload-survey-report-september-2014.pdf, accessed 21 January 2015.

NUT (2014b) *Year of the Curriculum, Reclaiming Our Curriculum*.

www.teachers.org.uk/files/yoc-reclaiming-a5-9625.pdf, accessed 21 January 2015.

Olson-Jones, B. (2014) 'Teachers' Working Conditions Are Students' Learning Conditions'. www.contracostatimes.com/opinion/ci_25480594/guest-commentary-teachers-working-conditions-are-students-learning, accessed 15 July 2015.

Paterson, K. (2013) '"We Are All Guerrero": Mexico's New Popular Revolt Takes on the State'. www.cipamericas.org/archives/9403, accessed 21 January 2015.

Pearson (2013) *Annual Report and Accounts 2013*. www.pearson.com/content/dam/corporate/global/pearson-dot-com/files/annual-reports/ar2013/2013--annual-report-accounts.pdf, accessed 21 January 2015.

Peck, J. (2010) *Constructions of Neoliberal Reason*, Oxford: Oxford University Press.

Peterson, B. (2015) 'If Teachers Can't Make Their Unions More Democratic and Social Justice-Minded, Public Ed Is Doomed'. http://inthesetimes.com/working/entry/17632/democratic_teachers_unions, accessed 15 July 2015.

Rincones, R., Hampton, E. and Silva, C. (2008) 'Teaching for the Factory: Neoliberalism in Mexican Education', in Compton, M. and Weiner, L. (eds) *The Global Assault on Teaching, Teachers and Their Unions: Stories for Resistance*, pp. 37–43. New York: Palgrave Macmillan.

Robertson, S. and Verger, A. (2012) 'Governing Education through Public Private Partnerships', in Robertson, S., Mundy, K., Verger, A. and Menashy, F. (eds) *Public Private Partnerships in Education: New Actors and Modes of Governance in a Globalising World*, pp. 21–42. Cheltenham: Edward Elgar.

Sahlberg, P. (2012) 'How GERM is Infecting Schools around the World'. http://pasisahlberg.com/text-test/, accessed 21 January 2015.

Simon, B. (1988) *Bending the Rules: The Baker Reform of Education*, London: Lawrence and Wishart.

Teachersolidarity (2008) http://teachersolidarity.com/blog/news-from-the-morelos-front-line, accessed 25 October 2016.

Teachersolidarity (2013) http://teachersolidarity.com/blog/urgent-invitation-to-solidarity-conference-in-mexico, accessed 25 October 2016.

Teachersolidarity (2014) http://teachersolidarity.com/blog/important-victory-for-london-parents-and-teachers, accessed 25 October 2016.

Teachersolidarity (2015) www.teachersolildarity.com, accessed 15 July 2015.

Vally, S. and Spreen, C.A. (2014) 'Globalisation and Education in Post-Apartheid South Africa: The Narrowing of Education's Purpose', in Stromquist, N.P. and Monkman, K. (eds) *Globalisation and Education: Integration and Contestation across Cultures*, pp. 267–283. New York: Rowman and Littlefield.

Weiner, L. (2012) *The Future of Our Schools: Teachers Unions and Social Justice*, Chicago, IL: Haymarket.

World Bank (2012) *Millennium Development Goals*. www.worldbank.org/mdgs/education.html, accessed 15 July 2015.

PART THREE

RANK AND FILE CHALLENGES TO TRADITIONAL UNIONISM

8 | 'UNGRIEVABLE' LABOUR AND 'UNRULY' POLITICS: NGOs, WORKERS' RIGHTS, AND THE 2013–2014 PROTESTS IN BRAZIL

Lucy McMahon[1]

On 6 February 2014, Tasman Amaral Accioly ran off the curb into Avenida Presidente Vargas and was fatally hit by a bus. He had been fleeing the police's flash bombs during one of the protests against rising bus fares in Rio de Janeiro. After his day shift working at a news stand, he had gone as normal to the Central station to buy the sweets he was to sell that evening in Lapa. Yet his sudden death initially went unreported, overshadowed by the death of cameraman Santiago Andrade. Santiago had been hit by a firecracker inside the station. Both were taken to Hospital Municipal Souza Aguiar, where according to reports a 'battalion of authorities and doctors were in place directing reporters and family relatives of Santiago' ('Aposentado Morreu' 2014). In contrast, Tasman's wife Ieda Accioly said that no one informed her about her husband's condition until after he had died hours later ('Aposentado Morreu' 2014). Santiago's death made headline news and was reported across the world. Tasman's death was reported first on Facebook, where a campaign finally managed to get the mainstream media to briefly notice a few days later. The differential treatment of the two deaths can be explained by two things: first the fact that Santiago's death could be attributed to protesters rather than to the police (although this is as yet unproven). But more importantly, because Santiago was a high-profile professional and Tasman was a street vendor.

The 2013–2014 Brazilian protest movement was a series of demonstrations across the country involving as many as two million people. Some trace the beginning to rises in bus fares in several cities (starting in Natal in August 2012) but by June 2013 the protests had become a multi-directional critique against inequality, corruption, privatisation, over-spending on mega-events and the everyday violence of the military police. These protests are often grouped along with a number of contemporaneous popular mobilisations – including the Egyptian revolution, Turkish protests and anti-austerity mobilisations in Europe – because of a common disaffection with such methods of political participation as parties, unions and established social movements (Nunes 2014: 7; Khanna *et al.* 2013: 9; Mendonça and Ercan 2015: 212). This chapter considers this disaffection as a product of an economic and political system that renders labour increasingly 'superfluous', and where – as demonstrated by the treatment of Tasman's death – lives are differentially 'grievable' according to their occupational status. In Brazil, as elsewhere, this differential grievability is being fought against by an assertive intrusion of new voices onto the political stage. Khanna *et al.* refer to these recent mobilisations as 'unruly politics': 'political action by people who have been denied voice by the rules of the political game', which 'take forms that are illegal, violent, disruptive of the social order, strident or rude' (2013: 14).

Compared to Egypt and Turkey, the protests in Brazil occurred under the 'progressive' government led by Dilma Rousseff of the Workers' Party (PT), which was elected on a platform of radical democratic and economic change (Mollo and Saad-Filho 2006: 99). While many claim that the PT merely pursues 'neoliberalism with a human face', others hold out hope that it provides at least some openings towards more systemic change (Petras and Veltmeyer 2006; Saad-Filho and Morais 2013). This hope was at least partly vindicated by Rousseff's response to the protests on 18 June 2013:

> Brazil today woke up stronger. The magnificence of yesterday's protests showed the energy of our democracy, the force of the voice of the street and the civility of our population . . . these voices of the streets need to be heard. They go beyond, and this remains visible, the traditional mechanisms of institutions, of political parties, of class entities and certain media. (Bonis 2013)

This prime time statement of support received international attention for being far more accommodating than the response of Recep Tayyip Erdogan in Turkey to similar demonstrations (Romero 2013).

In this chapter, I consider what 'unruly politics' means for street vendor labour struggles in Brazil. I draw from interviews with vendors and participant observation during 2013 and 2014 at the feminist workers' rights NGO, CAMTRA[2] to claim that street vendors have little reason to trust existing political institutions. Unionisation has rarely been effective and where it has worked it has been contingent on some kind of exclusion. Recent cash transfer programmes and contributory social security schemes initiated by the PT are seen mainly as palliative (Barrientos 2013: 892; Vannuchi 2015). As such it is not surprising that the forms taken by street vendor labour struggles in the recent protests have not involved unions but have been spontaneous and direct action. The chapter firstly asserts that the 2013–2014 protests were simultaneously the desperate acts of a disillusioned citizenry and the generator of a new, innovative and transformative politics. I then highlight the limitations to 'unruly politics' in the fight against social and political exclusion. As the case of Tasman shows, street vendors' participation in protest is shaped by the vulnerable space they occupy as citizens; street protest provides no immunity to social inequality, no privileged 'outside' space.

As many of the contributions to this volume show, unions, NGOs and political parties all have a role in inciting, shaping and responding to street protest. Several years of horizontalist anti-austerity and (at times) anti-capitalist street protest across the world have led in some countries to attempts to formalise this protest. Examples include Syriza and Popular Unity in Greece, Podemos in Spain, the rise of the Left Bloc in Portugal and Jeremy Corbyn in the UK. Brazil's protest movement provides important insights for the future of these European movements, because it provides an example of a state that professes – through the words of the president – to encourage such mobilisation, while employing dictatorship-era tactics to repress it, and continuing a regime of austerity (Assy and Ertür, 2014: 11; Trevisani 2015). In the third part of this chapter, I outline CAMTRA's response to this political challenge, and argue that it offers a new way of thinking about labour politics that seeks to avoid both the exclusiveness of traditional labour organising and the danger and short-termism of more spontaneous mobilisations. It both appeals to and protests against the state. There are three elements to CAMTRA's work that I suggest make an important contribution to any discussion about the future of informal sector labour struggles under neoliberalism. These are (1) the expansion of the term 'worker', which also expands an understanding of what constitutes 'worker's rights', (2) the assertion of a mutual relationship between personal and political empowerment and (3) the participation in new or 'unruly politics' while also working aspirationally inside existing political structures; or in other words, the adoption of two kinds of hope.

'Ungrievable' labour and 'unruly' politics

In *Frames of War: When Is Life Grievable?*, Judith Butler argues that contemporary politics is shaped by a distinction between lives that are treated as grievable, and those that, for whatever reason, are framed as 'not quite lives' in the first place, and hence unworthy of the status of mourning (2010: 1). The use of protest to assert the 'grievability' of lives is evident in the responses to the self-immolation of Mohammed Bouazizi in Tunisia, the police shooting of Mark Duggan in London and of Michael Brown in Ferguson among many others. Bouazizi's last shout 'How do you expect me to make a living?' is echoed also in the suicides of Dimitris Christoulas in Greece, whose suicide note claimed that the government 'has annihilated all traces for my survival' and who caused a wave of protest and awareness of other austerity-related suicides across Europe (Margaronis 2012). In the case of Bouazizi and Christoulas, protests were directed straight at an economic system that had left people without the means of dignified survival. Where individuals' deaths were associated predominantly with racism and police violence, the ensuing protests were also a response to economic marginalisation. It is here where the connection between labour mobilisation and a discussion on the 'grievability' of lives intersects. The adoption by many states of neoliberal economic growth models that push people into the individualised precarity of unemployment or the informal sector has rendered masses of people economically 'superfluous', which is reflected in a profound stripping of citizenship rights (Ferguson 2013: 231). Traditional unions have been subject to brutal legislation limiting their power while political parties have lost capacity and influence in part due to the dismantling of the state and increasing power of the private sector. To combat the social consequences of dispossession, states invest heavily in police, prisons and security forces (Abdelrahman 2014: 16). As a result, recent mobilisations call not for specific goals that appear feasible today but for the overturning of a whole system that renders so many people economically and politically 'superfluous' (Abdelrahman 2015: 7).

With little or no recourse to public funds, for most of the street vendors I interviewed, the face of the Brazilian state is the face of the police officers who loot their stalls and prevent them from working. Many vendors have to resort to selling in illegal spaces, keeping moving whilst selling in order to avoid being penalised and finding innovative ways to escape the police. This conversation I had with two sweet vendors is illuminating:

Jennifer: 'The life of a street vendor is very hard here. We are trying all the time to earn a living and then the police themselves steal your stuff and keep it for themselves'.

Beatriz: 'Yes there was an assault here on the road'.

Jennifer: 'We live with a lot of fear here'.

Me: 'You live feeling fear?'

Jennifer: 'Yes, all the time, of course. You don't know what could happen. I try to have ways . . . . I hide stuff here (points to lower part of trolley) but you have to stay strong, if I had a weak mind it would be very hard'.

Jennifer's emphasis on the need for a strong mind is emblematic of the claim that for many groups the main source of protection they have is their own bodies. One of the first questions I asked when I arrived at CAMTRA's offices was about their views on unionisation among the street vendors with whom they worked. Iara, the Project Coordinator replied that despite the attempts to create a more inclusive unionism through the Unified Workers Central (CUT), unions still tend to be dominated by men, and to be limited to campaigns that privileged the needs of the most secure of the members. Although Darby Igayara, the president of Rio's branch of the CUT claims that 'the CUT does not only represent its members but also other underprivileged groups', their support for the two organisations that actively campaign for the rights of street vendors, CAMTRA and MUCA,[3] is limited to periodic lending of their building, and charitable support for events (Movimentos Sociais: O Que a CUT Tem a Ver Com Isso? 2009). The CUT does not directly campaign on vendor issues, nor work towards unionisation or membership of vendors in existing unions.

By comparison, the street vendors union in Recife is relatively strong. I also interviewed vendors in Recife about their experience of the Union of Informal Sector Workers of Recife (SINTRACI). SINTRACI organised a number of protests with regard to the withdrawals of licences, including a large road blockade on 31 October 2013. Yet for those I interviewed in 2014, the union was a disappointment. Leo, an orange juice vendor explained:

> I'm not part of them. I used to be part of them, we had a big protest at the prefecture, but the government just paid off the union leaders . . . they [the union leaders] do nothing when government takes our stuff, so we always lose.

His colleague Rafael complained that the union had only ever managed to obtain a few more licences for a small select number of vendors. The forms of exclusion practised (inevitably or deliberately) by unions are also explored elsewhere in this volume by Daou for the case of Lebanon and Moyer-Lee in the case of the UK.

Street vendors and 'unruly' politics

Unsurprisingly, then, the political action of street vendors in Rio is spontaneous and relatively atomistic. For example, on 25 August 2013, the police arrived at Praça São Salvador in Rio and attempted to confiscate a kombi van from which a man had been selling sandwiches without a licence. A group of people who had been drinking in the square formed a human chain around the vendor in an attempt to protect him from the police. I heard anecdotally from vendors that this had started to happen quite frequently during and after the 2013 peak of the protest movement. In 2014 MUCA helped to organise two road blockades by vendors in Rio on Rua Uruguaiana in reaction to increased police violence towards vendors (Camelôs fazem manifestação na Rua Uruguaiana 2015; Maria dos Camelôs and Hertz Leal 2014). In my interviews, vendors asserted that only in protests was it possible to make demands that really addressed the severity and depth of the problems they faced. Mariane, who sells clothes in central Rio, told me explicitly that I should 'Focus on the protests – these were good. This is a good area for you to look at'. Her justification for this was: 'People do not have a voice in organisations or government. But the protests are one way . . . it is a way of speaking . . . these protests do show something – people woke up, you know?' Carolina, who sells sweets near the port, explained protest as something people could do if they did not have other opportunities to influence policy: 'We don't get listened to; there is no way we can change things in this position. But people should be protesting'.

The value of spontaneous street protest is not only its independence from exclusionary political institutions; it can also transform the way people conceive themselves as citizens in relation to the state. Flavia Vinhaes (2013) argues that protests evade cooptation by the state in part because their power is in the micro transformations that occur in temporary, explosive moments. Such transformative moments might include when protests confer a citizen status on people, for example the coordinator of CAMTRA, Eleuteria, argued that street children deprived of all rights put on a black bloc mask and instantly become citizens. It could also be a person's first experience of state violence, or a realisation that through collective action it is possible to block a road or occupy a building. There is some evidence that such 'moments' cause important shifts in collective opinion. For example, in Rio a widespread politicisation of public discourse was evidenced in one of CAMTRA's surveys with 120 female street vendors on their experience of 'mega-events'. Claims included 'the World Cup is for the rich, not for people like us', and 'they should be spending the money [instead] on education and health' (CAMTRA 2014). According to CAMTRA , this kind of politicised conversation with street vendors was rare before the protests, when women often tended to explain their difficulties in terms of their own failings or that of their families, rather than an adverse political situation.

The dangers of being 'nothing but human beings'

It is one thing to recognise this kind of action as potentially empowering, and symptomatic of a particular political and economic landscape. It is, however, quite another thing to then suggest that this is the 'ideal' type of political action (Agamben 2000). Hannah Arendt points out the dangers of abandoning institutional identity categories and 'expos[ing] ourselves to the fate of human beings who, unprotected by any specific law or political convention, are nothing but human beings' (1994: 118). The disrespect and non-recognition of lives that do not enjoy professional citizen status, even during a protest, is starkly demonstrated in the treatment of Tasman's death. No matter how much participants in a protest seek to act in a merely human capacity, they will be treated differentially according to their status by the police and the press. Furthermore, the disruption caused by protest also affects non-protesters according to their economic status. In a conversation during the bus fare protest in which Tasman was killed, the coordinator of CAMTRA, Eleuteria, expressed doubt at the tactics used, pointing to the long queues of non-air conditioned buses being held up in 50 degree heat; the suffering of precisely those hit hardest by the fare rises. A survey done by CAMTRA with street vendors revealed widespread support of the protests but criticism at the way in which protests made their lives much harder due to the increased presence of police on the streets. Luana, who sold swimwear in Recife, told me of her perceptions of the difference between vendors in Recife and in Rio, where she has relatives:

> In Rio the protests were more violent. Here people did protest, but they did it more calmly, through meetings and things. I think this is because the people there have more education, here the vendors who protest here have less education, fewer resources, so if they were to protest the police would treat them much worse. They would suffer more.

Luana narrates the ability to protest in an unruly manner as a privilege, as an outcome of having more education and security. This is the opposite claim to the idea that protest is the space for political representation of the most marginalised, or in the famous Martin Luther King claim 'a riot is the language of the unheard' ('MLK: A Riot Is the Language of the Unheard' 2013). Due to the state's violent response to protests by oppressed groups, perpetuated by the right-wing media, unruly politics can also have a disempowering effect. Imprisonment, death and simply the fear of being tear gassed can provoke a powerful transformation *away* from political involvement. An activist working in the Maré favela explained to me in an interview that 'I was gassed a lot, I didn't have the means to buy masks that some people were buying and I stopped going to the protests because I didn't have parents who would be able to pay if I were arrested'. At CAMTRA, Eleuteria acknowledged the importance of protest as a political expression, but suggested that a compromise needed to be made between the safety and accessibility of protest and its disruptive power.

This compromise is politically very difficult, as was demonstrated in the case of an International Women's Day protest that CAMTRA led. During this protest, a couple of men started to sexually harass the protesters, about which the onlooking police did nothing. Protesters immediately reacted to the men by yelling at them to leave. When the men refused to leave and the situation looked like it was about to escalate, CAMTRA's staff approached the police and asked them to respond, and the men eventually responded to the police's verbal warnings. Here is an example of a protest that is 'illegally' taking control of roads and blocking traffic, but at the same time drawing on the authority of the police. It demonstrates how difficult it is to escape engaging with the power of existing institutions, even as they are vehemently criticised. In Ieda Accioly's interview with the press she stated: 'My husband was a peaceful man. Want to protest? You must go to the Assembly, to the door of Dilma's house' ('Aposentado Morreu' 2014). This phrase both asserts the importance of protest, and argues that it must be directed straight at the most powerful institutions. Inside this is a belief – or at least, a hope – that existing political elites might be moved. It is not a statement to abandon or sideline traditional politics but rather to target it. There is, then, a dilemma facing those wanting to campaign for the labour rights of informal sector vendors, particularly in the specific case of Brazil under the PT. It does not make sense to operate only 'within' the current political structures, for example by campaigning for more licences or focusing all efforts on unionisation. Nor can all hope realistically (or safely) be placed in revolutionary street protest. In the remainder of this chapter, I suggest that CAMTRA's approach provides three key insights into the ways in which informal sector worker struggles could best operate in this challenging contemporary political and economic climate.

Expanding the concept of 'worker'

Street vendors are a diverse group with shifting occupations and shifting statuses between formal and informal. Their right to work, and to decent working conditions, goes beyond the simple legality of being able to sell in the streets but also their right to social security, to other choices of employment and training, to affordable public transport and to legal representation in the case of police appropriation of their merchandise. These kinds of citizenship rights are not associated with traditional union action, which, as mentioned above for street vendor unions, tends to focus almost entirely on licences. There is a need, therefore, to look beyond existing unions to create a more inclusive and ambitious labour movement, such as the social movement unionism discussed by Manzano in this volume. Another space where this might be built is in the work of NGOs, such as CAMTRA. NGOs do not have a membership to be democratically responsive to, and must instead be responsive to donor interests. Another problem is that they do not hold much political weight. Yet there is growing hope in the possibility of NGOs to support the initial stages of unionisation, or to fight for labour rights through alternative methods (Kabeer *et al.* 2013).

CAMTRA's way of linking worker's rights with the citizen rights that facilitate decent work is to assert that 'all women are workers', due to the domestic and caring responsibilities assumed by women even when they are not working for money. For CAMTRA, 'work' is the totality of labour done including caring, taking children to school or to hospital, cooking etc. As such, these kinds of work, too, need protection from exploitation. The ability to work, according to CAMTRA, requires freedom from violence in the home, at work and on public transport, education, affordable public transport and cultural and political respect. These elements are just as much 'workers' rights' as, say, the ability to strike or a minimum wage. As such CAMTRA removes the exclusivity associated with the category of 'worker' but at the same time incorporates the significance of work inside a campaign for equal citizenship. For CAMTRA, it does not matter that labour is 'superfluous' on the grounds of its use-value to contemporary means of production associated with the growth of GDP. Nor are their campaigns with informal workers based only on their abstract human rights. Instead, CAMTRA respects the daily emotional and physical work done by the women it works with as an essential contribution to human survival by (mostly unremunerated) labourers.

We can see one example of this approach in the introductory paragraph of one of the leaflets that CAMTRA gives out to street vendors, containing information about licencing, crèche and health contacts, and what to do when police appropriate merchandise:

Salutations to all informal workers and street vendors of Rio de Janeiro, who daily take to the streets and confront rain, sun and oppression to carry out their profession . . . marginalised from all workers' rights and services, in the daily fight to sustain their children. We salute the fight and courage of all women. Women who work in the home, young women and girls, young mothers, black women, women who work in the formal sector, domestic workers, agricultural workers.

In launching this material we reaffirm once again that 'All women are workers: in the home or in the street' independently of whether or not they are in the labour market, formal or informal.

Alongside this broad commitment, however, CAMTRA also recognises the strategic importance of organising within a particular occupational category for specific rights. They have particularly close connections with the Domestic Workers union (SINDIDOM); indeed in my interviews the staff of CAMTRA and SINDIDOM referred to each other as 'sisters'. CAMTRA provides links to unions on their material and participates in joint campaigns. It sees itself as providing a comradely partnership with unions on the grounds of shared goals. CAMTRA's particular contribution is to unite different workers' struggles in order to identify common goals that may exceed the traditional sphere of a union. It also – given the predominance of self-employed women they work with – decouples the association between labour rights and employer, placing most responsibility instead with the state.

CAMTRA provokes a radical re-evaluation of the value of labour, *not* on the grounds of abstract claims to being 'mere humans', nor on people's 'productive' value, but rather as a contribution of labour to social wellbeing. It combines this with a strategic alliance with more limited (but more targeted) worker struggles. CAMTRA works both to facilitate labour struggles as they currently exist, and to devise new conceptualisations of labour that could be used to unite people around a more collective struggle.

Personal and political

Sudden political transformations are not only experienced in street protest, they can also happen in private or in group settings. CAMTRA organises '*encontros*' that are workshops (with childcare and food provided), normally in schools in the northern favelas, that bring together people in a particular area to talk about a specific issue. This might be to do with work – as with an *encontro* they ran in Providência for self-employed young people (men and women), or with domestic relations or education. The *encontros* work on personal empowerment, consciousness raising and collective action. They bear some similarities with Paulo Freire's pedagogical framework and the groups organised by the Women's Liberation Movements across the world in the 1960s and 1970s, as defended in Carol Hanisch's seminal essay 'The Personal Is Political' (2006).

There were two significant events that I witnessed with CAMTRA that demonstrated the way they managed a fluctuation between the personal and the political. CAMTRA's protest outside Rio's municipal chambers on the Latin American Day for the Decriminalisation of Abortion involved a tent with information leaflets that we gave out to passers by and the unrolling of a very large banner that covered the entire staircase up to the building. There was also partner protest done by a group of feminist students who mainly chanted, played drums and sang songs. We gave out hundreds of leaflets about a new law against further criminalisation of abortion in the case of rape. Yet Eleuteria was particularly unhappy about this protest because the location and timing meant that far fewer people passed by than she would have hoped for. 'We are basically just talking to each other', she said at one point. Just before the end of the protest she called for everyone to sit down together in a circle. She told the story of a friend who was facing criminal charges for performing illegal abortions, and a number of other stories of women who faced abuse and death for their campaigning work. She created a moment of quiet introspection on the edge of one of the busiest city streets. Eleuteria then taught the group a Ciranda, which is traditionally danced by fishing women in her native Pernambuco. Cirandas are choreographed so as to permit any number of people to join or leave at any time. She turned what was an ineffective, outward looking protest into an act of powerful personal reflection that also drew on older traditions of community building.

At the *encontro* in Baixada, I saw the opposite shift occur in the structure of the daily activities. The first workshop began with a discussion of the body, pride and shame. One woman asserted that she would not have been able to talk openly before attending

CAMTRA's previous *encontro* and said that she wanted to share her personal experience to create a space where other people felt comfortable sharing theirs. This created a shift towards a more intimate and protective atmosphere in the group, and the personal became the basis from which political narratives were then developed. Through the day the sessions gradually grew more politicised, from the politics of sexual consent and freedom, through a film on the history of female sexuality to finally a discussion on how to take the ideas generated into their local communities.

The impact of CAMTRA's balancing of the personal and political in their strategies can be seen in the experience of Elaine, who at the time that I interviewed her was a sweet vendor who works on the trains. She said: 'CAMTRA helped me in days of my life that I most needed it'. Although the most significant impact CAMTRA had is on her personal life, Elaine has also become an active campaigner at CAMTRA's events and in her own community. Elaine is currently pregnant and has no access to social security (apart from $R295[4] a month from Bolsa Familia for her and three daughters). She is also affected by a new law in which people can only receive unemployment benefit after one year (instead of six months) of work in one place, which she says discriminates against people who are only hired on short-term contracts. I asked her about whether she thought a union would improve her working conditions, and she said that no, she felt that a union would do nothing except take a proportion of her salary. She said that CAMTRA was the only organisation she knew of that was fighting for the kind of citizen rights she said were important for street vendors like herself. When I asked her what these rights were she replied:

> To have more opportunities for employment, to be able to campaign for their rights and see them met, to have good health, to be able to go to the hospital and be attended, with none of these words like 'there is no doctor', or to go to find work only to hear 'there are no vacancies'.

CAMTRA are working with Elaine to support her efforts to invite other women from her neighbourhood to *encontros* and local campaign events. As a small and underfunded NGO it has little power to make the big changes that Elaine outlines. Yet their work on personal empowerment does translate into politicised critique and a shift in blame away from women's own decisions towards the political structures they must inhabit.

Two kinds of hope

For CAMTRA, the 2013–2014 protests were a way of shifting the consciousness raising and personal work they had been doing to a space where the kind of political change outlined in Elaine's comment above seemed possible. Staff talked about feeling reenergised after years of disillusionment, and joined the mobilisations throughout 2013 and 2014, sometimes with their own banners and sometimes as individuals. They supported the occupation of the town council building in Rio, joined others on the steps of the federal offices and organised their own marches and 'feminist blocks' inside the larger demonstrations. However, like the other NGOs, social movements, unions and political parties who participated in the movement, CAMTRA also sought to transform the protests into campaigns that made specific demands, even if these demands necessarily could never encompass the extent of political change that was perceived to be needed.

In her work on the role of protest in labour struggles, Sian Lazar proposes that one way to engage with the simultaneous need for and impossibility of the possibility of 'real' political transformation is through an exploration of different social experiences of time. Successes and failures can be situated on the one hand within a constantly progressing historical movement, and on the other hand as singular moments that have effect in and of themselves. A movement could be considered transformative only when seen as part of a much wider historical trajectory, or only in a single 'revolutionary' event, disappearing when things return to normal (Lazar 2014: 101–102). I will suggest here that these different kinds of time are reflected in CAMTRA's work alongside different kinds of hope: one kind that is pessimistic about the possibility of change within the current system and therefore aspires towards profound or 'revolutionary' change, and the other that is idealistic about the current system, and therefore pragmatic and reformist.

One example is their survey on the impact of mega-events on vendors. Anger at the Confederations Cup, World Cup and Olympic Games was a very prominent theme in the protest movement, and protests followed the schedules of the World Cup closely in 2014. The government and FIFA justify mega-events on the (as yet unproven) assumption that they will attract investment, and that this will consequently have an impact on citizens' wellbeing. Or alternatively that the mega-event itself will have a direct event on wellbeing, for example through better sports facilities, the (temporary) creation of jobs in construction and retail, or even a heightened sense of national pride (Steinbrink 2014). Of course, mega-events also conveniently allow policymakers to prioritise actions they might not otherwise be able to justify, for example on huge private sector infrastructure projects, slum clearance or zero tolerance policing.

CAMTRA's response to the mega-events works with two different kinds of hope: one that engages formally with the government rhetoric, aspiring towards slow changes in historical time, and another that rejects it entirely. CAMTRA's survey shows that not only did mega-events make no improvements to the lives of vendors, but in fact they made them worse. They publicised their results through a film. By revealing the experiences of women working in precisely the sector that should see economic benefits from increased tourists on the streets, CAMTRA presents material that counters the city government's claims. This work idealistically cooperates with the state's charade of claiming an interest in the social impact of the events, and in their supposed receptiveness to people's views. The outcomes to CAMTRA's survey may not be immediately apparent, but may provide very useful fuel for future campaigning in the lead up to the Olympics, forming a contribution in 'historical time'.

Yet very few people believed in the government's rhetoric about the mega-events. As one of CAMTRA's interviewees explained: 'The television, the newspapers say that it (the World Cup) is going to improve the lives of workers, but for the street vendor there is no change to be seen, only promises'. Most people of course know the truth about the real 'purpose' of the mega-events, for example as claimed by another vendor, that 'with the cup only those who already have money will earn' – but cannot do anything about it. In order to change anything CAMTRA has to do more than just prove that the mega-events are not beneficial, or actively harmful; it has to somehow destabilise the easy ability of a government to maintain its power based on a farce. It has to change a situation whereby huge numbers of people have no faith in the mega-events, but their opinions are considered superfluous. The way in which CAMTRA tries to do this is to combine the slow campaigning work of the survey with participation in the protests. The film specifically asserts the importance of protest in achieving the demands expressed by their interviewees. The closing credits provide a particularly rich insight into CAMTRA's balancing of two kinds of hope, and the personal and political. They begin with shots of the March Against the Genocide of Black People in the Manguinhos favela – which combines a feminist politics with anti-racism and the assertive mourning of young, black, often male lives. The scene then shifts to an anti-World Cup protest. The backing music meanwhile criticises the sexual objectification of female bodies. The film ends with an image of the train that runs from the northern favelas into the city. This ending defends the importance of existing service provision, while referencing protests that called for their radical improvement.

A similar combining of two kinds of political hope was evident at the aforementioned abortion protest. Although CAMTRA was there ostensibly to campaign, very modestly, against the further criminalisation of abortion, protesters' goals and messages went far beyond this battle, and also called for a 'feminist revolution', for women to have sovereignty over their own bodies and for free and universal family planning rights; all of which are far beyond the imaginary of the current political system, in Brazil and the rest of the world. A third example is in CAMTRA's more traditional 'NGO' action in their fortnightly sexual health stall, the 'Barraca de Direitos' (Rights Stall). The stall provides free male and female condoms, and staff distribute the condoms together with information and advice sheets about the events or campaigns CAMTRA is organising. First and foremost, the stall fulfils a practical need for better access to sexual health education and contraception among workers in the centre of the city. As Mayara Lemos, a vendor working in the area states:

> I think this work distributing condoms to prevent diseases like AIDS and others is important. It's this reason why I always call CAMTRA telling them when the condoms are running out, I don't want to hear about anyone with illnesses because they didn't use one. (CAMTRA 2016)

However, sometimes women come asking for the kind of support that CAMTRA is not in a position to provide. For example one woman came saying she was being evicted from her home. At this point CAMTRA can do little other than help her fill in forms and send her to the exact same government institution she came from.

In CAMTRA's view, the provision of condoms, sexual health and anti-violence advice should be the role of the state at public health posts, and the stall represents, in part, the NGOisation of public services (CFEMEA 2003; Alvarez 1999: 182). Yet at the stall, the limitations of 'humanitarian' action by NGOs are openly discussed and combined with a critique of the absent state. Eleuteria argues that CAMTRA's stall was only ever a 'lever for militancy'. It was set up in 1999 as part of a long-term campaign for a health post that meets *all* health needs in the centre of the city. Another of the key aims of the stall is to develop longer-term relations with vendors with the ultimate hope of supporting campaigns for workplace rights. Mayara is one of the vendors who have organised among their colleagues to come and collect boxes of condoms and leaflets for distribution among those working different shifts. Although it is only a fledgling step towards worker organising, the delivery of condoms does facilitate networks of support between and within shops and stalls. In addition, much of CAMTRA's written material, given out at protests, celebrates the work of militant communist and anarchist figures from history. For example, the International Women's' Day leaflet emphasises the roots of the day in the street protests of Russian textile workers in 1917, while the leaflet on domestic violence includes a paragraph that states: 'We will continue in the streets, occupying the squares, protesting until no more women are assaulted or killed'. In this way, the stall manages to provide practical support and work inside a system while also making a strong assertion against it.

Conclusion

Street vendors are excluded from state security, criminalised and attacked by the police and have little representation in labour unions or other institutionalised methods of political participation. It makes sense that their labour struggles must be directed not just at their immediate working conditions but at profound deprivations of citizenship that can seem so embedded in economic and political structures as to be immovable. Street protest and blockades can seem like the only – and the most appropriate – political response. Yet there is also an important place for more institutionalised organisation around labour rights, both in campaigns for immediate policy change and towards the deeper political and economic transformations necessary to shift a society that renders some lives more 'grievable' than others. I have suggested in this chapter that CAMTRA plays an important role in this work in Rio. It is worth ending with Eleuteria's justification for why she founded CAMTRA:

> I wanted to create a socialist and feminist revolution. So where, with whom was I going to leave my daughters in order to do all of this? My major revolution had been managing to bring up my daughters. It was then that I became aware of the lack of public policies for women, and I decided to found the House of the Working Woman.

In this statement, Eleuteria makes clear that her political involvement is rooted in her personal experience of balancing work responsibilities. She asserts both the practical need for childcare and her desire for revolutionary change. It is in this combining of the personal, the political, the pragmatic and revolutionary that CAMTRA's strategies offer important insights for the necessarily multi-dimensional struggle for informal sector labour rights across the world.

Notes

1 I would like sincerely to thank Elaine Dos Santos Vital, Eleuteria Amora da Silva, Iara Amora and Suellen Araújo from CAMTRA, all of whom contributed to this research.

2 Casa da Mulher Trabalhadora, or House of the Working Woman.

3 United Movement of Street Vendors – an organisation campaigning on behalf of street vendors – coordinated by Maria de Lourdes.

4 About £50.

References

Abdelrahman, M. (2014) *Egypt's Long Revolution: Protest Movements and Uprisings*, Abingdon, Oxon and New York: Routledge.

Abdelrahman, M. (2015) 'Social Movements and the Question of Organisation: Egypt and Everywhere', LSE Middle East Centre Paper Series, 08.

Agamben, G. (2000) *Means without End: Notes on Politics*, Minneapolis, MN: University of Minnesota Press.

Alvarez, S.E. (1999) 'Advocating Feminism: The Latin American

Feminist NGO "Boom'",
*International Feminist Journal
of Politics*, 1(2): 181–209. doi.
org/10.1080/14616749935988o.

'Aposentado Morreu Atropelado Em
Protesto, Após Se Assustar Com
Manifestação' (2014, 11 February)
O Globo. http://oglobo.globo.com/
rio/aposentado-morreu-atropelado-
em-protesto-apos-se-assustar-com-
manifestacao-11567715.

Arendt, H. (1994) 'We Refugees', in
Robinson, M. (ed.) *Altogether
Elsewhere: Writers on Exile*, pp.
110–119. Boston, MA: Faber and
Faber.

Assy, B. and Ertür, B. (2014)
'Supplements: Law and Resistance
– Turkey and Brazil', *Law
and Critique*, 25(1): 1–13. doi.
org/10.1007/s10978-013-9131-3.

Barrientos, A. (2013) 'The Rise of Social
Assistance in Brazil', *Development
and Change*, 44(4): 887–910. doi.
org/10.1111/dech.12043.

Bonis, G. (2013, June 18) '"O Brasil hoje
acordou mais forte", diz Dilma
após protestos' [Artigo]. www.
cartacapital.com.br/sociedade/
manifestacoes-comprovam-
democracia-no-brasil-diz-dilma-
7493.html.

Butler, J. (2010) *Frames of War: When
Is Life Grievable?* (Reprint edition).
London and New York: Verso.

'Camelôs fazem manifestação na Rua
Uruguaiana' (2015, April 13) *O Globo*.
http://oglobo.globo.com/rio/
camelos-fazem-manifestacao-na-
rua-uruguaiana-14061819.

CAMTRA (2014) *Pesquisa: Impactos dos
Mega Eventos na Vida das Mulheres
Trabalhadoras*. Rio de Janeiro:
CAMTRA. http://camtra.org.br/
images/mega-eventos-resultados-
fase1e2.pdf.

CAMTRA (2016) Depoimentos.
http://camtra.org.br/index.

php?option=com_content&view=art
icle&id=57%3Acamtra-depoimentos-
&catid=48%3Apublicacoes&Itemid
=79&lang=en, accessed 29 January
2016.

CFEMEA (2003) *As Mulheres na
Reforma da Previdência: O desafio
da inclusão social*. São Paulo: entro
Feminista de Estudos e Assessoria.
www.bibliotecadigital.abong.org.
br/bitstream/handle/11465/262/
CFEMEA_As_mulheres_na_reforma_
da_previdencia.pdf?sequence=1.

Ferguson, J. (2013) 'Declarations of
Dependence: Labour, Personhood,
and Welfare in Southern Africa',
*Journal of the Royal Anthropological
Institute*, 19(2): 223–242. doi.
org/10.1111/1467-9655.12023.

Hanisch, C. (2006) 'The Personal Is
Political'. http://carolhanisch.org/
CHwritings/PIP.html.

Kabeer, N., Milward, K. and Sudarshan, R.
(2013) 'Organising Women Workers
in the Informal Economy', *Gender
& Development*, 21(2): 249–263. doi.
org/10.1080/13552074.2013.802145.

Khanna, A., Mani, P., Patterson, Z.,
Pantazidou, M. and Shqerat, M.
(2013) 'The Changing Faces of
Citizen Action: A Mapping Study
through an "Unruly" Lens', IDS
Working Papers, 423: 1–70. https://
www.ids.ac.uk/files/dmfile/Wp423.
pdf.

Lazar, S. (2014) 'Historical Narrative,
Mundane Political Time, and
Revolutionary Moments: Coexisting
Temporalities in the Lived
Experience of Social Movements',
*Journal of the Royal Anthropological
Institute*, 20: 91–108. doi.
org/10.1111/1467-9655.12095.

Margaronis, M. (2012, April 5) 'Dimitris
Christoulas and the Legacy of
His Suicide for Greece', *The
Guardian*. www.theguardian.
com/commentisfree/2012/apr/05/

dimitris-christoulas-legacy-suicide-greece.

Maria dos Camelôs and Hertz Leal (2014, January 27) 'A resistência dos camelôs da Uruguaiana'. https:// movimentounidodoscamelos. wordpress.com/2014/01/27/ a-resistencia-dos-camelos-da-uruguaiana/.

Mendonça, R. and Ercan, S.A. (2015) 'Deliberation and Protest: Turkey and Brazil', in Fischer, F., Torgerson, D., Durnová, A. and Orsini, M. (eds) *Handbook of Critical Policy Studies*, pp. 205–221. Cheltenham: Edward Elgar.

'MLK: A Riot Is the Language of the Unheard' (2013, August 25) *CBS News*. www.cbsnews.com/news/ mlk-a-riot-is-the-language-of-the-unheard/.

Mollo, M. de L.R. and Saad-Filho, A. (2006) 'Neoliberal Economic Policies in Brazil (1994–2005): Cardoso, Lula and the Need for a Democratic Alternative', *New Political Economy*, 11(1): 99–123. doi. org/10.1080/13563460500494933.

'Movimentos sociais: O que a CUT tem a ver com isso?' (2009, July 28). www. bancariosrjes.org.br/informativos/ index.php?id=1643.

Nunes, R. (2014, July 25) 'The Worst Kind of World Cup Legacy: Brazil's New Political Prisoners'. www. huffingtonpost.com/rodrigo-nunes/the-worst-kind-of-world-c_b_5620976.html, accessed 4 January 2016.

Petras, J. and Veltmeyer, H. (2006) 'Whither Lula's Brazil? Neoliberalism and "Third Way" Ideology', *Journal of Peasant Studies*, 31(1): 1–44. doi. org/10.1080/03066150310000169116.

Romero, S. (2013, June 24) 'Responding to Protests, Brazil's Leader Proposes Changes to System', *The New York Times*. www.nytimes. com/2013/06/25/world/americas/ responding-to-protests-brazils-leader-proposes-changes-to-system. html.

Saad-Filho, A. and Morais, L. (2013) 'Mass Protests: Brazilian Spring or Brazilian Malaise?', *Socialist Register*, 50(50). http://socialistregister.com/ index.php/srv/article/view/20199.

Steinbrink, M. (2014) 'Festifavelisation: Mega-events, Slums and Strategic City-Staging – the Example of Rio de Janeiro', *DIE ERDE – Journal of the Geographical Society of Berlin*, 144(2): 129–145.

Trevisani, P. (2015, September 14) 'Brazil Unveils Nearly $17 Billion in Austerity Measures', *Wall Street Journal*. www.wsj.com/articles/ brazil-unveils-measures-to-balance-2016-budget-1442265652.

Vannuchi, M. (2015, June 28) 'The Social Security Tool in Brazil (MEI) and Its Relation with Street Vendors'. http://streetnet.org.za/show. php?id=605.

Vinhaes, F. (2013) 'A democracia Frankenstein', in *E O POVO REINVENTOU AS RUAS: Olhares diversos sobre as manifestações de 2013 – Vários autores | Livraria Antonio Gramsci*, pp. 53–62. Rio de Janeiro: Multifoco. http:// livrariagramsci.com.br/produto/e-o-povo-reinventou-as-ruas-olhares-diversos-sobre-as-manifestacoes-de-2013-cristovao-f-duarte-eliana-v-barcantes-flavia-vinhaes-flora-daemon-jose-antonio-sepulveda-kadu-machado-karla-varga/.

9 | THE EXPERIENCE OF GRASSROOTS SYNDICALISM IN GREECE: WORKPLACE RESTRUCTURING AND THE ROLE OF TRADITIONAL TRADE UNIONS IN THE TERTIARY SECTOR

Aris Anagnostopoulos and Angelos Evangelinidis

Introduction: looking back at labour organisation

The ebb and flow of mass movements in Greece in the 2000s This chapter is written during the expiry of the short-lived cooperation government between the left-wing party SYRIZA and the populist right-wing party ANEL in Greece, in the summer of 2015. It is a moment of pause and contemplation for most militants in Greece, not least because the shortcomings of the anti-austerity agenda ('anti-memorandum' as it is known nationally) and the resulting political forms it created have been bluntly exposed to public scrutiny and reflection. Such a moment is perhaps also important as a vantage point for the re-examination of recent cycles of struggle for social and economic justice in Greece in terms of their practical, everyday forms, as well as their international ramifications.

The social and political life of the last decade in Greece has been marked by multiple waves of movement participation. Starting with the anti-globalisation movement of 2003, precarious youths, especially during and after their undergraduate years, were increasingly involved in grassroots organising, both in the workplace, but also locally, in their places of residence and socialisation. The peak point for the radicalisation of an entire generation of young people was the student movement of 2006–2007. Students took to the streets *en masse*, protesting the proposed law that aimed to overhaul the university structure and introduce private interests to public universities, paving the way to tuition fees. The student protesters were brutally attacked by riot police, beaten, tear-gassed and arrested in great numbers. Widespread reactions and the reluctance of the government to press on with the reforms halted the proposed measures.

For all its internal strife and mutually hurled accusations of 'reformism' or conversely 'revolutionary wishful thinking', the student movement left a significant legacy of radical politics and questions of organisation that remain pertinent to the radical movement in Greece today.

The next phase was the spectacular riots of December 2008, which began when a 16-year old schoolboy was shot by a policeman in the bohemian neighbourhood of Exarchia in central Athens (Johnston and Seferiades 2012). Immediately, massive demonstrations were organised and violent clashes with the police became a common occurrence in the following month. While most commentators, in Greece and abroad, looked at the riots as merely a reaction to police brutality, or even the heavy-handedness of the neoliberal government, for the movement itself it was also a moment of setting up new structures, attempting new actions, and bringing together its newly-acquired experience with alternative political structures. Examples of this abound: in the neighbourhoods of Athens, local initiatives against big development or privatisation of public land turned into full-blown popular assemblies; occupations of university schools and public buildings started questioning the work and employment conditions of their occupants; the solidarity movement for the attacked syndicalist Konstantina Kouneva attempted to connect issues of class, race and gender by focusing on this case of a brutal assault of this Bulgarian female cleaner in the public transport of Athens.

In our view, the December 2008 events were probably the first public reaction to the deepening crisis in Greek society, whose 'official' onset was still some months in the making, but was already profoundly felt, particularly among younger generations of precarious workers.

Bringing labour back into the picture As Sian Lazar notes in the introduction, there has been in Greece, as elsewhere, a renewed attention to labour struggles both in academia and some media. As she correctly points out, this is not identical to a labour movement 'resurgence'. Class confrontation and labour struggles have in a way 'always been there', during the long decade that followed the anti-globalisation struggles and their pivotal role in re-invigorating the anti-capitalist and anti-authoritarian milieus in Greece. The difference with previous cycles of contention in Greece was mainly the changes in class composition, and particularly the increased participation of precarious youths, who devised new forms of unionising in response to the limited scope of existing trade unions.

In fact, worker's struggles are the missing link in the usually offered narratives of youth radicalisation in Greece of the 2000s; they are the connection between neighbourhood assemblies, a new generation of precarious workers, the events of the student protests of 2006–2007 and the riots of December 2008, as well as the massive demonstrations of the summer of 2011. In these mobilisations, the new generation of radicals attempted to turn the widely publicised gatherings of the big squares in Greece into decision processes grounded in neighbourhoods. In some cases, they also led struggles to directly improve working conditions and lower the costs of living for workers (e.g. by demanding free public transportation). In what follows, we try to show that the waves of mass participation in Greece were threaded through by persistent struggles at workplaces and in the neighbourhoods of Athens.

These struggles remain the untold story of the radicalisation of a significant proportion of Greek precarious workers. The main issue with studying the ways in which labour struggles have provided a meeting point for local activists, new grassroots unions and radicalised youth is the paucity of information on the incredible variety and number of small-scale labour struggles in the previous decade. They have been partly documented, if at all, in brief announcements in social media, word of mouth, leaflets produced by neighbourhood assemblies, grassroots unions or political groups. The near absence of primary literature remains a pressing question of movement memory and long-term strategy. It reflects a lack in bottom-up reconsideration of the motives, synergies, victories and shortcomings of collective action throughout the past decade or so. The question is obviously a very big one to be answered in a single book chapter. What we are going to do here is provide a glimpse of the ways in which these big events were sutured through the everyday struggles at places of work and influenced the unionisation attempts of young precarious workers.

The literature available to academics and activists mainly focuses on low union density among young precarious workers and offers valuable overviews for the relations between young workers – especially in the tertiary services sector – with traditional trade unions in Greece (Kretsos 2011b; Mattoni and Vogiatzoglou 2014). The inability of these unions to cater for the needs and demands of these new jobs has been sufficiently demonstrated (Kretsos 2011a). Besides this, existing literature highlights the novel and very impressive proliferation of grassroots unions that have developed a diverse repertoire of political action and mobilise an impressive percentage of younger working people (Vogiatzoglou 2011).

This literature is to a great degree written from a sympathetic – or altogether partisan – view that regards these grassroots organisations as important players in social change. It lacks however the perspective of workers' experience of organisation, especially in sectors where traditional trade union representation is unable, or unwilling, to organise workers into collective bargaining for better work conditions, wages, or control over their free time. We argue here that a critique that is useful for activists and militants on the grassroots level should focus more insistently on the lived experience of working subjectivity if we are to produce a socially relevant academic discourse that may be useful to the subjects of this research themselves as well as social research in general.

As a case-study, we examine autonomous syndicalism at call centres in Greece, a process in which one of us was involved for a long period in the aftermath of the student movement of 2006–2007 and the events of December 2008. We adopt this perspective as a bottom-up approach, an attempt to speak for ourselves as active subjects in the circles of contention that emerged in the 2000s and in the implementation of novel forms of collective action and political thought. This is part of an on-going project of auto-ethnography (cf. Reed-Danahay 1997; Maréchal 2010; Marshall *et al.* 2009) whereby we propose to use our personal experience to understand the context in which we were produced as socially (in)formed subjects of struggle. As militants, we participate in an assembly that employs the tool of militant research, or co-research, to frame our interaction and participation in struggles (Evangelinidis and Lazaris 2014).

Looking back in such a manner at our involvement with the activities of grassroots unions and assemblies in Greece, it is possible to engage critically with existing periodisations of recent struggles in Greece, which aim to match the peaks and troughs of youth radicalisation and union participation, leading to a skewed picture of political organising. Most commentators saw in the December 2008 riots a spontaneous eruption of new organisational forms; some even theorised about a 'subject non-subject' that emerged from these protests (Gavriilidis 2014: 67). As we will discuss here, the apparently spontaneous forms of political action and organisation were in fact the result of a much longer process of engagement, spearheaded by anarchist and ultra-left-wing milieus, joined by new generations of precarious youths.

It is indisputable that the radicalisation brought about by the student protests of 2006–2007 and the riots of December 2008 inspired a great number of activists to resort to apparently spontaneous and novel forms of grassroots (or 'autonomous') unionising and as a node where incentives and resources for further mobilisation could be produced and circulated. Shortly after the December Riots, there was a sudden increase in the numbers of unions of precarious workers: to quote the list provided by Vogiatzoglou (2011), unions were formed by translators and editors, courier workers of the Achaia region, informatics employees, show business employees, fixed-term contract workers in the Postal Office, employees in NGOs and the call centre workers of the Greek Telecommunications Organization (OTE), who formed two different unions, one in Athens and one in Thessaloniki. All told, the number of precarious workers' unions in Athens more than doubled, from eight unions before December 2008 to 17 in early 2011.

However, these particular forms and methods as well as their rationale were an effect of an older phase of struggle (or, more technically, cycle of contention) that emerged out of the experience of precarity and the effects of neoliberal labour restructuring in Greece, especially in the early 2000s. Attempts at grassroots organising may have become more visible by increased participation, but they were not new. They were based on the shared experience and political networking of a number of people, who were instrumental in building up the know-how necessary to organise in precarious conditions of employment, in terms of strategies, movement repertoires and networking activities.

Trade union participation in the social-democratic state In order to put this turn in perspective, we need to look at developments in trade union participation in the last two decades of the twentieth century. 'Traditional' trade unions, which progressively came to represent an older social arrangement tied to stable work relations and a more or less developed welfare state, were increasingly unable to incorporate young workers, causing a fall-out of young precarious workers (cf. Kretsos 2011a). This dissolution was an effect of three not necessarily interrelated processes: the crisis of large trade unions in Greece, the proliferation of service jobs, and the radicalisation of youth in conjunction with the rise in youth unemployment. We will examine these in turn below.

The crisis of state-sanctioned trade unions reflected the expiry of the 1980s social-democratic arrangement. The social-democratic government of PASOK in the early 1980s recognised trade unions as the only legally representative organisations on a federated level. Officially, trade unions are not affiliated or financed by any political party. Nevertheless, the newly introduced statutes concerning unions combined with the long stay of PASOK in power during the 1980s and its clientelist politics gradually turned these unions into party-affiliated political organisations. This meant that official trade unions and their confederations had an ideological or party political link. Significantly, all GSEE (General Confederation of Greek Workers) presidents in the last 30 years were members of PASOK.

The Greek trade union movement mainly consists of the GSEE and the Greek Confederation of Public Servants (ADEDY) who together represent all trade unions of the country. GSEE in particular is directly involved in negotiations with employers' organisations for collective bargaining. Both confederations are under party control by PASOK although during austerity times their influence has been reduced due to their inability to prevent austerity measures (GSEE 2013). Following the transnational trend, union density in Greece is estimated to have dropped from 34 per cent in 1990 to 21.3 per cent in 2012 (OECD 2014), but their institutional role in mediating with the government and lending legitimacy to worker mobilisations has remained in place.

The bureaucratic nature of both confederations, their organisational structure, which reflects past industry (and union) boundaries and their lengthy affiliation to the two main parties, the centre-left PASOK and the centre-right New Democracy have created an image of distrust and compromise along with a loss of credibility during the last 30 years. Their biggest problem, however, was their consent to labour market deregulation laws and neoliberal reforms. Indeed, the credibility of the two trade union confederations has been further weakened during the anti-austerity protest cycle of 2010–2012, owing to their weak opposition to austerity policies. One aspect of the protest wave of Greek *indignados* was against the bureaucratic trade unions. The same was reported in the case of the Spanish *indignados* (Flesher Fominaya 2015 and Martí i Puig and Aparicio Wilhelmi this volume).

The form of official trade unions in Greece emerged as part of an earlier class settlement, and reflected older forms of employment contracts and workfloor organising. Recruitment patterns for the two decades between 1980 and 2000 are indicative: Greek official unions were not interested in recruiting new members, especially among the younger generations of workers. Membership in large unions was automatic in some, important cases, such as the DEKO companies (State-owned, Public Benefit Corporations – in electricity, transports and telecommunications mostly), and therefore their political goals focused more on fractional struggle and less on campaigning or recruiting new members. Furthermore, their organisation was geared towards 'older' forms of labour relations: for example, union representatives were present as a norm at the boards of these corporations. This means that unions had a *de jure* institutional recognition. It also means, however, that novel work relations, such as rented workers, training/apprenticeship contracts, fixed/short-term contracts, self-employment taken up by a significant number of educated young professionals, were 'invisible' to organised union members and officials. These latter groups in fact lacked official representation in the workplace or in the collective bargaining process since established union rules only permitted the recruitment of full-time, open-ended contract, regular employees as members.

The second process, that came to change this established pattern, and led to decreased union participation amongst younger employees, was the proliferation of low-wage service jobs in the last part of the 1990s – as part of the neoliberal regulation of work in late capitalism. In practice, this meant that new, flexible employment contracts were introduced, which, in combination with a dated welfare provision service, constituted the picture of precarious work in Greece (cf. Papadimitriou 2009; Triantafyllou 2008). As Vogiatzoglou notes

(2010), union participation for this new precarious workforce was very low. In some cases, this was because established unions did not represent workers in newly established sectors; in others, because in sectors where flexible labour was introduced, union representation and militancy was already low.

On the shop-floor level, an important implication was the divide between precarious workers and workers with more permanent job contracts, a divide that was reflected in union participation and militancy. State reforms to promote labour market flexibility initially did not affect the employment rights and benefits of those already in standard employment. It affected young entrants to the labour market, who were less able to bargain collectively for their wage, employment arrangements and work conditions. Participation in grassroots unions and their relationships with the more established unions representing the 'standard' full-time workforce was therefore fraught with tension ever since the first surge in grassroots unionising after the December 2008 events (Vogiatzoglou 2014).

To better understand the nature of precarious work in Greece, and the relationship of precarious workers, especially of younger generations to the established unions, we need to see precarity as a continuation and an expansion of an already existing profusion of informal job contracts. Precarity did not come to abolish the norm of widespread permanent job posts among younger workers, for they simply did not exist. The proliferation of 'unofficial' job posts had already been noted before the onset of the financial crisis (Giannakourou 2006). These jobs were handled on a one-to-one basis between contractors or entrepreneurs and workers, and strayed from the legally established job contracts, and various other legal requirements regarding social security, wage and compensation (Giannakourou 2006). In some sectors, this 'unofficial' employment was – and still is – the norm, and this affects youth employment the most. The prospective employee will 'talk it out' with the shop owner, for example, and a verbal agreement will be reached; the wage per shift will be agreed on the basis of the usual wage in 'the market' and no social insurance will be offered; no contract will be signed, so that the employee will not be visible to the tax office or the national insurance bodies, and the worker will be paid cash in hand. The jobs that are available to young students or graduates are more frequently jobs that are based on such 'unofficial' or even verbal contracts or agreements, rather than permanent posts with the usual provisions and legal sanctions of official job contracts (cf. also Kouzis 2009 and Kretsos 2011a: 458–459).

To complete this picture, we should add that official statistical data have a blind spot for the unofficial forms of work we have mentioned above. Jobs like that are not recorded in the data provided by social security institutions, simply because they do not provide any social security at all. Empirical observation, however, points to a proliferation of such jobs as a part-time measure that enables tertiary-skilled university graduates to 'wait out' unemployment in hopes of a better and more permanent post. These posts, combined with family support for young undergraduates, enable this social group to deal with the high-risk nature of the job market in Greece (Kretsos 2011a: 457). Structural analyses of the Greek job market have pointed to the increased number of university graduates in Greece, and the inability of the job market to accommodate them, especially after the onset of the latest financial crisis (Tubadji 2012). On the contrary, there are no studies that examine the strategic use made of such posts by graduates in the first years of their careers. Precarious work, marked by part-time contracts, such as those we are going to discuss below in the call centre industry, are also seen by these generations of workers as a temporary wage, and working experience in view to more secure employment in the future. The experience of the call centre industry for university graduates who are faced with precarious work or no work at all, and at the same time have a certain degree of radical political affiliation is instrumental for the understanding of a new subject that more often than not participates and motivates the struggle of the new surge of grassroots unions.

The third factor that shaped this picture was the radicalisation of younger generations described at the beginning of this chapter. Following the events of December 2008, and their seriously overlooked aspect of worker-oriented action and organising, a great part of the anarchist and extreme left milieu turned to workplace syndicalism as one of its principal practices. While it is true that this turn to syndicalism from below is unique for its mass participation and dynamism, it would not be clearly understood if we did not examine it in the light of previous recent attempts to form organisations of precarious workers, both within and outside the workplace. Furthermore, the continuity between these grassroots unions and a dynamic radical student unionism is empirically testified but not sufficiently studied in the relevant literature (Kretsos 2011b).

With the most marked examples being the courier service and the book trade, throughout the 2000s, groups and individuals proposed an aggressive, non-institutional syndicalism, based on collective action for the consolidation of individual workplace victories, with the ultimate aim of gaining workers rights for 'new' types of workers, marginalised by state-sanctioned trade unions. It is the experiences and social networks of these groups and individuals that effectively led to the consolidation of circles of struggle, when conditions of mass participation changed the picture of grassroots syndicalism (Kretsos 2011b).

In what follows, we examine the example of call centre syndicalism to show how successive efforts to organise led to the consolidation of techniques and modes of intervention for young precarious workers.

Grassroots unions in the Greek call centre industry

The student connection The call centre industry in Greece appeared in the late 1990s and swelled during the 2000s, following the growth of the ICT sector and, more generally, the burgeoning of the services sector. The first decade of the new millennium marked a tremendous boom for telecommunications firms, which invested heavily in infrastructure and saw their earnings skyrocket. In the first quarter of 2009, however, it was already obvious that the earnings of the telecommunications sector in Greece were plummeting, due to the late onset of the economic crisis in the country (ICAP and EUA 2011). The responses of the companies to the diminished returns on their investments were to curtail investments in infrastructure and human resources, while trying to keep prices of their services at a competitive rate. In a work environment already developed through precarious work relations, this meant further reductions in wages, less job security and much greater intensification of tasks in call centres.

Given the relatively late application of neoliberal policies in the country, call centres were initially staffed following an older model of employment, called the 'standard employment relationship'. This meant that employees there enjoyed the protection that full-time employment guaranteed for most workers in other sectors. However, in the early 2000s the first measures were implemented that introduced part-time work, flexibility and precarity. At the same time, the composition of the call centre workforce gradually shifted to mostly overqualified young graduates or undergraduates. The deteriorating working conditions and intensification of labour made young adults the most desirable workers for this kind of position. This age group was more vulnerable to exploitation at work, since it lacked work experience – and therefore was less knowledgeable about its rights and the ways to demand them through unionising and industrial action.

Given both the aversion of younger generations towards established unions and the refusal of the latter to cover new precarious forms of work, such businesses were intentionally staffed with university graduates to create a syndicalist void where individual job contracts substituted for collectively bargained ones. The result was that young graduates familiar with student syndicalism and often political activism became the most active poles of this emerging precarious subject.

We emphasise this connection between university education and the rise of a new precariat, not simply because it has been empirically noticed in the relevant literature (Tubadji 2012). We want to bring to the fore the emergence of certain individuals and groups within this demographic category that understood themselves from very early on as a distinct precarious and politically active subject. In a characteristic move that highlights this connection, in 2007, during the massive student demonstrations that rocked the country, a group of about 70 university students occupied the main OTE Telecommunications building in Thessaloniki in solidarity with their militant companions who were either laid off or moved due to their unionising efforts in the company, issuing at the same time an open call to workers in the call centre to support the students' struggle (AntiCallCentre 2008).

Earlier attempts to organise call centre workers were also characteristic of the political allegiances of the workers involved in struggles for better work conditions and pay. In the Thessaloniki call centre of OTE, some 450 workers – most of whom were university students or graduates aged between 20 and 25 – were employed on part-time contracts in 2005. Their supervisors, in contrast, were employed on permanent contracts. Workers organised by starting an assembly that met periodically, and making plans for the creation of a grassroots union. The main thrust of this assembly was to clarify those workers' rights that were mostly withheld by the company, and make them publicly known to all workers in the centres. At the same time, they began industrial actions to demand the right to leave during university exam periods, as well as the two-day monthly leave that is usually ensured by Greek legislation (AntiCallCentre 2008).

Characteristics of participation and chosen modes of action Two characteristics – and limits – of grassroots efforts to organise this new precariat then became visible and are both powerful tools and common concerns for rank and file union members to this day: one is the assembly form and the other is the high turnover (due to short employment time) that makes the organisation of permanent institutions much more difficult.

To begin with the last point, it is by now plainly visible that the most serious limitation of traditional unionisation forms in the workplace of precarity is the combined short-term contract with the increased turnover of new workers. The contracts of OTE, in 2005, in Thessaloniki and elsewhere, lasted a mere eight months, and were seldom renewed. The assembly form worked only as far as successive 'generations' of workers came in contact with each other and ensured the continuation of struggle. Indeed, after the first batch of militant workers left the call centre, the most active elements in the remaining few were either moved to other sectors or forced to resign – the latter were students and their line managers simply moved their allocated shifts to the mornings, when they knew they had to attend their school (AntiCallCentre 2008). This is a very strong factor both in turnover and in the effectiveness of grassroots unions within the tertiary sector that is not usually addressed in existing, macroscopic studies of such phenomena.

The first rank and file effort that tried to organise call centre workers collectively finally culminated in a grassroots union. It addressed solely call centre workers of the main telecommunications provider in Greece, OTE (state-owned and at the time under privatisation). The union formed in 2009, in the aftermath of the 2008 riots.[1] The workers who created it were university students who worked part-time with short-term contracts. At that time OTE hired only undergraduates as call centre workers. In contrast, permanent employees in the company – commonly middle-aged – received high wages and enjoyed many privileges. These same employees staffed some of the most bureaucratic unions that denied union membership to call centre workers.

A serious event marked the formation and action of this early attempt at call centre organising, and is indicative of the way in which part of the established syndicalism responded to grassroots unions. On 9 May 2009, a delegation of the grassroots union went to the regular conference organised by OME-OTE, the official union of permanent employees at OTE, and demanded to speak at the proceedings. OME-OTE had deemed the formation of the grassroots union 'incompatible' with syndicalism in the company, and denied them access to the podium. The grassroots union delegation handed a printed communiqué to participants, and loudly protested their ostracising. Members of the right-wing DAKE (official union representatives of the right-wing party Nea Dimokratia) physically and verbally attacked the three-strong delegation. Syndicalists from left-wing parties tried to stop them and demanded that the grassroots union should be given some time to address the conference. They in turn were attacked and chaos ensued in the hall. The attack was denounced by a series of other grassroots unions and left-wing organisations.[2]

A year later (2010), a collective of call centre workers was born, named 'No dial zone', that included those working in the private sector. It was an anti-hierarchical assembly of precarious workers, mostly with connections to the extra-parliamentary left and the autonomous antiauthoritarian milieu that participated in general strikes side-by-side with the grassroots union already formed by student precarious workers in OTE. They focused mostly on subcontracting schemes between the main company, the outsourcing company and the worker, whereby the worker signs a short-term contract that is renewable every few months. They criticised recruitment for call centres that employed temporary and seasonal workers who were laid off a few months later, only to be replaced by other precarious workers. Some of the members also circulated between short-term contracts. Additionally, they distributed leaflets outside various call-centre companies against lay-offs and promoting all workers to join in.

One similar short-lived attempt followed, labelled '*eksegermena akoustika*' (riot headphones). They tried to connect with the wider anti-austerity mobilisation and introduce labour-related claims in the movements' agenda. The group dissolved after a year, faced with the realities of shop-floor organising in call centres. The flexible time schedule, the logics of consent and resignation along with individualisation and neoliberal ideals, are serious obstacles for the organising efforts. Right now, one identical assembly exists, following on the same path, named '*proledialers*', organising call centre workers against lay-offs, abuse by supervisors and so on.[3]

The main organisational structure of all these attempts in the call centre sector is the members' assembly, borrowed from the culture and legacy of decision-making in the student assemblies during the movement of 2006–2007; they are based on direct-democratic procedures, where no leadership can be identified. This is a profound shift from the traditional decision-making processes of established unions in Greece, who worked through elected representatives and limited participation in decision making by its members. In general, it can be said that the majority of the membership of these new precarious unions are militant, meaning that they are actively engaged in decision making and the implementation of all actions decided.

Most actions taken by these unions and call centre collectives follow the traditions of direct action activism, such as occupations of offices or blocking the entrance to selected offices or outlets while distributing leaflets to passers-by. While 'traditional' forms of union action, such as strikes or street marches are not shunned, shop-floor action is the defining characteristic of these unions, which sometimes earns them the dubious title of 'case-specific unionism'.[4] Due to the difficulty of creating unions in precarious working conditions and acting from within the workplace, the call centre collectives were forced to follow forms of direct action in order to be heard. In addition, they put pressure on the employers by publicising the anti-worker politics of a specific company, or sharing worker's experience across the sector or individual contractors.

Participation in these grassroots collectives is not marked by formal entry processes. It is usually sufficient to show up regularly in the meetings and participate actively. To create a union or association, the law requires a governing body of five members and a minimum of 20 participants in order to constitute a union.[5] While in the majority of traditional small-scale unions and associations this was the extent of participation required, in new forms of grassroots syndicalism this is usually a technicality. The board of the union rarely decides on its own, and the assembly is in practice the governing body.

The choice of direct action and open participation in decision bodies can be partially explained by the practical-ideological constitution of the individuals who usually begin such collective initiatives. Undergraduate students or early graduates, with experience in student assemblies and activism, and usually of an anarchist/autonomous political background, show marked preference towards horizontal forms of decision making and direct action as a political tool to effect changes in the workplace. To fully conceptualise this, we need to look at the simultaneous development of direct action and grassroots assemblies, especially in the neighbourhoods of Athens before and after the December 2008 events (an occurrence only marginally examined in recent literature, e.g. see Kretsos 2011b). While the assembly form and direct action were forms of struggle adopted by earlier attempts at grassroots unionising (Kretsos 2011b), these acquired a new momentum in the aftermath of the December riots.

The relation between such forms of organisation (direct action and union participation) is also a response to very palpable shortcomings of traditional unions in new workplaces, as well as a pragmatic response to the deregulated workers' rights legislation. The creation of a grassroots union in a sector, or even a single company (as is often the case with call centre workers) does not mean that bosses are forced to recognise it as a representative of the workers in a collective bargaining process. The ease of legally setting up a union makes for a profusion of grassroots unions, but does not guarantee their bargaining power as a collective body. However, it grants workers in a sector or workplace the legal right to protest, distribute printed material and call for industrial action. While, therefore, the union as a form of organising is seen by many participants as obsolete, it arises as a need by the demands of shop-floor direct action: for example the presence of fellow union representatives brings the blocking of a shop entrance into a legislative grey area that enables workers to negotiate work conditions at the shop-floor.

Shop-floor organisation: issues of organising and bosses' counter-tactics To better grasp the methods and aims of grassroots unions and assemblies in the telecommunications sector, we must look more carefully at what they were organising against. In the terrifying climate of an unprecedented financial crisis, with real wages dwindling dangerously, and familial means of social reproduction for working people irremediably hit, the spectre of lay-offs was the main weapon that telecommunications companies wielded against their employees in order to force rises in productivity and reduce production costs. Using this, they further intensified work in call centres. This meant a series of directives that focused on the management of time in the workplace, as for example, floor managers pressing for a decrease in 'call time', therefore getting more phone calls made in a shift. Most companies introduced 'elastic' scheduling, which set shift commencement and duration times according to the company's needs. Shifts could be set in the morning or in the afternoon, on weekends or national holidays, without a fixed pattern, again according to productivity needs. Finally, the wave of layoffs that constituted the first response to the crisis meant the intensification of work for the remaining workers, as well as an expansion of work tasks. Therefore, a call operator would not only take more calls, but s/he would also have to take up tasks from departments who were dismantled as part of company restructuring.

At the same time, the work environment of call centres became increasingly taxing for the individual worker. Phone booths are stacked in tight rows, with very poor soundproofing. Equipment is cheap and malfunctioning: chairs, computer screens and headphones do not make work any easier. Call centre workers are allowed a ten-minute rest for lunch in eight hour shifts, which of course is not enough to have a decent meal. Every movement is watched by shop-floor managers, walking on catwalks above the booths. Work behaviour – i.e. call time, the successful completion of a customer demand, logging in and out of the system, operational errors, breaks, etc. – is logged on company computers and compared weekly. HR departments usually publish results and celebrate the 'agent of the month', i.e. the most productive call operator, creating a climate of competition and antagonism between co-workers.

Work conditions in call centres make unionising, or even simple acts of resistance, such as sabotage or skiving, very difficult. Outsourcing by large telecommunications firms also makes collaboration and unionising between departments much more difficult. In the same call centre workers may be working with very different wage scales, different shifts and different outlooks for future employment, serving different companies (especially in the call centre customer service sector). Outsourcing results in further fragmentation of working contracts: instead of eight-hour contracts, of indefinite conclusion, companies can now hire workers in four-hour shifts, with much less pay and more precarious working conditions, without fear of industrial action by the unions. Besides the obvious obstacles that short shifts pose for unionising, even meeting your co-workers, part-time employees are usually overworked individuals who rely on several jobs to earn a decent wage.

Besides the climate of competitiveness that prevails in call-centres, there is also the cultivation and dissemination of a familial-collaborative narrative that is shared by managers in one-to-one meetings and pep talks. The company is presented as one big family, in which more established members (the managers) really look after the more precarious ones (the workers), while they strive united together for the good of the mother company that guarantees the well-being of everybody. This climate enables managers to go ahead with company restructuring by selectively laying off workers. By enforcing almost surgically precise redundancies, instead of across-the-board ones, the company is then able to justify each individual case in personal terms, by spreading rumours about the person in question and his or her ability on the job.

We now turn to discuss a specific example, from the technical support department of a large telecommunications firm in Athens during the winter of 2013.[6] There, the firm implemented various forms of work intensification as described earlier. Furthermore, salary reductions were preceded by circulated rumours, while at the same time managers continuously disparaged the effectiveness of the technical department. Simultaneously productivity figures both individual and collective soared, which enabled the managers to effectively use the diminution of work quality against the workers. The increase in call volume received by individual workers, as well as the broadening of the spectrum of potential issues an operator was faced with, created a larger margin for error and unresolved issues. In this case, a shortcoming of managerial restructuring was again rolled over to the workers in the call centre, perpetuating the threat of layoffs and further instigating a competitive climate between them.

In the customer care department, an experienced female co-worker was laid off, under the pretext of 'low productivity', the latest in a line of layoffs from several departments for the same reason. While tensions and complaints were rising inside the company, it took this event to force politically active members of her department to call for a general assembly of the company union. Here the union itself was not the negotiating body intervening between workers and management, as is usual with large trade unions in Greece or elsewhere. The union acted as a legal 'cover' to call what was the real decision body, the general assembly, without risking retributions from the company. This particular meeting discussed the layoffs, the employment of new workers with severely decreased wages, and health and security conditions inside the call centre. It gave the opportunity to many workers who were not politically active or had not expressed grudges before to step up and share their dissatisfaction.

The final decision was to implement a work stoppage for four hours, starting at eight in the morning a few days later. Work stoppages in such precarious workplaces need to be protected against attacks by company-friendly employees, furious managers and their cronies, or even the police, called in by the company. For this reason, most work stoppages effected by grassroots unions are accompanied by a rally at the company gates, which blocks entrance to the workplace. This is also a good opportunity for participants to meet co-workers who have not been convinced or approached and try to discuss their issues once again.

There are a number of issues that arise from such a course of action. For one, blocking the entrance to a company building constitutes an action that is carried out in a 'grey area' of the law, and the reaction of the police depends on the policies that the police leadership – and in continuation, the government itself – follows at a specific time. In this balance, the presence of officially elected union leadership is a factor that weighs in significantly. In this case, the police were called in, to protestations from the elected union leadership, who managed to turn the policemen away. On other occasions, especially during the rule of the right-wing New Democracy party, union protests like these were brutally attacked by riot police. The next step for the company was that shop-floor managers started calling workers (who had joined the rally in their vast majority), to convince them to return to work. When this failed, managers came to the rally in person, and pulled people aside to coax them back to work. Finally, they put pressure on younger workers, freshly employed, as the weakest link most likely to give in. Every step of this offensive was met by the official protests of the union leadership, supported by the people in the picket line with howls, whistles and slogans.

At the picket line, the union called for a new general assembly, which decided on the continuation of the work stoppage for the next day. The same afternoon, managers called individual workers from the following shifts, and tried to convince them to stop the protest. Many experienced, politically active younger workers were present and pressed the management with specific questions about work conditions, layoffs and pay scales, which the management either responded to vaguely, or altogether dismissed. The next day, the management imposed a series of moves to break the workers into smaller, more manageable groups. It changed the shift schedule, and moved many shifts to other buildings, away from that where the picket line was formed. It also pressed other employees to work from home for the specific shift. As we have pointed above, outsourcing to several call centre providers gives the managers an opportunity to break protests like this, simply by moving employees around. The result in this case was that the picket line was guarding the entrance to a central company building empty of managers and workers. Nonetheless, this mobilisation ended with a partial victory as the wave of lay-offs was stopped. Perhaps a more important outcome was that the experience of organising an action from below created a 'culture of solidarity' (Fantasia 1988) that troubled the company management for some time and forced its hand to try and dismantle it later on by moving people around posts and outsourcing whole departments.

Concluding remarks

We have offered this narrative to show different aspects and peculiarities of grassroots union formation in sectors characterised by precarious work. We have also concluded with a glimpse of the issues emerging in organising and acting at the grassroots level, in order to impart some insights that are usually left out of the discussion on youth participation in unions. Grassroots unions in this picture emerge as formal organisations that in a way mimic the statutes of large trade unions in Greece. This is in many ways a legalistic precaution, which must be interpreted as a weapon in the arsenal of collective action. To see how union participation is employed at grassroots level qualifies conundrums that have been impervious to the usual approaches mustered to explain Greek unions. The union form becomes, therefore, subsumed to other political forms of action and organisation, such as the assembly or the network of politically active militants and their connections to a larger base of individuals and collectives in political struggle. We offer therefore an alternative mode of explanation of macroscopic peculiarities of grassroots unions in Greece, by proposing that what is really at stake here is not the formal mustering of a repertoire of organisational forms, but a response to very palpable issues at the workplace and the rigidity of work legislation in Greece. The way in which grassroots syndicalism employs the union form points precisely to this direction. That union participation is not the goal, but a means that enables militant subjectivities to react *ad hoc* to the restructuring of work and the worsening of conditions for workers at the place where it matters the most, namely the shop-floor.

Notes

1 See the texts in http://swmateiostonote.blogspot.de/ (last accessed 27 January 2015). This union, created in the wake of December 2008, was called 'Konstantina Kouneva', after the female cleaner syndicalist who was attacked with acid by thugs in December 2008.

2 http://swmateiostonote.blogspot.de/2009/05/blog-post_228.html and http://swmateiostonote.blogspot.de/2009/05/blog-post_22.html (last accessed 27 January 2015).

3 http://proledialers.espivblogs.net/ (last accessed 27 January 2015).

4 This is an accusation usually aimed at union-minded militants by groupings and people, especially of the anti-authoritarian and anarchist milieu, who favour direct action as part of a more general agenda that purportedly enables them to intervene in the 'central political scene'.

5 At least 20 persons who have worked more than two months in a specific post constitute the founding members, which then have to elect a five-strong governing body, and compile a statute, which then has to be accepted by a tribunal.

6 To protect the participants in this action, the company will not be named.

References

AntiCallCentre (2008) About Anticallcentre and OTE (a brief post in English). https://anticallcentre.wordpress.com/about-anticallcentre-and-ote-a-brief-post-in-english/, accessed 27 January 2015.

Evangelinidis, Angelos and Lazaris, Dimitris (2014) 'Workers' Inquiry in Praxis: The Greek Student Movement of 2006–2007', *Ephemera*, 14(3): 413–429.

Fantasia, Rick (1988) *Cultures of Solidarity*, Berkeley and Los

Angeles, CA: University of California Press.

Flesher Fominaya, C. (2015) 'Debunking Spontaneity: Spain's 15-M/Indignados as Autonomous Movement', *Social Movement Studies*, 14(2): 142–163.

Gavriilidis, Akis (2014) 'Laissez Faire, Security, and Liberalism: Revisiting December 2008', in Brekke, Jaya Klara, Dalakoglou, Dimirtis, Filippidis, Christos and Vradis, Antonis (eds) *Crisis-Scapes: Athens and Beyond*, pp. 67–71. Athens: Crisis-Scape.net.

Giannakourou, S. (2006) 'Chronos ergasias kai atypikes morfes apasxolisis: nomika zitimata' [Timework and atypical forms of employment: legal matters] (in Greek), *Epitheorisis Ergatikou Dikaiou*, 65(21): 1265–1283.

GSEE (2013) Press Release – 'Results of the Elections Held during the 35th Conference of GSEE', 24 March 2013. http://www.gsee.gr/news/news_view.php?id=2022, accessed 27 January 2015.

ICAP and EUA (Economic University Athens) (2011) *O Klados tis kinitis Tilefonias sto Neo Perivallon* [The sector of mobile phone providers in new environment] (in Greek). www.vodafone.gr/portal/resources/media/downloads/public-policy/9_ICAP_Study_on_Greek_Mobile_Industry_2011.pdf, accessed 27 January 2015.

Johnston, H. and Seferiades, S. (2012) 'The Greek December, 2008', in Johnston, H. and Seferiades, S. (eds) *Violent Protest, Contentious Politics, and the Neoliberal State*, pp. 149–156. Farnham: Ashgate.

Kouzis, Yannis (2009) 'The Panorama of Job Insecurity and Precarious Employment', *Epoxi*, 52, 22 November 2009.

https://entosepoxhs.wordpress.com/2009/11/22/episfaleia-ths-ergasias/, accessed 27 January 2015.

Kretsos, L. (2011a) 'Union Responses to the Rise of Precarious Youth Employment in Greece', *Industrial Relations Journal*, 42(5): 453–472.

Kretsos, L. (2011b) 'Grassroots Unionism in the Context of Economic Crisis in Greece', *Labour History*, 52(3): 265–286.

Maréchal, G. (2010) 'Autoethnography', in Mills, A.J., Durepos, G. and Wiebe, E. (eds) *Encyclopedia of Case Study Research*, vol. 2, pp. 43–45. Thousand Oaks, CA: Sage.

Marshall, Yvonne, Roseneil, Sasha and Armstrong, Kayt (2009) 'Situating the Greenham Archaeology: An Autoethnography of a Feminist Project', in Hamilakis, Yannis and Anagnostopoulos, Aris (eds) *Archaeological Ethnographies. Public Archaeology* 8 (2–3).

Mattoni, A. and Vogiatzoglou, M. (2014) '"Today, We Are Precarious. Tomorrow, We Will Be Unbeatable": Early Struggles of Precarious Workers in Italy and Greece', in Chabanet, D. and Royall, F. (eds) *From Silence to Protest: International Perspectives on Weakly Resourced Groups*, pp. 67–82. Burlington, VT: Ashgate.

OECD (2014) Trade Union Density. Stat Extract Online Database. http://stats.oecd.org/Index.aspx?DataSetCode=UN_DEN#, accessed 27 January 2015.

Papadimitriou, K. (2009) 'Ergodotikes apofaseis en opsei tis oikonomikis Kriseos', *Deltion Ergatikis Nomothesias*, 65(1549): 1377–1383.

Reed-Danahay, Deborah E. (1997) 'Introduction', in Reed-Danahay, D. (ed.), *Auto/Ethnography: Rewriting the Self and the Social*, pp. 1–17. Oxford: Berg.

Triantafyllou, C. (2008) 'Precarious Work in Greece', in Network of Refugees and Immigrants Social Support (ed.) *Discussion on Precarious Forms of Employment*. Athens: Network of Refugees and Immigrants Social Support.

Tubadji, Annie (2012) *Youth Unemployment in Greece*, Bonn: Friedrich-Ebert-Stiftung.

Vogiatzoglou, M. (2010) *Precarious Workers' Unions in the Greek Syndicalist Movement*, Rethimno: University of Crete.

Vogiatzoglou, M. (2011) 'Precarious Workers' Unions in the Aftermath of a Student Rebellion', presentation at ECPR General Conference, Reykjavik.

Vogiatzoglou, M. (2014) 'Die griechische Gewerkschaftsbewegung: Protest- und Sozialbewegungen im Kontext der Austeritätspolitik', *WSI-Mitteilungen*, 5(2014): 361–368.

10 | DILEMMAS OF TRADE UNIONISM AND THE MOVEMENT OF THE UNEMPLOYED UNDER NEOLIBERAL AND PROGRESSIVE REGIMES IN ARGENTINA

Virginia Manzano

Translated by Lucy McMahon

Introduction

The unemployed workers' movement – the *piqueteros* – became one of the most significant actors in the popular mobilisations and protests opposing neoliberalism in Argentina at the turn of this century. Thousands of people occupied bridges, roads, squares and governmental buildings, demanding food and work. Workers were facing industrial restructuring programmes, layoffs, the flexibilisation of labour and the austerity programmes that were prescribed for Latin America by the Washington Consensus.[1] The *piqueteros* formed part of what became known as 'the multiple and diverse' ('lo múltiple y lo diverso') during the days of 19 and 20 December 2001, when the multitude stormed the streets, confronted armed troops and forced the resignation of two national presidents in seven days. This set in motion a profound crisis in neoliberal governance and paved the way towards the consolidation of what were globally recognised as progressive governments in Latin America. This chapter considers the complex formation of the unemployed into a political and social movement and the subsequent inclusion, fragmentation and redefinition of this movement under progressive governments in the region.

Mass media reports[2] presented the *piqueteros* as unemployed, poverty stricken and desperate. Their actions were perceived to be far from the realms of trade unions and political parties, and a source of social unrest prompted by the slow response of government to their demands. Social scientists have attempted to counter this mechanistic understanding of the protests as simply a spontaneous reaction against unemployment and poverty (Auyero 2002). Studies emphasise the high level of negotiation between the *piqueteros* and the state, the independence maintained by their leaders from the traditional Peronist party and the use of autonomous organisational strategies based around horizontalism and the assembly (Svampa and Pereyra 2003).

These interpretations leave little room for an analysis of the role of trade unionists and leaders of grassroots urban movements in the organisation of the unemployed. Yet, the emergence of the unemployed movement also represents the consolidation of a form of social movement unionism adopted by the Argentine Workers' Central Union (Central de los Trabajadores de la Argentina, CTA), modelled on Brazil's Unified Workers' Central (Central Única dos Trabalhadores, CUT). This unionism was strengthened by public sector workers affected by neoliberal reforms who, together with leaders of urban land occupations, joined the unemployed, and extended the scope of their own trade union action from the workplace to the neighbourhood. Women and young people massed to join a union that was distinct from the classic Argentinian trade unionism based on the male industrial worker affiliated to one single state-legitimated union. Coordinating with this model of social movement unionism was a union based around '*clasista*' traditions.[3] This was embodied in the Combative Clasista Current (Corriente Clasista y Combativa, CCC) that also organised the unemployed, inspired by the insurrectionary events of urban class struggle of the 1960s and 1970s and supported by the structures of the Maoist-orientated Revolutionary Communist Party of Argentina. Both organisations rejected an understanding of unemployment as an inevitable result of technological change in capitalist labour methods; instead converting it into powerful grounds for resistance to neoliberalism.

Building a social movement union is not a simple task, and some analysts insist on defining it more as a process towards confronting global capitalism than an already defined institutional form (Moody 1997). Union activists are faced with the challenges of balancing these new union models with the daily practical demands of factory work; of building communitarian methods of struggle while simultaneously seeking to minimise immediate exploitation in the workplace (Mollona 2009). Since it is usually assumed that union activism begins among organised workers and then extends in a linear process to those who are less organised, it is rare to recognise the difficulties of those workers who – conversely – joined the movement of the unemployed. In this article I will discuss the main challenges that such activists faced. I will outline two conflicting trends that emerged in the organisation of the unemployed in Argentina. First, the emergence of state policies that facilitated, albeit in different ways, the organisation of workers and the unemployed. Second, the historical understandings of work that retained a strong popular legacy and limited the ability of unions to bring together struggles in the work place with those in the neighbourhood or domestic sphere.

Conditional cash transfer programmes facilitated the organisation and participation of the unemployed as beneficiaries of state policies. The rise of the unemployed as a social movement therefore represents both a process of confrontation with the state and, at the same time, the emergence of the unemployed as collective subjects of economic policies. Progressive governments initiated income redistribution policies and the stimulation of the domestic market, and the consequent confrontation and negotiation with centrally organised state initiatives by workers led to a complex process of union inclusion and fragmentation. The challenge of organising the unemployed also had to deal with deeply held popular conceptions of what constituted work, that had an impact on the form of unionism that could develop in this scenario. In particular, unemployed men held a specific understanding of formal work as the inclusion into a masculine social order, sustained daily in the factories and represented politically by Peronism,[4] which undervalued the strong participation of women in the unemployed movement.

In this chapter I draw from an ethnographic study in the district of La Matanza,[5] in the West Zone of Buenos Aires. Between 1940 and 1960, textile, metallurgy and automotive industries were established in this area, attracting migrant groups from various provinces in Argentina. In 2000, when I visited the area for the first time, people evoked images of La Matanza's past as a working city, and its present of 'National Capital of Pickets (*piquetes*)'. Two neighbourhoods on occupied land became centres for the organisation of the unemployed in the CTA and the CCC respectively. In this chapter I focus on the daily life of these places in order to provide an account of the unemployed workers' movement, which evolved as a model of social movement unionism in the case of the CTA and as a form of class struggle in the CCC. These groups coordinated across territories and both faced fragmentation in the context of progressive governments.

Trade unionism and the formation of the unemployed movement

Union activists helped to organise the unemployed from the mid-1990s. In 1989, the Peronist Carlos Menem was sworn in as president, winning the elections with the promise of a 'productive revolution'. Instead, collective memory associates his administration with policies of deindustrialisation, monopolistic concentration of the economy, structural reform of the state, a decline in labour conditions, poverty and rising unemployment. According to official surveys, the unemployment rate in metropolitan areas expanded exponentially in two decades, from 2.4 per cent of the economically active population in 1975 to 20 per cent in May of 1995, and dramatically to 24 per cent in 2001. In this context, some trade unions supported the neoliberal model while others rejected it. They paved the way for the initial grouping of the unemployed, under the motto 'From the factory to the neighbourhood' ('De la fábrica al barrio'). To achieve this they created new associations, such as the CTA and the CCC.

The CTA designed a model of social movement unionism, taking considerable strength from public sector workers such as teachers and state employees unionised in CETERA (Confederación de Trabajadores de la Educación de la República Argentina – Confederation of Education Workers of the Republic of Argentina), and ATE (Asociación de Trabajadores del Estado – Association of State Workers), respectively. These workers suffered intensely as a result of the transformations of the state, which included processes of privatisation, decentralisation and threats to their jobs. They faced layoffs in the form of voluntary redundancies, early retirement, wage freezes and the proliferation of temporary contracts (Duhalde 2009; Manzano 2013). A meeting of union representatives held on 17 December 1991, known as the 'Encounter of Burzaco', laid the foundation for the formation of the Congreso de los Trabajadores de la Argentina (Workers Congress of Argentina) in 1992, which was reorganised as the Central de los Trabajadores de la Argentina (Workers Central of Argentina, CTA) in 1996. Their goal was to construct a 'new union model' as part of a new social and political movement that was open to other social organisations engaged in campaigning for the multiple demands of the 'popular sectors' and reflected the reality of five million Argentinians with employment problems (Debate para la Organización de los Trabajadores, 1991). Unemployment became the basis for the fight, and was understood as a consequence of a process of profit accumulation by elite economic groups. Consequently, the movement aimed to extend union representation towards the entire workforce, including those active, retired and unemployed, while using union practices as much in neighbourhoods as in the workplace. The movement promoted an orientation towards unity, solidarity and labour mobilisation in the fight for health, education, land and housing rights (Documento del Primer Congreso Nacional de Delegados CTA, 1996).

This type of union activism required a different structure to that of classic Argentinian trade unionism. With the accelerated process of import substitution industrialisation and the decreasing influence of anarchism and socialism among workers in the middle of the twentieth century, the Argentine trade union model was sustained through the centralisation and unification of the workers' movement in unions that enjoyed legal state recognition, monopolised industrial representation and controlled financial contributions from workers. This union model was facilitated by the expansion of the formal sector, the strength of industrial workers in the Argentinian social structure in comparison with other Latin American countries, and by the political climate of Peronism (Doyon 1984; Villarreal 1985). In contrast, the union model embodied in the CTA promoted direct affiliations built around federations. In April 1998, the Federación de Tierra Vivienda y Hábitat (Federation of Land, Housing and Habitat, FTV) was formed in a squatter settlement in a district of Matanza; it became the principle tool for mobilising the unemployed within their neighbourhoods. This type of affiliation was committed to the ideas of democracy and to union autonomy from parties, the state and economic interests.

Alongside the CTA, the CCC also converted unemployment into the basis for political and trade union organisation during the 1990s. The CCC was affiliated with the '*clasista* current' inside the Argentinian workers' movement, whose most immediate predecessor was found in the 'Cordobazo', a worker-student rebellion in May 1969, which became a global landmark for urban class struggle. The CCC organised itself as a politicised current that ran through various unions and workers' centres and aimed to bring delegates closer to grassroots activists. In the 1990s, the Revolutionary Communist party identified a triple crisis – economic, social and political – the cause of which was understood to be the overproduction of the capitalist system at a global level, which would ideally lead to a rebirth of mass organisation and insurrection. The party therefore proposed the abandonment of participation in elections and promoted uprisings ('*puebladas*') understood as fights for an *Argentinazo* on the model of the Cordobazo. It was as a result of this that the CCC unemployed wing also formed in an occupied neighbourhood of La Matanza. The unemployed were considered part of the working class together with workers and the retired.

Public sector workers, especially teachers, nurses, doctors and state administrative workers, took on the task of organising the unemployed alongside leaders of neighbourhood organisations. These leaders had emerged in the mobilisations around urban land occupations at the beginning of the 1980s and many of them had affiliations to Peronism or Maoism. They campaigned for land rights and mobilised workers living in the occupied areas. Residents participated in networks of community reciprocity and formulated strategies for making demands on the state for the expansion of public services, such as street maintenance, electricity, running water, schools and health centres. In this way they expanded the presence of the state at the local level, which was apparent in the number of public sector workers who arrived in the new neighbourhoods.

Public sector workers who worked towards organising the unemployed did not live in the poorer neighbourhoods but by the nature of their work undertook daily tasks in these areas, generating closeness and respect among the communities. In studies of teaching unions this dynamic is widely recognised (Compton this volume) but it can be extended to include health workers such as doctors and nurses. In the mid-1990s, when these unions began to organise the unemployed, it was common for people to respond to the loss of their jobs by drawing on resources from their previous life experience, for example converting trades learned in the factories into odd jobs, establishing new family arrangements or resorting to connections with the Peronist Justicialist Party branches in urban areas (Quirós 2008). Organising the unemployed, therefore, involved working through the variety of trajectories connected to the neighbourhood in order to form a politicised subjectivity in relation to the state. For example, union activists and neighbourhood leaders went about the task of measuring unemployment levels in different districts of La Matanza, making use of classic state tools, such as surveys and census data.

These tools contributed to the building of relationships between neighbours, since data collection allowed for conversations that created personal connections. The results of censuses made visible a social category, the unemployed, which served as evidence for legitimating further demands on the state. Censuses, as mechanisms used to register phenomena about the population and to convert social situations into social problems, constitute one of the key levers of the 'art of government', that, as in the Foucauldian formation (Foucault 2006), has the population as its target (number of deaths, illnesses, births etc.).[6] In this case, the census results were specific modes of power-knowledge that became proofs of a reality that could be understood and interpreted by the government, making use of a common language that favoured opening channels of dialogue.

The censuses also helped make the unemployed into a political movement, as thousands of residents accompanied leaders to present the results of the censuses to public offices. In addition, they set up camps in squares and occupied public offices, waiting to dialogue with government authorities. Based upon their census data, they demanded food and work, appealing to conventional understandings about necessary state response to poverty, such as the distribution of food to poor families. Those first meetings with government authorities played an important role in establishing negotiations between the state and those organisations that represented the unemployed.

To confront and negotiate: the unemployed as subjects of neoliberal politics

The Argentine government, at different scales (national, provincial and municipal), responded to rising unemployment rates and numbers of demonstrations (pickets) with policies of workfare or conditional cash transfer. These policies were financed by the World Bank and offered 50 US dollars a month to unemployed families with children of school age, who submitted to particular health care regimes. This cash was offered in exchange for daily chores at productive or communitarian projects, such as popular kitchens, urban infrastructure, small gardens, to name a few. These kinds of programmes were first implemented in 1996 and, in 2002, they had reached 2 million 'beneficiaries'.

Paradoxically, the emerging unemployed movement became a central actor in relation to the state, transforming the unemployed into the subject of public policies. The unemployed movement turned the above policies into objects of collective demand and used them in everyday life. Members of trade unions (CTA and CCC) and local leaders fought to enrol thousands of unemployed families on state-sponsored rosters in order to obtain small amounts of money. They also fought to maintain these kinds of benefits over time, since their longevity and stability were threatened by the conditionalities of international loans and structural adjustment. For that, they blocked roads, occupied bridges and organised marches to central public offices.

In the late 1990s and early 2000s, the picket was a key form of protest in so far as it presented to the public both the struggle and the suffering of the unemployed. At its most basic level, the picket involved road occupations in which families affiliated to CCC and FTV-CTA set up camps and remained for days or even – in a few cases – for months. The pickets started as ritualised events where people sang the national anthem, chanted slogans opposing the government and waved flags. The most important organisations prohibited their members from consuming drugs and alcohol. They also promoted solidarity and cooperation through sharing food, games and dances. The picket developed in the face of threats of force based on the Penal Code, which criminalised the obstruction of free traffic. In several cases, *piqueteros* were brought to trial, some imprisoned and others killed by police forces.

Alfredo, a member of CCC, told me that the movement didn't offer him – and others – a place of work, but a place of struggle ('el movimiento no ofrece un puesto de trabajo sino de lucha'). People joined the movement through bonds of kinship and neighbourhood ties. Their aim was primarily to gain access to conditional cash transfers, but they also committed themselves to a broader struggle. This commitment was formalised in a scoring system that consisted of a monthly average of attendance at mobilisations, assemblies and daily tasks involved in the projects. Most families combined that participation with informal jobs (street vending, waste-picking) and with other ways of accessing money, including small loans among relatives. In this context, becoming a beneficiary of a government-sponsored programme was transformed into the product of a collective fight won by the people in light of their suffering on the roads. As they told me, 'we stay days and nights on the roads, under heat and cold, intense sun, heavy rain and wind. In summer, we fainted. In winter we caught pneumonia'.

The administration of unemployment and poverty was partially reinvented when the unemployed movement agreed that 'collective struggle' was the principal strategy for access to welfare provision. Unionised teachers and state employees together with leaders of the unemployed workers' movement collaborated with the unemployed in each neighbourhood in order to facilitate their access to these policies, for example they helped to obtain and arrange health and school documentation. The movement also designed the projects so that the community activities could be completed in four hours of work a day. Moreover, the movement worked month after month to organise the community work conducted in exchange for the cash transfers. Some members of the movements (most of them women) specialised in this, in daily contact with public servants. In a contradictory way, the neoliberal policies expanded their scope because of the collective struggle while the movement also expanded through the collective administration of these policies.

At the same time, people recounted recurrent experiences of profound physical and psychological suffering that were resolved collectively. The unemployed movement made sense out of these stories and experiences, asserting the value of the collective. They de-individualised the experiences through public testimonies in weekly assemblies, through personal meetings with leaders of the movement and therapeutic-pedagogical interventions provided by doctors, nurses, psychologists and teachers who were members of the unions linked to the CTA and CCC. These interventions consisted of workshops against domestic violence, refuges for women who had been beaten, the formation of self-help groups for young people with addiction problems, cultural projects and school support. In this way, the unionised public sector workers made use of their expert knowledge within the unemployed movement in order to temper the effects of government policies, accentuate the value of collective struggle and hold back the deterioration in living conditions.

The movement expanded significantly around the fight for policies of conditional cash transfers through the medium of collective struggle. Unionised teachers, nurses, psychologists and social workers made use of their expert knowledge to prepare documentation and to design, direct and shape projects. As the beneficiaries of these types of programmes increased, so too did the number of temporary contracted workers in the public sector, who the unemployed supported in their campaigns to various national ministries for more job stability.

The meaning of work and limits of union representation

Locally, the expansion of the unemployed movement took the form of multiple everyday interactions, as thousands of people came together to carry out tasks in the offices of the movement or in private homes of local leaders. The movement organised everyday tasks in ways that people were already familiar with, from their previous involvement in formal employment; forms that had been dramatically cut short but that re-surfaced among the unemployed. For example, they organised shift work, and established patterns of weekly breaks and summer holidays. Likewise, people were expected to learn particular trades and skills, and also to incorporate an affective component into their activities, something apparent in the significance that toy distribution acquired in the contexts of the Christmas season, for example.

The daily meetings articulated around these activities promoted sociability and solidarity. Some women, for example, told me that they enjoyed talking with others while participating because they could 'unburden' themselves of intimate problems. Conversations covered common life situations such as diseases, relationships, parenting, domestic violence, drug use and imprisonment of their children. In sum, partially through the activities promoted by government policies, the unemployed movement was also able to intensify affective bonds between its members.

People involved in the unemployed movement explained those daily tasks in different ways. For some, especially for the leaders of urban struggles, this regular work was useful because it helped to improve the infrastructure of popular neighbourhoods and raise the standard of living for residents, which was especially significant given the self-constructed nature of these zones. Women particularly valued these tasks as a way to help children and young people. However, for most former industrial workers the daily chores within the movement were an insufficient substitute for 'productive' labour, which they viewed as useful for the wealth of the nation as well as for their personal benefit.

The link between productive labour and social utility indicates the complexity of organising a labour force that included the unemployed; amongst them many women and young people. It demonstrates the barriers that the historical understanding of work and unionism in Argentina imposes on this type of organisation. For many, work was understood to be useful in so far as it was productive, that is, as much as it brought wealth to the nation. This belief was firmly entrenched and widely held among a generation of men who had arrived in Buenos Aires from different provinces from the interior of Argentina during the 1960s and 1970s, to be employed as manual workers in factories. This form of productive work meant that the spaces of the factory and the home were clearly delimited; a divide that the social movement unionism and class-based movements merged in their opposition to the effects of neoliberal structural adjustment.

The reification of productive work also led many to oppose state assistance policies for people who were physically able to work. Policy interventions on poverty, indigence and unemployment were seen as part of a historical narrative that categorised and separated the poor who were incapable of work (elderly, disabled or children) – who were seen as legitimate recipients of aid – from the poor who were able to work and who became the target of repressive projects aimed at making them productive (Castel 1997; Gautié 1998). As a result of Peronism, in the case of Argentina, industrial development, the expansion of employment and the institutional recognition of organised labour meant that the range of rights associated with the category and condition of formal sector worker were widely supported (Grassi 2003). The historical background that extolled the value of productive work and stigmatised the unemployed poor who were physically able to work had a particular influence over those older workers who became unemployed and became recipients of assistance policies.

Productive work was seen as diametrically opposed to state assistance and was also incorporated into the movement as part of the demand for *real work*. This was connected to ideas about production, the development of the internal market, the establishment of fair salaries, and a set of rights that were usually associated with formal work in Argentina, such as social protection, education, health, housing and leisure time. In a conversation with Marcelito, a leader of the FTV-CTA, he emphasised 'We, *piqueteros*, the people (*pueblo*), must be the protagonists of wealth distribution'. The leaders of CCC, affiliated with Maoism, also thought that this model allowed for the return of the male workers to the factories, which they considered the epicentre for re-thinking the possibility of social revolution.

The demand for *real work* connected the experience of workers with Peronism, which grew in importance in a context where successive governments brutally attacked the historical victories of the workers' movement. Since Perón took control of the National Ministry of Work and Social Provision, he encouraged the unionisation of workers and oversaw collective negotiations that were reflected in agreements that regulated salary scales, labour regulations and social security (sick leave, maternity leave and paid vacations among others). The definition of citizenship during the first Peronist governments incorporated a vision of the working class as a social and political force, which is to say they were recognised as more than simply workers in the sphere of production and as atomised individuals in the political arena (James 2010). Under the remit of Peronism, the working class became a legitimate participant – through its unions – in such national issues as economic development, national sovereignty and social justice (James 2010).

This historical link between work, unionisation and Peronism posed a challenge to the politics of social movement unionism that blurred the distinctions between factory and neighbourhood, men and women, economics and emotions. This new understanding of work was amplified by the policies launched by the Kirchner governments (2003–2015), which decisively influenced the model of social movement unionism.

Union revitalisation and fragmentation under Kirchnerism

The governments of President Néstor Kirchner (2003–2007) and President Cristina Fernández de Kirchner (2007–2011 and 2011–2015) shared with those in other Southern Cone Latin American countries the 'progressive' label.[7] Kirchnerism – as a kind of governance – developed in the context of intense social protests during the 1990s, in which *piqueteros*, social movement and class-based unions played a key role. The Kirchnerist regimes subsequently established 'normality' through incentivising the labour market, collective bargaining and the recovery of the state after its dismantlement in the 1990s (Pérez and Natalucci 2012). Between 2003 and 2008, 4,2000,000 jobs were created, of which 3,100,000 were registered by labour institutions (Armelino 2012; Abal Medina 2015). In 2005 the National Council of Employment, Productivity and Minimum Salary (Consejo Nacional del Empleo, la Productividad y el Salario Mínimo, Vital y Móvil) was formed, and became the primary space where wages were negotiated between business entities, industry unions and the state (Armelino 2012).

These policies had a profound impact on trade unionism, provoking a process of reinvigoration and fragmentation that some authors perceived as governmental co-optation (Svampa 2005; Battistini 2007). Unions in the private and industrial sector, mostly grouped together in the General Confederation of Work (Confederación General del Trabajo, CGT), that represented traditional trade unionism, gained strength in campaigns for wage increases and distribution. In contrast, social movement unionism led by the CTA was debilitated by the fragmentation of its membership and the alienation of urban leaders who coordinated the unemployed movement. Among the reasons for this weakness was the low participation of the CTA in the industrial sector, which was a key impediment to its being granted recognised trade union status by the state.

In this context two opposing tendencies developed in the CTA, which progressively led to its fragmentation as a union body in 2010. One of these promoted the building of a unified workers centre, in response to the creation of jobs during the Kirchner period. It also questioned the prioritisation of the unemployed movement at the expense of organising in the industrial sector. It proposed to organise formal sector workers first, and gradually to create a collective agreement through which the informal sector could participate (Abal Medina 2015). This tendency considered it appropriate to make union action independent from politics, and therefore proposed the creation of a political party similar to the Workers' Party of Brazil. This suggestion was rejected, and various leaders of the

CTA, including the leaders of the FTV, became members of the government Frente para la Victoria (Front for Victory) coalition as a gesture of support to Kirchnerist policies. Some of them were elected as deputies and others were given executive roles in various state institutions (Armelino 2012; Pagliarone 2012; Da Silva 2012).

Another position in the CTA maintained an understanding of union action as a social movement. It perceived that precarious workers had been neglected, and so precarious workers became a central concern for a union strategy that also served to unify the private and public sectors. In the case of the public sector, precarisation became a central concern in the work of the ATE, focusing on the variety of those contractual forms associated with the 1990s that had been retained in the state sector (Lazar 2012). This tendency continued to assert the value of autonomy from political parties and from the state, promoting a form of social movement through campaigns for referendums and participatory budgeting.

In this context, the unemployed movement also started to change and rearticulate its principles. A considerable number of those who were integrated in the FTV-CTA and the CCC, especially men, returned to employment in small and medium-sized enterprises that had taken off through governmental measures that promoted new forms of industrial development.[8] The unemployed workers' movement was mostly being run by women and young people, who were the objects of policies that promoted partnership between microenterprises and cooperatives for the construction of houses, urban improvements and various other productive enterprises (Manzano 2013). In addition to these policies, in 2009 the Universal Child Benefit was launched, a measure that transferred money to the unemployed, informal workers and domestic workers who earned less than the minimum wage.

The nature of work in cooperatives was a subject of debates and different political strategies between the FTV-CTA and the CCC. For the FTV, cooperatives represented a version of employment creation, albeit of a precarious character, that would be progressively institutionalised and would achieve a fair salary (Manzano 2013). The CCC, in contrast, adopted a position of confrontation towards the Kirchnerist policies, understanding work placements in cooperatives as palliatives for poverty and unemployment, rather than productive work that was subject to the set of rights won through historical workers' struggles. The nature of work became a point of political conflict for the CCC, frequently in coordination with the tendency of the CTA that continued to fight for social movement unionism.

Beyond the discrepancies about the nature of work, both the CCC and the FTV-CTA struggled to maintain the jobs that had been created in connection to the cooperative development strategies. These included the community promotion of healthcare, childcare, housing construction and urban infrastructure, textile enterprises, footwear and food preparation. The CCC revised the protest strategy of their confrontations, notably reducing the frequency of pickets and focusing instead on engagement with government agencies and the exhibition of products (such as clothes, foods, handicrafts) at markets held in politically strategic places.

In the case of the FTV-CTA the situation was more complicated. Some of its members were given administrative and legislative roles in government, which resulted in a process of personal distancing and ruptures in some relationships. In my meetings with those members of the FTV who continue to organise cooperatively, I noticed that they were constructing their demands in a more subtle language than that employed by the CCC, and focused on the kinds of precarity that affected poorer neighbourhoods, such as problems with the environment, landfill, the paucity of infrastructure and violence. When they talked about these problems they frequently commented to me that compared with the 1990s, 'now resources fall from above'. This showed a perception of the state – particularly of the national government – as strong and dynamic. This image of the state also led to an image of collective organisation as 'punctured', which is to say, as fragmented and without dynamism, which was attributed to the challenge of being part of the state while at the same time being part of collectives that campaigned against this same state. In these meetings, I noticed the effort made to search for a language that was distinct from earlier languages of collective struggle. However, the value of collective struggle that had been magnified through the unemployed movement retained a strong emotive role, in the ways in which people thought about themselves, in small daily meetings, in the circulation of photos of road occupations and marches, or in the sharing of daily tasks associated with the conditional cash transfers.

All these processes led to the decoupling of union activity from politics, fragmenting especially the social movement unionism of the CTA while the industrial unions grouped in the CGT were revitalised, especially at the national level.

Conclusion

Both the CTA and the CCC converted unemployment into the basis from which to build opposition to neoliberalism. Both accentuated the political causes of unemployment, displacing the perception that it was an inevitable consequence of new technologies incorporated in capitalist labour processes. They reconceptualised the figure of the worker – which in Argentina was usually associated with the male industrial worker, unionised and politically represented by Peronism – in order to include the unemployed, women and young people in union-based forms of representation. The CTA gave life to the model of social movement unionism and the CCC practised a tradition of class-based unionism associated with left-wing parties. Public sector workers, deeply affected by administrative reforms, undertook the task of organising the unemployed in neighbourhoods. In this way alliances were created with leaders of land occupation movements, and the neighbourhoods became the base for the unemployed workers' movement.

The unemployed workers' movement created a powerful tool in the fight against neoliberalism through adopting practices and bio-political discourses to ensure that its protests and demands for food and work would be noticed and listened to. The state responded to unemployment by promoting an alternative form of organisation of the unemployed through conditional cash transfer programmes, financed by the World Bank. As a result of these types of policies, the unemployed movement organised the daily life of the unemployed in their neighbourhoods, asserting the value of collective struggle and establishing cooperation, solidarity and relationships. It is common for both popular and academic discourse to overestimate the effects of individualisation and privatisation on social relations under neoliberalism. It is not my intention to deny the devastating effects of neoliberal economic policies in Argentina, but I am inclined to maintain, as Sian Lazar (2013) observed for the case of Bolivia, that these policies do not only produce a society of individuals competing with each other and isolated from collective processes. Rather, they paradoxically also build collective subjects and social relations with considerable social and political weight.

In Argentina, neoliberalism ended the expansion of 'productive' work and weakened the historical model of social and political integration of workers through industrial work and Peronism. The daily actions of the unemployed movement ended up being profoundly biopolitical, visceral, emotive and communicative. Women took advantage of this opportunity to build social relations and solidarity with other women but also fought together with men to re-establish the potential for 'genuine work', into which masculine power was notably inscribed. The understanding of 'genuine work', that is to say, what was considered to be real work, came from the politics of the factory and the traditional workers' movement, and for the fight for the recuperation of a set of protections linked to wage labour, and enshrined in the first Peronist governments. It also referred to a particular kind of gender relation because its policies concerned only men, while women's role was presumed to be outside of this in the world of care, the home and the neighbourhood. This understanding brought tensions to the attempts by the social movement to merge these two spaces.

The unemployed movement helped to bring about a crisis in government and create a new terrain for popular politics of income redistribution. Kirchnerism, like the agendas of other progressive governments in the region, spurred industrial development, the internal market and wage agreements between businesses and legally recognised unions. Those who remained outside these arrangements were recognised through cooperative programmes or through campaigns for formal work. Unions referred to this group as 'precarious workers'. The Kirchner governments also incorporated union leaders and those from the unemployed movement into various executive and legislative roles in the public sector. This type of relationship is often interpreted as cooptation, indicating the domestication of the disruptive power of social movements and its subordination to the power of the state.

I suggest that it is better not to use the term cooptation as it is often used in Argentina, where it has a strong instrumental or mechanistic understanding, for example through the provision of state resources in exchange for demobilisation. Instead I would like to highlight that the involvement of the unemployed movement with Kirchnerism was affected by narrow understandings about what constituted work, which could not easily encapsulate the profound mutations of capitalism. These understandings of work had a strong influence over methods of organising workers. For this reason, progressive governments generated a process of fragmentation, dispersion and disorganisation. Social movement and class-based unionism was outstandingly effective in finding points of opposition to neoliberalism through the organisation of the unemployed, but did not manage to find the appropriate language to make collective demands on progressive governments. In my opinion the search for this language of demands was achieved on the local level but did not manage to become generalised as it had in other contexts.

These scenarios expose the existence of categories of workers who cannot easily be represented through classic union relations based on the industrial workers' movement: namely, the unemployed, precarious, cooperative workers. These categories provoke a more profound debate about the functioning of contemporary financialised global capitalism, and its particular manifestations in the peripheries of the Global South. It is here where the work of Hardt and Negri (2002) is informative, not so much for their conclusions but rather for the debates that they provoked about the weakening of industrial workers, the extension of capitalist exploitation into all forms of social cooperation, and the multitude as a positive affirmation, as a creative power, of the figure of the new immaterial worker (Hardt and Negri 2002; Colectivo Situaciones 2002; Negri et al. 2010). These debates promote new understandings about methods of work, about the possibility for collective organisation, and establish the importance of a more serious consideration of the power that national states still possess.

Hardt and Negri (2002) argue that Empire creates itself through the weakening of the nation-state, but far from being nostalgic for old forms of state domination and the Fordist factories, they celebrate this as a new possibility for forces of emancipation. However, as Moody claims (1997), despite capitalist globalisation, workers are still governed in national spaces. In Argentina, the state's role as an interlocutor for demands and as an organiser of work and life survived severe neoliberal restructuring during the 1990s and gained new impetus under progressive governments in the first decade and a half of this century. This posed a serious challenge for the organisation of workers and for the construction of unions, especially for social movement unionism.

An important legacy of the *piquetero* experience was the perspective that collective struggle was necessary to produce social transformation and to improve the lives of poorer groups. This is summarised in the famous song sung in the pickets 'As in La Matanza and Tartagal, our hope lies in popular struggle'. On 10 December 2015, the businessman Mauricio Macri became the new president of Argentina. He won by two points against the Frente para la Victoria, whose candidate was Daniel Scioli (Cristina Fernández de Kirchner could not stand again for reelection). Within weeks, the Macri government undertook a series of measures to reinstate a strong neoliberal agenda, dismantling the progressive policies of the previous governments. There were two principle attacks on workers: the reinstatement of temporary contracts in the public sector under a new rhetoric of state modernisation, and threats against cooperatives (such as non-payment of benefits, depending on the recipients' prior relations with the Kirchner regimes, and the arrest of one of the most popular movement leaders in the country while protesting in favour of cooperatives). Hundreds of temporary workers in the public sector symbolically embraced the buildings in which they worked, as a sign of protest, while cooperative workers camped in front of provincial and municipal buildings in order to campaign for the renewal of their positions. It is still too early to know with any certainty how this situation of protest will evolve, what kinds of political subjecthood will be articulated in this new configuration of social relations and if the language of collective struggle inherited from the unemployed movement will reemerge. However, it is undeniable that Argentina has started to write a new page in the story of collective struggle against global capital, precarity and neoliberal agendas in Latin America.

Notes

1 The measures imposed on (and by) Latin American governments, outlined in the document written by the economist John Williamson in 1990, include fiscal discipline, tax reform, financial liberalisation, the reform of exchange rates, foreign direct investment, privatisation and deregulation (Llistar 2003).

2 *Diario Clarín*, 16 May 2001.

3 In the Argentine context, 'el clasismo' refers to a tendency within the world of unions that was especially important from the late 1960s until the middle of the 1970s. It was associated with new leftist parties of the time (e.g. the Maoists), as well as with armed urban guerrilla groups, and proposed a take-over of state power by means of insurrection. This tendency opposed dictatorial governments and centralist unions, promoting democratisation

and rank and file union participation in the factories. It was influential in the industrial city of Córdoba, especially in automobile plants like FIAT and Renault; and it was central to an insurrection in 1969, known as the Cordobazo. Furthermore, it was innovative in developing new repertoires for union action, through active urban stoppages and occupations of factories (Ortíz 2010).

4 Peronism is the political movement that developed in support of Juan Domingo Perón, Minister for Labour in 1943, and president from 1946 to 1955, and 1973 to 1974. Subsequent Peronist governments have been those of Carlos Menem, 1989–1999, Eduardo Duhalde, 2002–2003, Néstor Kirchner, 2003–2007 and Cristina Fernández de Kirchner, 2007–2015.

5 The last national census from 2010 registered a total of 1,775,816 inhabitants in La Matanza. In 2001, the district of La Matanza had 1,249,958 inhabitants, while the Greater Buenos Aires region had 11,460,575 inhabitants.

6 In Argentina, the modern state was established over the course of the second half of the nineteenth century. It began to produce quantitative data to inform government action, which replaced census forms inherited from Spanish colonisers. This new system was established through the creation of state agencies, the use of scientific notions to direct principle and action, the secularisation of data collection and the creation of institutions of professional statisticians (Otero 2006).

7 In the Southern Cone these include the governments of the Andean zone, like Bolivia, Ecuador and Venezuela, as well as the governments of Brazil, Uruguay and Argentina, and the administrations of Lugo in Paraguay and Bachelet in Chile. These governments addressed the crisis of neoliberalism in the region and attempted to fight the poverty and social exclusion that had been caused by structural adjustment. They also committed to the recovery of the state that had been dismantled by neoliberalism.

8 According to estimates, in 2003 unemployment was at 20.4 per cent while in 2010 it had dropped to 7 per cent (Armelino 2012).

References

Abal Medina, P. (2015) 'Dilemas y desafíos del sindicalismo argentino. Las voces de dirigentes sindicales sobre la historia argentina reciente', *Trabajo y Sociedad*, 24: 53–71.

Armelino, M. (2012) 'Kind of Blue. Las vicisitudes de la Central de Trabajadores de la Argentina (CTA) durante los años kirchneristas', in Pérez, G. and Natalucci, A. (eds) *Vamos las bandas. Organizaciones y militancia kirchnerista*, pp. 101–126. Buenos Aires: Nueva Trilce.

Auyero, J. (2002) *La protesta. Retratos de la beligerancia popular en la Argentina Democrática*, Buenos Aires: Libros del Rojas-Universidad de Buenos Aires.

Battistini, O. (2007) 'Luchas sociales en crisis y estabilidad', in Villanueva, E. and Massetti, A. (eds) *Movimientos sociales en la Argentina de hoy*, pp. 95–103. Buenos Aires: Prometeo.

Castel, R. (1997) *La metamorfosis de la cuestión social. Una crónica del salariado*, Buenos Aires: Paidós.

Colectivo Situaciones (2002) 'Por una política más allá de la política', in *Contrapoder. Una introducción*, Buenos Aires: Ediciones de Mano en Mano.

Da Silva, M.L. (2012) 'Cooptados por las ideas. El Frente Transversal Nacional y Popular (2003–2011)', in Pérez, G. and Natalucci, A. (eds) *Vamos las bandas. Organizaciones y militancia kirchnerista*, pp. 83–101. Buenos Aires: Nueva Trilce.

Debate para la Organización de los Trabajadores (1991) Encuentro de Organizaciones y Dirigentes sindicales reunidos en la localidad de Burzaco (provincia de Buenos Aires) el 17 de diciembre de 1991. http://lae.princeton.edu/catalog/ 1d6p7#?c=0&m=0&s=0&cv=0&z=- 0.1608%2C-0.078%2C1.3215%2C1.5597, accessed 28 October 2016.

Documento del Primer Congreso Nacional de Delegados CTA (1996) 4 y 5 de noviembre. www. bibliotecacta.org.ar/bases/pdf/ BIT00671.pdf, accessed 28 October 2016.

Doyon, L. (1984) 'La organización del movimiento sindical peronista 1946–1955', *Desarrollo Económico*, 24(94): 203–234.

Duhalde, S. (2009) 'La respuesta de los sindicatos estatales al neoliberalismo en Argentina (1989–1995)', *Trabajo y Sociedad*, 13: 1–13.

Foucault, M. (2006) *Seguridad, territorio y población*, Buenos Aires: Fondo de Cultura Económica de Argentina.

Gautié, J. (1998) 'Da invenção do desemprego à sua deconstrução', *Maná*, 4(2): 67–83.

Grassi, E. (2003) *Políticas y problemas sociales en la sociedad neoliberal. La otra década infame (I)*, Buenos Aires: Espacio Editorial.

Hardt, M. and Negri, A. (2002) *Imperio*, Buenos Aires: Editorial Paidós.

James, D. (2010) *Resistencia e integración. El peronismo y la clase trabajadora argentina 1946–1976*, Buenos Aires: Siglo XXI Editores.

Lazar, S. (2012) 'A Desire to Formalize Work? Comparing Trade Unions Strategies in Bolivia and Argentina', *Anthropology of Work Review*, 33(1): 15–24.

Lazar, S. (2013) *El Alto, ciudad Rebelde*, La Paz: Plural Editores.

Llistar, D. (2003) 'El consenso de Washington una década después', in Ramos, L. (ed.) *El fracaso del consenso de Washington. La caída de su mejor alumno: Argentina*, pp. 11–20. Barcelona: Icaria, Más Madera.

Manzano, V. (2013) *La política en movimiento. Movilizaciones colectivas y políticas estatales en la vida del Gran Buenos Aires*, Rosario: Prohistoria Ediciones.

Mollona, M. (2009) 'Community Unionism versus Business Unionism: The Return of the Moral Economy in Trade Union Studies', *American Ethnologist*, 36(4): 651–666.

Moody, K. (1997) 'Towards an International Social-Movement Unionism', *New Left Review*, 1(225): 52–72.

Negri, T., Hardt, M., Cocco, G., Revel, J., García Linera, A. and Tapia, L. (eds) (2010) *Imperio, multitud y sociedad abigarrada*, Buenos Aires: CLACSO ediciones and Waldhuter editores.

Ortíz, M.L. (2010) 'Apuntes para una definición del clasismo. Córdoba, 1969–1976', *Conflicto Social*, 3: 59–83.

Otero, H. (2006) *Estadística y Nación. Una historia conceptual del pensamiento censal de la Argentina moderna 1869–1914*, Buenos Aires: Prometeo Libros.

Pagliarone, M.F. (2012) 'Piqueteros y funcionarios. Transformaciones de la FTV en el kirchnerismo', in Pérez, G. and Natalucci, A. (eds) *Vamos las bandas. Organizaciones y militancia kirchnerista*, pp. 55–81. Buenos Aires: Nueva Trilce.

Pérez, G. and Natalucci, A. (2012) 'El kircherismo como problema sociológico', in Pérez, G. and Natalucci, A. (eds) *Vamos las bandas. Organizaciones y militancia kirchnerista*, pp. 7–26. Buenos Aires: Nueva Trilce.

Quirós, J. (2008) 'Piqueteros y peronistas en la lucha del Gran Buenos Aires. Por una visión no instrumental de la política popular', *Cuadernos de Antopología Social*, 27: 113–131.

Svampa, M. (2005) *La sociedad excluyente. La Argentina bajo el signo del neoliberalismo*, Buenos Aires: Taurus.

Svampa, M. and Pereyra, S. (2003) *Entre la Ruta y el Barrio. La experiencia de las organizaciones piqueteras*, Buenos Aires: Biblos.

Villarreal, J. (1985) 'Los hilos sociales del poder', in Jozami, E., Paz, P. and Villarreal, J. (eds) *Crisis de la dictadura argentina. Política económica y cambio social, 1976–1983*, pp. 197–281. Buenos Aires: Siglo XXI.

11 | FROM INVISIBLE TO INVINCIBLE: THE STORY OF THE 3 COSAS CAMPAIGN

Jason Moyer-Lee and Henry Chango Lopez

Introduction

As recently as the spring of 2011, the University of London's outsourced workers went largely unnoticed. Nearly 400 cleaners, porters, security guards and caterers earned just barely above the minimum wage. They didn't have occupational sick pay, they had the legal minimum for holidays and most didn't have a company pension. Management abuse was rife, unlawful deductions of wages were the norm and people were sacked without recourse to any procedures. And virtually none of these workers were members of a union.

Just three years later the situation had changed dramatically. Wages for cleaners had gone up by 49 per cent (from £6.15 to £9.15 per hour), none of the outsourced workers earned less than the London Living Wage, workers were entitled to up to six months of occupational sick pay per year and 33 days holiday (depending on length of service) and many were offered the opportunity to buy into the same pension scheme as their managers. Cofely – the University of London's main subcontractor – had been taken to an employment tribunal for discrimination, and the majority of Cofely workers were unionised. All of these achievements occurred against a backdrop of government austerity, pay cuts and redundancies, implemented by the government most ideologically committed to neoliberalism in recent UK history.

This chapter will tell the story of the changes that occurred in the three years between the spring of 2011 and the spring of 2014. The story starts with UNISON, the large UK public sector union. UNISON's English classes, recruitment drive and London Living Wage campaign got the ball rolling. However, the story will also tell how UNISON ignored many of the needs of the workers, worked at a glacial pace and then later tried to block worker activism. The workers' relations with UNISON sheds light on some of the internal struggles of the UK trade union movement today. The Independent Workers' Union of Great Britain (IWGB), the small militant union that the outsourced workers joined after a mass exodus from UNISON (discussed below), became a symbol for the 'new trade unionism', contrasting sharply with UNISON's more traditional style. This story is one of union struggle, as opposed to the living wage campaigns that have become increasingly associated with civil society organisations such as London Citizens.

In the next section we shall tell the story of UNISON at the University of London, from the first recruits and English classes to the decision to leave *en masse*. The following section will describe our experience in the IWGB, from the early days of writing the branch constitution to our two-day strike in November 2013, which led to a ground-breaking victory on terms and conditions. The conclusion will reflect on our experience and the implications of this for the battle between old and new trade unionism.

Old trade unionism: UNISON

The perfect storm The story begins at the University of London (UoL)[1] in the spring of 2011. By this time, like many other universities and public sector entities more generally, the UoL had decided to outsource its 'non-essential services'. As occurred in other institutions throughout the country since the 1980s, with the outsourcing came the degradation of terms and conditions, and the creation of a two-tier workforce, with the 'public sector' direct employees on the one hand, and the new 'private sector' outsourced workers on the other. It is this outsourcing that was the root of the problem and the origin of legitimate grievance of UoL workers. The outsourcing created the opportunity for institutions to propagate the deceptive narrative of 'they are not *our* employees', thereby fomenting a justification for not only a legal, but also a moral, abdication of responsibility towards these workers by their former employer.

At the time the UoL was outsourcing with two companies: Aramark and Balfour Beatty Workplace (BBW). Aramark is an American multinational that specialises in catering and runs the cafes and cafeterias at the UoL. BBW[2] – the facilities management arm of the multinational construction giant Balfour Beatty Group – held a total facilities management contract whereby it provided cleaning, portering, maintenance, post room, security and other services.

These outsourced workers were almost entirely migrants. Indeed whilst there were a handful of British workers, the majority of catering and security workers were from Asia, Africa and Eastern Europe. Bar a significant minority of Polish workers, nearly all of the cleaners and porters were from Latin America. And all of these workers were earning well below the London Living Wage, some as little as £6.15 per hour. The majority were only entitled to the legal minimums of statutory sick pay (SSP) and 28 days holiday, and did not have a pension. This labour force was also non-unionised. In the spring of 2011, out of around 350 workers, fewer than 20 were members of UNISON, one of the UK public sector unions.

On the surface this picture appears quite bleak from the perspective of trade union activism and workers' rights. However, behind the scenes a perfect storm of pro-activism conditions was gathering. The composition of the cleaner workforce – the workers that became by far the most active in the UoL unions and campaigns – had been changing over recent years. Prior to 2011 there had been plenty of undocumented Latin American workers. These workers had come directly from their home countries and often worked with fake papers, thereby creating an enormous risk for these workers to be involved in militant and public campaigns against their employer. However, by the spring of 2011 the workforce shifted to become mainly composed of *second wave* migrants, Latin Americans (mainly from Ecuador and Colombia) who emigrated to Spain in the previous decade. They obtained Spanish citizenship and hence were EU citizens with the right to work in the UK. So when the economic crisis hit Spain (an excellent exposition of which can be seen in Martí i Puig and Aparicio Wilhelmi in this volume) they moved to London in search of work. Having fled economic and/or political crises in their home countries, many were able to obtain a comfortable middle-class lifestyle in Spain, some of them owning flats or cars, able to afford holidays, etc. There was no language barrier and social integration was easier to achieve. Yet when these workers came to London their lifestyle took a major hit. They were often crammed into shared flats, began cleaning jobs at five or six in the morning, earned poverty wages, and due to the language barrier were isolated from the rest of society. Therefore the story of their move to London is one of a degradation of living standards compared to what they had previously been accustomed. This shock change contributed to a genuine sense of grievance about their work situation at the University of London. And as they could not be deported due to migration status, there was less risk for them to fight about their grievances.

Around the same time as the composition of the workforce was changing, student and trade union activism in the UK was on the rise. Responding to an economic crisis and hit in living standards, austerity and a tripling of tuition fees, trade union and student activists started to mobilise nationally. This was particularly prevalent in Bloomsbury, where the UoL headquarters is situated, for example the 'Justice for Cleaners Campaign' at SOAS, which had won the London Living Wage and a voluntary recognition agreement with UNISON in previous years.[3] The new wave of student militancy culminated in 2012 in the election of a socialist president and vice-president of University of London Union (ULU), the University of London student union, which counted over 120,000 members. The new leadership of ULU later went on to have an enormous influence on the 3 Cosas Campaign, which will be seen below. In addition to the broad context outlined above, there was also a group of keen individuals who happened to be in the right place at the right time. This group started attending UNISON's (UoL) London Living Wage campaign meetings, which became the incubator for trade union activism at UoL.

The UNISON honeymoon: English classes, recruitment and the campaign One of the first steps towards trade union activism at UoL came in the mildest of forms: English classes. As many of the Latin American cleaners were recent migrants from Spain, English skill was a major barrier to integration in society and there was abundant interest in learning the language of their new country of residence. The classes began small but they soon went on to become a proper English language course that was open to cleaners at a number of the Bloomsbury colleges, had a budget of around £10,000 (funded by local UNISON branches), and had teachers from SOAS and the Workers' Educational Association (WEA). UNISON was fully behind the English classes, both financially and logistically, and the project was spearheaded as a team effort by Jason Moyer-Lee and the then Educational Officer and Vice-Chair of the UNISON branch at UoL.

In addition to English classes, recruitment to UNISON also quickly became one of the first priorities. Activists made a series of visits to the intercollegiate halls of residence to recruit the Latin American women who cleaned there and the Senate House porters recruited their colleagues. By far the most effective recruitment selling point was the provision of free English classes. Within a matter of months membership among BBW workers at UoL had soared from fewer than 20 to over 100.

As the Latin American cleaners learned the basics of English grammar and pleasantries, and as the UNISON membership forms continued to flood in, the London Living Wage campaign meetings kept taking place. The ground work had been done and now people were ready for *action*, something that the campaign meetings didn't always produce. After a few months it was decided that the campaign would be officially launched at an event at SOAS in July 2011. This was the first UNISON event aimed at outsourced workers at UoL and it was attended by a collection of cleaners, UNISON officials, local activists, students and even the local Labour MP Frank Dobson (as a guest speaker). By the end of the meeting people were fired up and enthusiasm with UNISON was reaching dizzying heights. From being virtually invisible, workers were now taking free English classes, beginning to fight for a dramatic increase in wages and had the unconditional support of the second biggest trade union in the United Kingdom. Or so they believed.

From malcontent to victory: strike, recognition, and the London living wage One of the difficulties UNISON had in dealing with its new recruits was the inability to engage with issues that didn't fall within its four-pronged agenda of recruitment, recognition, English classes and the London Living Wage. Whilst this agenda was popular with the new recruits, it did not encapsulate all of their needs and aspirations. For example, one of the most pressing industrial issues at the time was non-payment of wages. Here we do not refer to the fact that the workers were paid poorly, but rather to the fact that sometimes they were not paid *at all*. Some workers would work up to two or three months and not get paid anything. Others would get paid half of what they were owed. Still others would be paid too much one month and then have an enormous amount deducted from the subsequent month's pay packet. Our firm belief is that this was not a deliberate effort on the part of BBW to defraud the workers but was rather due to incompetence which, to our eyes, continues to characterise Cofely's management and administration to the present time. Compounding this was BBW's seeming lack of interest in resolving pay problems for employees.

Had those of us who were activists at the time had the knowledge of employment law then that we do now, we simply would have submitted a series of unlawful deduction of wages claims to the Central London Employment Tribunal. However, given that many of us at the UNISON branch were new to the struggle and had no employment law or trade union rep training, we were reliant on UNISON officials to resolve the pay issues. Unfortunately, and despite the best of intentions, the UNISON officials were entirely ineffective. Months were spent gathering pay slips and attempting to have courteous conversations with BBW managers. However no grievances or employment tribunal claims were filed. And unsurprisingly, the pay issue went largely unresolved.

By the end of August 2011, frustrations were at boiling point. UNISON was coming to be seen as friendly but incompetent, and the union's priorities paled in comparison to the pressing needs of workers to pay their rent. Finally, the workers decided to go on an unofficial strike. The picket line was supported by local trade union activists and a group of Bloomsbury students. This was the first strike or protest ever staged by outsourced workers at Senate House, and it is important to note that the strike was not about demands for improved wages or terms and conditions, but rather it was about enforcing the legal right to be paid for work done. In other words, the strike was about 'the right to have rights' (Peano, this volume). The shock factors of the event's novelty, the boldness of low-paid migrant workers taking unofficial action and the disruptive nature of the drumming and shouting all led to a quick resolution. The strike was called off and within three days BBW paid out £6,000 in overdue wages.

It is difficult to overestimate the magnitude of the impact of 1 September 2011 on the following three-and-a-half years of activism at UoL. First, the bold action and quick victory boosted the confidence of the workers. Having taken unofficial action and won with no negative consequences, participating in peaceful and lawful protests outside of working hours therefore seemed like a minor undertaking. Second, the UoL outsourced workers popped up on the radar of local trade union branches, colleges and students. The strike established that there was now another place – in addition to SOAS – where militant cleaners were standing up and fighting back. Third, the strike showed that UoL was incredibly susceptible to pressure. Indeed UoL was deeply involved in the negotiations between the strikers and BBW that ended the walkout. And fourth, the strike showed BBW that *the workers*, rather than *UNISON*, was the force to be reckoned with.

After the strike the workers also stepped up efforts in the London Living Wage campaign. The role of UNISON officialdom in the campaign began a steady recession into the margins of relevance as the campaign increasingly focused on the confrontational tactics that the union so abhorred. Noisy protests were called where MPs blasted the UoL for paying poverty wages, leaflets were distributed and petitions were signed. Within a month the UoL made an offer to phase in the London Living Wage by raising salaries in four stages – starting in October 2011 – and fully implementing the London Living Wage in July 2012. In a striking precursor to the tensions between workers and UNISON that were to follow, UNISON signed off on the offer whereas the campaign – which by this time had become entirely autonomous from UNISON bureaucrats and local branch leadership – rejected the offer as a joke and continued to push for immediate implementation. Although more campaign events and protests were held – including on the UoL's prestigious Foundation Day at the end of November 2011, which resulted in Princess Anne cancelling her visit – the UNISON/UoL deal had taken the wind out of the campaign's sails and the efforts for immediate implementation ended up fizzling out.

The tensions rise: committee, the 3 Cosas Campaign and branch elections One of the results of the BBW/UNISON recognition agreement at UoL that resulted from the strike was facilities time for BBW workers. This means that BBW reps were occasionally given paid time off during working hours in order to engage in union duties, for example in order to attend UNISON branch committee meetings. Prior to the recognition agreement the UNISON (Senate House) branch committee met once per month and was composed almost entirely of British, university-educated, direct employees of the UoL.

However, with the BBW recognition agreement the composition, content and style of the committee changed dramatically overnight. Now half of the committee's participants were Latin American cleaners and porters. Most of these workers did not speak English so committee meetings were interpreted (which means they took twice as long). Instead of debating who should be the branch delegate to the conference in Manchester the topics of the day became pay problems and campaigns.

Needless to say, the abrupt change to the committee described above led to increasing tensions between the local branch leadership on the one hand and the outsourced workers' reps on the other. Used to dominating the show with a rubber-stamp committee, the local leadership now had to contend with an unruly bunch of activists who weren't keen on being domesticated.

In July 2012 the London Living Wage was finally implemented and the workers evaluated the next step. The BBW reps met in the summer of 2012 with supporting activists and the group discussed a campaign for improved terms and conditions, in particular for sick pay, holidays and pensions. A debate within the group took place about whether to wage a 'Back in House' campaign where the case would be made for the UoL to end the outsourcing and bring the workers back as direct employees, or a campaign merely for the terms and conditions regardless of employer. In his case for a campaign for terms and conditions only, Robinson – a leading worker/activist – repeatedly stated: 'Tenemos que luchar por las tres cosas' (We have to fight for the three things). In the end the decision was taken to launch a campaign for terms and conditions and call it the 3 Cosas Campaign.

The campaign was to be a more intense and improved version of the London Living Wage campaign. The 3 Cosas Campaign sought to emulate the successful confrontational tactics of the previous campaign for wages but also to learn from mistakes of the past. For example, whilst the previous campaign had enjoyed lots of support from workers at protests and major events, workers were not at the heart of the strategy and planning of the campaign. Rather, planning meetings were often dominated by local students and activists. In order to address this it was decided that campaign meetings were to take place once per week and be limited to outsourced workers only (with the exception of Jason Moyer-Lee who was working essentially as a full-time volunteer organiser).

The 3 Cosas Campaign was launched in September 2012 and immediately started making a presence on social media. Within the first few months Reel News produced a video on the campaign,[4] the campaign achieved a unanimous vote of support from the ULU Senate (the body that represents the student unions of all of the UoL's constituent colleges), workers had once again become enthusiastic about fighting for their rights and, most curiously, UNISON's (national) head office took an interest in the campaign. Indeed, activists met with various officials at UNISON's head office and were even invited to speak alongside David Miliband MP at an event in parliament.

All of the above was achieved without money and without backing from the UoL UNISON branch, both of which were problematic. The campaign therefore put together a modest budget of just over £2,000 with the intention of presenting it for a vote at the branch committee meeting of 4 November 2012. In the weeks leading up to this committee meeting the UNISON head office had also been in touch to say that it could no longer support the campaign if the campaign did not have the official backing of the local branch. So a motion on official support for the campaign was added to the list of issues to be voted on at the next branch meeting. However, at a heated meeting, the local leadership prevented this coming to a vote.

At this stage there was a lot of debate among the workers about whether to stay in UNISON or not. Indeed, Sonia Chura, a recent Bolivian migrant and leading figure in the campaign, was an early advocate of leaving the union altogether. However, it was decided that people would stay but that we would attempt to take over the branch democratically in the upcoming branch elections in the spring of 2013. It had become clear that it was no longer sufficient to have a majority of votes on the committee, but rather we needed to take control of the key leadership positions as well. We therefore put together a slate of pro-campaign candidates. Our candidates were both direct employees and outsourced workers.

UNISON engaged in what could only be called voter suppression tactics in this branch election, for example, deciding that the vote would be conducted via postal ballot despite the fact that in the past the elections had always been conducted via show-of-hands votes. Our protestations that this move would disproportionately disenfranchise a precarious and highly mobile group of Latin American cleaners whose membership records were not up to date due to language barriers were ignored; and a number of cleaners did not receive ballots on the day they were meant to. Other complications were documented by a SOAS PhD student in a student newspaper.[5] Finally, on the day the election results were to be announced, UNISON issued a communication announcing a postponement due to on-going investigations; and roughly three weeks later, they invalidated the elections and refused to release the results.

The day after the announcement on the invalidation of the elections was made we held a protest at the UNSON head office.[6] UNISON responded by calling the police[7] – the final straw for many members – and within weeks the outsourced workers had voted to leave UNISON and join the IWGB.[8]

¡Hasta la victoria!

Once we left UNISON we suddenly found ourselves with an abundance of free time, which had for the previous months been invested solely in fighting our former union's vicious bureaucracy. This section will discuss the arrangement we made with the IWGB, as well as various of the successful campaign tactics used, including collaboration with students, collaboration with other organisations, campaign videos, protests, press coverage and industrial action. We will also discuss the important 3 Cosas victory. Rather than give a chronological blow-by-blow of everything the campaign did – which could fill a book rather than a chapter – this section is structured around themes that we believe are intrinsic to the 3 Cosas Campaign.

The IWGB When we decided to leave UNISON there was really only one union that we considered joining and this was the IWGB. After our experience with the UNISON bureaucracy we were weary of the big unions. Therefore the idea of joining UNITE or GMB *en masse* was little more than a fleeting thought. Second, we believed that IWGB had a similar history and approach to us. They had come out of a big union (UNITE), were militant and not averse to confrontational tactics. Indeed we had come to know the IWGB people mainly in the streets. They came to the London Living Wage and 3 Cosas protests and some of us went to their protests and pickets.

Despite this, we had been burned so badly with the UNISON experience that we wanted to join the IWGB with as much autonomy for our new 'University of London Branch' as possible. We were able to negotiate this autonomy in a number of important areas such as our own ability to set membership rates and our ability to retain 75 per cent of the membership contributions of our members. Once the deal was in place we drafted a branch constitution and started recruiting. Within the first two weeks of creating the new branch roughly 60 UNISON members left to join the IWGB. Most of the rest of the outsourced workers who were members of UNISON followed suit and we soon became the biggest union among outsourced workers at UoL. A month or so after joining the IWGB we held the branch's first AGM, where Henry Chango Lopez and Sonia Chura were elected Branch Chair and Vice-Chair respectively, and Jason Moyer-Lee was elected Branch Secretary.

It is important to understand that the new members of the IWGB did not see the solution to UNISON's over-bureaucratisation being a union with no structures. In a similar way to how Bolivian coca-growing trade unionists scoffed at the amorphous and disorganised Occupy movement (Grisaffi, this volume), the new IWGB members focused from the get-go on creating officer positions, rules, democratic and regular meetings and so on.

Student support One of the most important elements of the 3 Cosas Campaign's success was the support of UoL students. This support was seen at the grassroots level – e.g. the majority of protest participants were often students – as well as at the institutional level, through student unions and campaigns. Nowhere was this support more visible and substantive than from the University of London Union (ULU) and its vice-president, Daniel Cooper. Among other things he helped facilitate a number of student events designed to raise awareness of the campaign. He also helped organise donations and support from other student unions. However, perhaps most importantly, ULU granted office space to the IWGB. Although it was small, this space helped immeasurably with the administrative organisation of the IWGB branch and provided a headquarters for the campaign.

One of the more creative ways in which students and workers collaborated was through the 'Summer of Action' in 2013. At this time a number of 'action weeks' were designated, with some actions being led by workers and others by students. For example, in the workers' action weeks they called protests and had an information stall. The students had two action weeks. In the first one they dressed up in beach gear, complete with towels, snorkels and music, and invaded the Senate House lobby unannounced. They set up an impromptu holiday camp – which was recorded and a video later posted on YouTube[9] – to highlight the fact that outsourced workers did not receive sufficient holiday entitlement. In the second action week the students pulled a similar stunt, this time some of them dressed as sick or injured cleaners and others as the UoL Vice-Chancellor (including masks depicting the Vice-Chancellor's face), and again showed up with no warning at UoL to put on a sketch about exploited cleaners with no sick pay.[10]

Finally, students were also instrumental in raising money for the IWGB strike fund. Indeed the fundraising effort was entirely led by students and was incredibly successful, raising thousands of pounds for different strikes. The students raised so much money that every participant in the first official outsourced workers' strike in November 2013 (more on which below) was compensated with what they would have earned had they gone to work on those days.

Working with other organisations The IWGB actively sought and obtained the support of a number of important organisations and individuals. Indeed, similar to Compton (this volume), the IWGB identified 'building alliances with communities' as one of its key routes to success. For example, shortly after leaving UNISON, the 3 Cosas Campaign started participating in meetings run by the Coalition of Latin Americans in the UK (CLAUK[11]), a coalition of Latin American NGOs in the UK. One of CLAUK's three core objectives is to improve Latin Americans' access to labour rights, hence there was major scope for collaboration. The forum CLAUK was attempting to organise included representatives from cleaners in local trade union branches as well as some Latin American NGOs. The forum's work culminated in a joint protest on May Day in 2013 as well as a video on the various cleaners' campaigns.[12]

Another organisation that collaborated with the 3 Cosas Campaign was Labour Start, an online organisation that runs electronic campaigns in support of trade union struggles.[13] Labour Start has thousands of supporters on its mailing lists and campaigns effectively by asking them to email the managerial targets in a given campaign calling on the relevant manager or government official to implement the requested policy or action. In this manner local disputes can result in managers or governments receiving thousands of emails from the trade union's supporters from around the world. In our case, the Labour Start campaign resulted in over 1,400 emails being sent to the UoL Vice-Chancellor, calling on him to implement improved sick pay, holidays and pensions.

Finally, we had the support of various high-profile figures such as Natalie Bennett, leader of the Green Party of England and Wales. Natalie has come to speak at various of our protests and union events and has participated in campaign videos.[14] She has also written statements or articles of support[15] for the campaign and wrote the UoL Vice-Chancellor calling on him to improve sick pay, holidays and pensions. Of course, having the support of high-profile individuals does not win the campaign by itself; however, it does help to construct the narrative that what we were campaigning for was not some extreme objective of a militant minority, but rather something behind which a broad cross-section of society – from workers to students to politicians – was rallying.

Videos As mentioned above, Reel News made a series of campaign videos for the 3 Cosas Campaign. In addition to simply telling the story of the campaign, the videos collectively serve three important purposes. First, the Reel News videos dramatise an injustice in an extremely effective manner. Rather than offering statistics on low pay, inequality or outsourcing, the videos contained firsthand accounts of the effects of all three. The videos took a group of workers previously characterised by their invisibility and launched them onto the iPhones of UoL students and desktop computers of university HR managers. In addition to recording the workers' eloquent articulation of the demand for improved terms and conditions, the videos also contained a number of anecdotal horror stories. For example, in one video a woman explained how she suffered from chronic back pain yet couldn't afford to stay home without sick pay and hence would end up lying down and crying on the beds of the student residence halls she was meant to clean. In appealing to people's emotions the videos were able to communicate the objectives of the campaign in an unprecedented manner.

Second, the videos created bad publicity for the UoL. Universities are increasingly focused on their public image and are exceedingly preoccupied with avoiding bad press. Having professionally-made videos posted on YouTube and readily accessible to anyone who had heard of their existence was in itself a form of public pressure on the UoL.

Third, the videos were a call to action. In addition to being used to inform the public and pressure UoL, the videos were also geared at a target audience: activists, trade union supporters, students and workers. The videos often contained rock music designed to pump up the viewer and usually ended with the announcement of the next campaign event, usually a protest.

In addition to the Reel News videos, another outfit, Novara Media, also made a couple of videos, this time to raise money for the strike funds.[16] The short punchy videos worked in a similar way to the Reel News ones, only that in these the call to action was to make a PayPal donation to the IWGB strike fund. As seen above, the strike fund efforts were highly effective.

Press Favourable press coverage played a fundamental role in the 3 Cosas Campaign. Not only does press coverage help spread the message of the campaign but it hits the UoL where it hurts: on reputation and image. Whilst the aim had always been *The Guardian* – the universities' daily of choice – the 3 Cosas Campaign has been written about in a number of fora, from student newspapers[17] to political party papers,[18] to the *Times Higher Education*,[19] to the Latin American press.[20]

The campaign was also able to obtain mainstream national press coverage on a few occasions, sometimes due to the campaign's efforts, and other times due to the UoL's incredible lack of astuteness when it came to strategy. The UoL committed a few blunders that resulted in favourable press for the campaign, from having a student arrested for writing a pro-campaign slogan in washable chalk on a plaque on the wall outside Senate House[21] to attempting in July 2013 to ban protests on UoL grounds.

The 3 Cosas Campaign and its student supporters defied the protest ban and the resultant clash with UoL management and the

Metropolitan Police led to significant press coverage.[22] By the end of 2013 clashes with UoL management and with the police had intensified, culminating in the violent eviction of student occupiers of Senate House and multiple police arrests of student activists. The UoL in turn responded by obtaining an injunction against sit-in protests for six months. Students responded by organising a massive protest, which counted some 3,000 participants. The police made no appearance at that protest. Student protesters forced their way onto UoL property and set afire the injunction papers that had been posted up all around the outside of Senate House. After this the UoL retreated from its untenable position of banning protests, but not before attracting another onslaught of negative press coverage.[23]

¡Huelga! Back in the first London Living Wage campaign meetings in the early days of UNISON, the UNISON regional organiser explained that a campaign should move in escalating stages. Events and tactics should start small and then gradually increase in impact. This was probably the only good piece of campaigning advice ever offered by UNISON officials. And this was indeed the strategy of the 3 Cosas Campaign. The campaign started with social media, then videos and protests, then press coverage, etc. We had left for the end what we considered to be potentially one of the most powerful weapons of all: official industrial action. However, by the autumn of 2013 we were ready. We followed all of the strict anti-trade union strike laws and indeed attempted to use these laws to our advantage. For example, we used each stage of the pre-strike action (notice of dispute, ballot, announcement of ballot result, etc.) as an excuse to ramp up publicity about the impending action. With a 97 per cent 'Yes' vote on a roughly 70 per cent turnout, the union had a strong mandate to call for strike action. After receiving the ballot result and the announcement of two days' strike designed to coincide with the UoL's Foundation Day event and the visit of Princess Anne, BBW parted with its unwritten rule of not speaking to us and invited us to negotiations at ACAS.[24]

The ACAS negotiations were not as fruitful as we had hoped and as no deal could be made, the strike went ahead on 27 and 28 November, starting each morning at 6 a.m. We rented a sound system and so had Russell Square jiving to Latino beats throughout the day.

Coffee, tea and food were offered to participants and supporters, and the picket line was visited by a number of local trade unionists, students and direct UoL employees. There was also a solid turnout of over 60 outsourced workers. Given the participation, noise, media coverage, energy and enthusiasm, it felt like the strike was a major success, even if we didn't expect a victory on terms and conditions at that stage.

On the afternoon of the second day of the strike the two of us were in the union office at ULU with Sonia Chura. Having packed up everything we were sitting around, exhausted and discussing the strike, when Jason's phone rang. On the other end of the phone was a *Times Higher Education* journalist wanting a comment on the UoL's announcement of improved terms and conditions. This was the first that we had heard of any announcement so Jason asked the journalist to send the announcement over to us and to call back in ten minutes. The statement said that from January 2014 all BBW employees would be given the option of receiving up to 33 days' holiday and six months' sick pay, depending on length of service, and have access to the same pension scheme as BBW managers. We stared at the screen for a few minutes waiting for it to sink in. When it finally did we were ecstatic. The new terms and conditions meant an additional week's holiday per year and the ability to fall ill or become injured without being financially penalised. Whilst these terms and conditions were still not as good as UoL direct employees, they were better than virtually all outsourced cleaning jobs in London and would have a serious impact on the things the campaign had been fighting for. When the journalist called back Jason said 'it was great progress' and 'a good first step, but certainly not good enough'.[25]

After the conversation with the journalist Sonia and the two of us started calling the dozens of workers who had been on the picket line that day to tell them about the victory. People were thrilled. After almost a year-and-a-half of protests, participating in videos, giving interviews to journalists, collaborating with students, working with other organisations and finally participating in industrial action, it had all paid off. BBW workers at the UoL were finally going to achieve improved holidays, occupational sick pay and access to a pension.

Conclusion

The dramatic implications of the 3 Cosas victory at BBW Whilst our focus had always been more on BBW than Aramark (due, among other things, to much higher membership levels at BBW), the 3 Cosas Campaign had been fighting for the rights of *all* outsourced workers, not just BBW workers. Having secured a victory on the back of industrial action at BBW, the campaign was then free to focus its efforts on Aramark. A few months after the BBW win, Henry wrote a letter to the Aramark regional manager asking her when she planned to implement similar terms and conditions for Aramark staff. She responded by meeting up with the two of us in the tiny IWGB office. In preparation for the office visit we printed off a poster with the Aramark logo with the words 'ARAMARK we're coming for you!', and pinned it up on the wall. In the meeting the manager told us that within a couple of months Aramark workers would be offered the same sick pay and holiday entitlement as BBW workers. This is despite the fact that the Aramark workers didn't go on strike and no protests specifically targeting Aramark had been held.

Roughly six months after the BBW victory, the SOAS cleaners also achieved a similar victory after days of industrial action and a vibrant Justice for Cleaners campaign. After the SOAS victory came the Birkbeck cleaners' victory, which resulted in the same terms and conditions as those won by SOAS cleaners. And following on from this came another IWGB victory on sick pay and holidays for cleaners at the London School of Hygiene and Tropical Medicine (LSHTM). Indeed, what we have seen with improved terms and conditions is a domino effect in higher education institutions similar to that of the London Living Wage, albeit on a dramatically smaller scale. When SOAS cleaners can say 'cleaners across the street at UoL do the same job as us but get decent sick pay and holidays', SOAS more quickly runs out of arguments and justifications that hold water with the public. The other aspect of the domino effect is the amount of effort that needs to go in to each subsequent victory. Whilst the 3 Cosas and the SOAS campaigns were long and arduous, the Birkbeck campaign was on a significantly smaller level, and the LSHTM campaign was non-existent.

However, beyond specific and concrete improvements in terms and conditions for IWGB members at the UoL, and beyond the similar improvements enjoyed by workers at other workplaces that benefited from the domino effect of the 3 Cosas victory, the 3 Cosas Campaign also achieved less concrete and tangible results. The starting point for evaluating the more intangible impacts is to take stock of what the 3 Cosas Campaign achieved in light of the political and economic context. The campaign – which garnered much public sympathy and support – was led mainly by migrant workers at a time when anti-immigrant rhetoric and sentiment was on the rise, stoked by political parties of all stripes. The UoL outsourced workers achieved a pay rise when real wages were stagnating and the government was implementing reductions in real pay for many public sector workers. The UoL workers avoided redundancies when the government was laying off thousands of public sector workers. The UoL workers unionised and maintained a high level of union density when the trend in recent decades has been one of declining trade union membership in the UK. The UoL workers took effective strike action, more than once, when the trend has been a massive reduction in strike days per year in the UK since the advent of the anti-union Thatcher laws. The UoL workers were able to *improve* their overall employment conditions when the nearly universal trend of outsourcing was one of a reduction in employment conditions. And finally, the UoL outsourced workers were able to be noticed, visible and assertive, when their counterparts in other universities had virtually disappeared from their institutions' radars.

Can old trade unions implement new trade unionism? Having lived through the UNISON saga one is struck by the obstructiveness of a coterie of UNISON stalwarts seemingly hell-bent on destroying any endeavour to unite, fight and win. However, the danger one runs in over-fetishising the courage and determination of the low-paid migrant workers who took on a union bureaucracy and then left the union to build their own, is to come to the conclusion that (1) but for union bureaucracies cleaners would be fighting and winning all over London and consequently that (2) low-paid workers would be better off outside of the big unions. Whilst one could certainly be forgiven for coming to these conclusions, we would argue that the biggest problem facing cleaners and other low-paid workers in London is not a union bureaucracy attempting to crush local activism, but rather that there is rarely any activism to crush! Our biggest beef with UNISON is that all too often in places where it has low-paid members, it does *nothing*.

As much as the IWGB is keen to grow and spread its reach and campaigns, the lesson of the 3 Cosas Campaign should not be that one must be a member of a small trade union in order to achieve results. The lesson should be that the tactics used by the 3 Cosas Campaign can and should be replicated in other trade union struggles. Many of the big unions in the UK have come to be seen as focusing excessively on their comfort zones, e.g. full-time, English-speaking, middle-class workers (similar to the focus of traditional unions in Greece, described by Anagnostopoulos and Evangelinidis in this volume). The confrontational and publicity-focused tactics we have described are replicable by both big and small, old and new, trade unions. Likewise, a campaign structure where the voice of the workers concerned in the campaign is that which guides strategy is also replicable. The implications of our approach entail a fundamental re-think of strategy and purpose for some of the UK's big unions. *New trade unionism*, we believe, is about ideas, approach and tactics. It is not about *new trade unions*.

Notes

1 The University of London is a federal university with 17 constituent colleges and 10 institutions. The federal structure has an administrative hub in the Senate House building off Russell Square, and runs the Senate House library, a few other academic buildings, and various intercollegiate student halls of residence. All references to University of London in this chapter refer to this federal admin hub.

2 BBW was bought out in its entirety in December 2013 by Cofely UK (owned by the French GDF Suez). Therefore the UoL currently has an outsourcing contract with Cofely Workplace Limited.

3 For more on this, see the Facebook page: Justice for Cleaners SOAS.

4 www.youtube.com/watch?v= W5j3zxXEl34.

5 http://roarnews.co.uk/wordpress/ ?p=3425.

6 For the Reel News that which documents the UNISON saga and includes footage of the protest at UNISON HQ, see www.youtube.com/ watch?v=Fw6E4z4Alfo. For pictures of the protest, see http://lucaneve. photoshelter.com/gallery/27-03-2013-Senate-House-Cleaners-Protest-outside-UNISON/GoooomNpg7RXV_IM/ CooooGPpTqAGd2Gg.

7 For a short article on this, see www.workersliberty.org/unisonpolice.

8 For more on the UNISON scandal, see https://bloomsburyfightback. wordpress.com/2013/04/03/ unison-vs-the-workers/, www.lrb. co.uk/blog/2013/04/09/harry-stopes/miembros-no-numeros/, www. workersliberty.org/story/2013/04/10/ unison-officials-sabotage-democracy, and http://libcom.org/forums/news/unison-vs-workers-university-london-07042013.

9 www.youtube.
com/watch?v=epK3okUxUUg.

10 www.youtube.
com/watch?v=qZhtxti1s1Y.

11 For more on CLAUK, see www.
clauk.org.uk/.

12 www.youtube.
com/watch?v=WCpo8R3FFQk.

13 For more on Labour Start, see
www.labourstart.org/news/.

14 For example, www.youtube.
com/watch?v=DfWuP8JxVpk.

15 For example, see https://
camdengreenparty.wordpress.
com/2013/04/11/strong-support-for-
university-of-london-cleaners-3-cosas-
campaign/.

16 For example, see www.youtube.
com/watch?v=6lxUoM-Wg7A.

17 For example, see http://roarnews.
co.uk/wordpress/?p=3757.

18 For example, see www.
workersliberty.org/story/2012/11/21/
cleaners-revolt-continues, www.
socialistparty.org.uk/issue/743/15727/21-
11-2012/london-uni-cleaners-fight-for-
basic-rights, www.morningstaronline.
co.uk/news/content/view/full/132355
and http://socialistreview.org.
uk/378/strike-your-rights.

19 For example, see www.
timeshighereducation.co.uk/news/
university-of-london-protest-seeks-rights-
for-outsourced-workers/2001333.article.

20 For example, see www.
theprisma.co.uk/2013/04/21/cleaners-
without-rights-and-unable-to-get-ill/.

21 For example, see www.
independent.co.uk/student/news/
police-accused-of-disproportionate-
force-at-ulu-chalking-arrest-8713380.
html, www.timeshighereducation.
co.uk/news/university-of-london-
chalk-protest-sparks-arrest/2005792.
article, www.workersliberty.
org/story/2013/07/17/university-
london-calls-state-thugs-arrest-3-
cosas-activist, www.huffingtonpost.

co.uk/james-burley/protest-
as-student-chalke_b_3697641.
html, www.timeshighereducation.
co.uk/news/university-of-london-
criticised-over-students-chalk-slogan-
conviction/2012124.article and www.
standard.co.uk/news/education/
student-criticises-university-of-london-
for-800-fine-after-senate-house-chalk-
protest-9204798.html.

22 For example, see www.
independent.co.uk/student/university-
of-london-bans-student-protests-
8740462.html, www.theguardian.
com/politics/2013/jul/31/hugh-muir-
diary-union-humphrys, www.lrb.co.uk/
blog/2013/08/06/oscar-webb/protest-
or-trespass/, www.studentrights.org.uk/
article/2111/protest_ban_at_university_
of_london_highlights_hypocrisy, www.
huffingtonpost.co.uk/2013/08/06/
university-of-london-bans-student-
protests_n_3713285.html?utm_hp_ref=uk-
universities-education and roarnews.
co.uk/wordpress/?p=8060.

23 For example, see www.
theguardian.com/uk-news/2013/
dec/05/three-arrests-student-protest-
university-of-london, www.theguardian.
com/commentisfree/2013/dec/05/
students-protests-police-repression-
university-of-london?CMP=twt_gu,
www.channel4.com/news/university-
of-london-student-protest-ban-senate-
house-occupy, www.theguardian.com/
education/2013/dec/09/intimidation-
seat-of-learning and http://blogs.
channel4.com/paul-mason-blog/
policing-student-protest-political/153.

24 ACAS is the Advisory,
Conciliation and Arbitration Service, a
government organisation that, among
other things, mediates in disputes
between employers and unions.

25 Read the *Times Higher Education*
article here: www.timeshighereducation.
co.uk/news/cleaners-to-continue-
outsourcing-fight/2009463.article.

AFTERWORD: BRINGING MANIFESTOS BACK IN?

Peter Waterman[1]

Emancipatory social movements and manifestos

I have two reasons for here not doing the conventional round-up and conclusion to this path-breaking compilation.

The first lies in the Introduction by Sian Lazar, which seems to me a more than adequate summary of and reflection on the chapters that follow. Both the introduction and the succeeding chapters strongly suggest there is a new wave of labour militancy worldwide. The compilation is, wisely, not a set of labour 'area studies': much of its value rests precisely on the awareness of the authors of what is going on elsewhere. Sian also surpasses the common distinction – or Manichean opposition – in recent global labour studies between those primarily focused on the traditional union institutions, national or international[2] and those primarily focused on the autonomous new labour movements in place or in space.[3]

The second reason for taking off from the compilation lies in its comparatively limited address to what might be called the 'What Is To Be Done Question'; remembering here that a 'question' for Marxists is something for which they didn't (or don't) have an answer: the Woman Question, the National Question, the Negro Question, the Jewish Question. Lenin, customarily credited with this question (actually the title of a novel by the nineteenth-century Russian socialist Chernyshevsky) had no problem answering it. Our authors are, however, more modest.

Indeed, only one of the contributions goes back to Lenin's 'What is to be done?'. This is by Walid Daou and his quotation might be found somewhat oracular (Daou, however, is also the only contributor to deal substantially with women's labour and organising). Most contributions portray a complexity that classical Marxism never had to come to terms with, even though the consciousness and behaviour of then existing working classes was as varied as it is now. But such variety was of less consequence to socialist thinkers or organisers than what History or Theory prescribed. This was of the transformation – the 'reduction' – of the mass of the rural poor, the semi-proletariat and the 'wavering' petty-bourgeoisie to proletarian status as capitalist industrialisation spread worldwide. And then of this proletariat becoming (under the guidance of an intellectual/political vanguard) the privileged social agent of internationalism and revolution.

Our authors, rather, show us the wide variety of working classes or categories, the regional/national differences between them, and the great variety of ways in which movements based on such differences express themselves. No assumption is made of their vanguard status, actual or predictable. This revelation of variety does not, however, lead to what we might call 'pessimism of the will'. In so far as these workers, their unions or their alternative forms of self-articulation are seen as existing way 'beyond the factory gates or the union office' (see here Haworth and Ramsay 1984), this implies the imbrication, or overlapping, of worker movements with those for not only democracy or nationalism (long recognised) but with urban, educational, rural, indigenous, migrant and cultural movements, as well as those for 'another possible world'. Moreover, the variety, the differentiation, does not deny the existence of common underlying trends within capitalism, or of common hegemonic state or political tendencies, and therefore the appearance of analogous labour movements, of the reproduction or borrowing of others' experiences, nor of transnational solidarity. The recognition of complexity is to be welcomed. This was, after all, always there, if in other forms. And we need to recognise that it was the failure of the left to see this, or its tendency to reduce the complexity to a set of binary or Manichean oppositions, that has led to the current crisis of this left.

So, perhaps our authors are being not so much modest as cautious?

Caution, as already suggested, is a welcome alternative to one or more teleological traditions in labour studies that knew *exactly* what was – or is – to be done, or would inevitably happen, and whose analyses were – or are – marked by conclusions that proceed from theory (consider here Charles Post 2016 and, by way of dramatic contrast, Burgmann 2016). On the other hand, however, this caution means that we seem to lack declarations, discussion documents, manifestos, charters or even scenarios with which we could engage, and which could – by their brevity and force – encourage the engagement of their putative public(s). Such were common to the early labour movement and are common to the newest wave of global emancipatory movements. Let us consider these in turn.

From post-revolutionary France came a number of utopian socialist declarations, and then the worker- (and women-) oriented one of Flora Tristan, *The Workers' Union* (1843). Then, from an industrialised Britain came *The Communist Manifesto*, inevitably linked with the names of Marx and Engels (1848). From Russia came the *Programme of the Social-Democratic Emancipation of Labour Group*, linked with the name of Plekhanov (1884). From the United States came the anarcho-syndicalist *Preamble and Constitution of the Industrial Workers of the World* (1905/1908) the preamble being publicised under the slogan, 'Education, Organisation, Emancipation'.[4] In Japan, 1914, we find Sen Katayama's *Japanese Manifesto* (1914). Hopefully this is sufficient to suggest the commonality of this early labour movement form of self-expression.

As for the equally common practice coming from, or interpellating, the newest social actors and movements, consider only these: a *World Charter of Migrants* (Global Migrants Action 2011); two feminist charters, the *Women's Global Charter for Humanity* (World March of Women 2004) and a *Political Manifesto for the Emancipation of Our Bodies* (13th Feminist Encounter 2014),[5] both of which make detailed reference to labour; an indigenous/ecological declaration (REDD 2012); *The Sixth Declaration of the Lacandon Jungle*, of the Zapatistas (2005). And I cannot but mention a charter directly addressed to an increasingly significant category of 'labour's others', *A Precariat Charter: From Denizens to Citizens* (Standing 2014b). This ends with 29 points – surely a major provocation to debate, discussion and – hopefully – labour movement dialogue?[6] Then there is a manifesto intended to update the Communist one for the age of Information Capitalism (though proposing primarily a radically-democratic cyberspace property relationship), the *Telekommunist Manifesto* (Kleiner 2010). And here is one not afraid of the S word, *Manifesto for a Socialist Alternative* (Lievens 2011).

Finally, I note a *commons-orientated* site that provides an apparent do-it-yourself kit for commons-orientated manifesto writers, *Globalcommonstrust* (see 'References and resources' below). Most of these are movement-produced or movement-orientated efforts, of a broadly radical-democratic family, addressed to either a particular or a universal public. Most of them are also either explicitly or implicitly expressive of emancipatory principles and in dramatic conflict with hegemonic ones. And in conflict, of course, with the hegemonic commonsense. Indeed, it now occurs to me, the manifesto form is intended *primarily* to transform the commonsense.

Contemporary union or labour charters: still within the iron cage?

The most widely spread union campaign of the present moment is that for 'Decent Work' (see ITUC website, and 'References and resources' below). Dreamed up, actually, by neither a labour movement body nor by a socialist intellectual,[7] it was gifted to the International Trade Union Confederation-Global Unions (ITUC-GU) family by the inter-state International Labour Organisation.

The ITUC-GU swallowed it, hook, line and two smoking barrels. This has, surely, to be itself an expression of the movement's ideological and moral dependency.[8] But the ITUC-GU and its forerunners have long been suspended from above by an inter-state agency in which union representatives (25 per cent), are vastly outweighed in political-economic terms by 'employers' (25 per cent) plus 'governments' (50 per cent). So this chalice was offered to the unions (actually 'representing' *not more than 10 per cent* of the world's workers)[9] by an institution representing (without sceptical quotation marks), for 75 per cent, capital and state. Given the 'tripartite' discourse and ritual surrounding labour's participation in the ILO, one might apply to it the concept used of the United Nations: 'a sacred drama' (Cruise O'Brien 1968), even though he might not have shared my scepticism concerning the sacred.

'Decent Work' (DW), assumes the past, present or future existence of Decent (unionised? unionisable?) Workers, working for Decent Capitalists, under the stern, but paternal, eye of a Decent State.[10] So powerful an appeal has the anodyne DW campaign that it has been adopted or adapted by, for example, the ITUC's Stalinist nemesis, the World Federation of Trade Unions (2013). Here it reappears as 'Decent Life':[11]

> Decent live [sic] presupposes that popular masses will have stable work, a good salary-good pension, public social security, free and public education. A decent present and future for

the new generations is to have stable work connected to their knowledge.

The WFTU's thoroughly incrementalist agenda is, of course, embedded in anti-imperialist and anti-capitalist rhetoric, but with no mention of – far less a challenge to – the 'wage slavery' common to early labour movement rhetoric.

A qualification is, however, here in order. New labour movements have been riding this wooden horse for possibly more significant purposes. This is, I would like to suggest, the case with both domestic workers and street traders, both predominantly women. There are networks and/or organisations (or networked organisations?) for both of these immense categories of the previously invisibilised workers. And each of them has achieved new standards at the ILO, in which 'Decent Work' is a keyword.[12]

I recognise that (unlike the original wooden horse) such declarations might be of positive *use* to the previously unprotected workers they cover. I stress 'use' since I would want to distinguish this from *faith*, though I am sure this significant distinction is not made by the activists concerned. However, like the Trojan horse, this one is far from a magnificent but harmless gift. The profound ambiguity of such ILO declarations is guaranteed by their incorporation within the institutions and ideology of social-liberal industrial relations. They might be reasonably considered as much a sign of desperate twenty-first-century 'outreach', by otherwise depleted and self-isolated unions, as a victory of the relevant workers themselves. A further doubt about the emancipatory potential of these victories lies, however, in their joint concern for transitioning from the 'informal' to the 'formal' when a globalised and informatised capitalism is still travelling, at computer speed, in the opposite direction.[13]

There are, however, charters more autonomous of the institutionalised labour movement, national or international. One might be the Global Labour Movement Charter of Australia-Asia Worker Links (2010). But this, despite its relative institutional autonomy, reproduces the ITUC-GU formulae, including the DW phrase. Its only additional element might be its mention of indigenous and land rights. There are other such. A more-challenging and autonomous declaration would surely be that of Argentinian Housewives in 2002 (see again 'References and resources' below).

Or that of the Peruvian, Carlos Tovar (2007), whose *21st Century Manifesto* includes a strong argument for a four-hour working day. Or the declaration of European sexworkers (International Committee on the Rights of Sex Workers in Europe 2005). Possibly yet more radical is that of the Puri Declaration (2013) of the All India Union of Forest Working People. This one covers not only labour but ecological, indigenous and women's rights, it attacks Brahminism, capitalism and imperialism, and is explicit in its internationalism. It bears interesting comparison with the kneejerk anti-capitalism/anti-imperialism of the WFTU.[14] And then there was this conference call, 2015, concerning less a labour than a general social strike in Europe (ConnessioniPrecarie 2015a). Not without significance (I mean for charters as provocations to dialogue) this call resulted in an immediate critical/alternative reaction, published on the same site (ConnessioniPrecarie 2015b). The same site also carries a Strikers' Charter.

I have a particular sympathy for the manifesto of Erik Forman (2015). This is not because I unconditionally endorse it but because it is on a 'unionism beyond capitalism'. Hereby Forman means a unionism breaking *now* with its subordination to capitalism (compare Waterman 2014). One has surely to admire a manifesto that offers us not 10 Commandments, 11 Theses or even 21 Conditions but 49 Clauses! My first qualification to the piece might be that whilst Forman recognises the necessity for a holistic social movement within/against/beyond contemporary capitalism, he largely repeats a workerist strategy of the Industrial Workers of the World from the period of capitalist industrial development that not only marginalised the IWW but also produced the kind of unionism he wishes to surpass. My second qualification would be that he does not recognise the existence of cyberspace – never mind discuss the labour and radical-democratic disputation of this new found land. Somebody, or some body, has nonetheless to confront his formidable challenge.

Finally, I must refer to an autonomist labour declaration, possibly forgotten in everything that has followed (or failed to follow) from the social movement wave in Greece. This is the call 'For the Regeneration of a Social-Labour Movement from the Base for Emancipation' (Drasi 2013). Even if some of the language or references might be comprehensible only to those familiar with Greece, the beginning surely evokes other countries or world areas:

The old era of a labour movement based on negotiating the price of its labour power; one recognised and integrated as an institutional actor in the smooth reproduction of labour power, and ultimately of capitalism itself, has come to an end.

Let's see it as a historic challenge and 'opportunity' for a rebirth of a labour movement based on self-organisation, direct democracy and lasting combative competition with capital and the state. A 'chance' for a break from all the things that were holding the labour movement dependent and ultimately subservient within the established order, transcending mere protest, claims and negotiations, and now creating our own world of solidarity and collaborative activity.[15]

In conclusion, here, it seems that some labour charters/manifestos/ declarations/calls for action, are at the edge of, or escaping from, the 'globalized and informatized cage of capitalism and bureaucracy' (again Waterman 2014) within which most of the international labour organisations are self-imprisoned.

A global labour charter as a dialogical process

In mentioning my own Global Labour Charter Project below I take encouragement from the cautious but determined note in this compilation (in its revelation of both the extent and variety of the new labour militancy worldwide), as well as from such recent labour and other social movement charters as are mentioned above.

More particularly do I take encouragement from one of the latest global labour studies,[16] this time a monograph inspired by the energetically re-emerging anarcho-syndicalist tradition. This is *Worker Resistance and Media* (Dencik and Wilkin 2015). Its attraction lies not only in the attention it accords the (digital) media but in its (re)presentation of labour's past, present and hypothetical future in the light of the anarcho-syndicalist/autonomist tradition. Bringing these two elements together, providing four relevant case studies of new worker movements (one of them being that of the above-mentioned domestic workers), and recognising, but qualifying, the role of digital media, the book concludes on the possibilities provided by an articulation of (1) the traditional global unions, (2) social movement unionism, (3) labour-community unionism and (4) the specifically anarcho-syndicalist tradition (in place and in cyberspace). So it does argue for what is to be done, if without a manifesto. Though it occurs to me that it would not be difficult to produce a manifesto from the authors' Conclusion (Dencik and Wilkin 2015: 213–220).

The history of my own Global Labour Charter Project is short . . . and sobering. Launched initially around 2005, it has been published in academic journals and labour magazines, in Western Europe, the USA, in Peru, Colombia, Hongkong and South Africa. It has been present online, and taken by me to various World Social Forums. After ten years it has yet to receive even the honour of a published *dismissal.* My best friends and comrades seem to prefer to give me a conciliatory pat on the back than to tell me that it is utopian. I think that it is *realistically* utopian but that the utopian principle – *The Principle of Hope* (Bloch 1954–1959) – has been largely lost in the labour movement and labour studies since – when? – 1945? 1968? 1989?[17]

Yet Boaventura de Sousa Santos somewhere insists, in this new century, that in the face of dystopia we are *condemned* to being utopian. Norman Geras (2000) argues for a 'minimum utopia', in ten theses, that surely ought to be entertained by the anti-utopian comrades. And Oscar Wilde – a century before Geras – said that 'a map of the world that does not include Utopia is not worth even glancing at'.

So, if the labour movement *is* to be worthwhile being *at least* glanced at, it would seem it is likewise condemned to being utopian. This is being slowly recognised around, if not in the union heart of, the labour movement. As is suggested by the special issue of the *Socialist Register* (2000) on 'Necessary and Unnecessary Utopias', by Chris Carlsson's *Nowtopia: A New Politics of Work* (2008), by Dinerstein (2014) on 'On Good and Bad Utopias'.[18] There are also various websites on ICT (information and communication technology) clearly oriented toward the emancipation from waged labour and inspired by early-labour/socialist utopianism.[19]

Whilst not going into detail on my own Global Labour Charter (Waterman 2009), I will reproduce the process there proposed:

6. The novel principle of such a charter should be its conception as a virtuous spiral – that it be thought of not as a single, correct,

final declaration, which workers, peoples and other people simply endorse (though endorsement could be part of the process), as for its processual, dialogical and developing nature. This notion would allow for it to be begun, paused and joined at any point. Such a process would require at least the following elements: information/communication, education, dialogue, (re-) formulation, action, evaluation, information.

7. It is the existence of cyberspace (the internet, the web, online audiovisuals) that makes such a Global Labour Charter for the first time conceivable. We have here not simply a new communications technology but the possibility for developing non-hierarchical, dialogical, equal relations worldwide. The process will be computer-based because of the web's built-in characteristics of feedback, its worldwide reach, its low and decreasing cost. An increasing number of workers and activists are in computerised work, are familiar with information and communication technology and have web skills. Given, however, uneven worker computer access, such a process must also be intensely local, imply and empower outreach, using the communication methods appropriate to particular kinds of labour and each specific locale . . . .

8. Networking can and must ensure that any initiators or coordinators do not become permanent leaders or controllers. There is a growing international body of fulltime organisers and volunteer activists, both within and beyond the traditional inter/ national unions, experienced in the GJ&SM, who could provide the initial nodes in such a network. Networking also, however, allows for there to be various such labour charters, in dialogue with each other. Such dialogue should be considered a normal and even necessary part of the process and avoid the authority, dependency or passivity associated with traditional manifestos.

Now, once upon a time, there was an international campaign for the Eight-Hour Working Day. Actually, it was quite a long time, since the idea might have been first proposed by Robert Owen in the early nineteenth century. Later it was intimately connected with the origin of Mayday as International Workers' Day and with the establishment of international trade union organisations. Attempts by the union internationals, after the First World War, to 'maintain' the campaign, with the help of the new ILO, failed (Heerma van Voss 1988). So legal limits on the length of the working day were never universalised, never referred to women's second day of work, nor to those without a 'standard employment contract', and have been arguably reversed even for the 'formal sector'.[20]

Whilst this could be considered proof of the *irrelevance* of the struggle for such a standard (or of union dependence on the ILO), it could also be understood as providing a lesson for us on the possible inter-relation between a deeply-felt worker need and a campaign; between a campaign and a movement; between the national and the international; between one stage of labour movement development and another. Perhaps the most important lesson would be not to entrust such a campaign to institutionalised union internationals and their lobbying of an inter-state institution issuing non-enforceable norms.

Have I strayed too far from the compilation with which this chapter began? I hope not. And, indeed, the Sian Lazar introduction encourages me in that thought. Because, as she suggests, the terrains of contemporary labour struggles are multiple, as are their sites, scales and forms (within the union leaderships, at the base of the unions, beyond the unions and autonomous of the unions?). All of which might again suggest both the need for overarching visions and for those independent of any specific existing labour movement form or issue: therefore beyond *both* the shorter working day (a single-issue campaign) and 'Decent Work' (with its multiple dependencies on national and interstate hegemons and ideologies).

All arguments, I would have thought, for an autonomous, local-to-global, cyberspatial, multi-faceted, global labour charter movement – or various of these. In dialogue. And,

if not now, when?[21]

Notes

1 90 per cent of the research on which the paper is based exists only online, and many of the manifestos or related projects are inevitably also digital in form. The solution, here, can only be to provide the URLs in eye-legible form so that they could be written down and then searched for online. There is an original draft in digital form (Waterman 2015). Thanks to Gina

Vargas and Sian Lazar for responses to earlier drafts.

2 For example, Pons-Vignon (2011); Harrod and O'Brien (2002); Webster *et al.* (2012); Fairbrother *et al.* (2013); Serrano *et al.* (2011); Mustill (2013).

3 For example, Dinerstein (2014); Ness (2014); Waterman (2007); Dencik and Wilkin (2015); Digital Humanities Network (2015).

4 Launched in the USA, the IWW spread to Latin America, The Philippines, Australia and South Africa.

5 Here in English: www. dropbox.com/s/opeh5ej6c1fldgr/ Manifesto13thEncuentroEnglish2014. docx?dl=0.

6 Even before his Charter, Standing's original precariat book (2014a) was forcefully challenged by, amongst others, Jan Breman (2013) and Ronaldo Munck (2013). And then forcefully responded to by Standing (2014b). I would expect further dialogue about Standing's Charter.

7 Not to here deny the intellectual capacities and socialist background of the ILO's then Director-General, the Chilean Juan Somavia. But Somavia arrived at this position via a heavily Northern-funded international NGO, various inter/national diplomatic posts, then as coordinator of the UN's World Social Summit (at which the international unions found themselves reduced to the role of just another kind of NGO).

8 Charters or Manifestos of Labour Movement Self-Subordination, as we might call the species, did not begin with 'Decent Work'. Consider this one, from 1914, approving military conscription, in the interest of the British capitalist state, and at the expense of any previous anti-war internationalism of the national labour movement (Parliamentary Committee of the Trades Union Congress 1914).

9 It seems reasonable to put 'representing' within sceptical quotation marks, since one has to doubt whether most of the unionised 10 per cent know more of the ILO than its name, if that.

10 A political-economic condemnation of the ILO/DW, in its address to 'development', can be found in Selwyn (2015). He places it within a hegemonic set of elite development strategies, stating that 'Common to all these conceptions of pro-poor or "inclusive" growth is the axiom of labour as a factor of production, where its use is to be determined by profit-oriented corporations'.

11 'Decent Life' also appears to have been added to 'Decent Work' by the ITUC, 'with the financial assistance of the European Union'. www.ituc-csi.org/ IMG/pdf/decentwork.pdf.

12 These are 'Convention 189' for domestic workers (see Equal Times 2013) and a standard for 'The Transition from the Informal to the Formal Economy' ('Formal/Informal' being other chapters or verses in the Gospel of Decent Work). www.ilo.org/ilc/ILCSessions/104/.../ informal-economy/lang.../index. htm.

13 Yet further qualification of such international achievements is strongly suggested in a chapter on domestic workers in Dencik and Wilkin (2015: ch. 6) – of which more below. Dencik and Wilkin stress the tensions between not only the international and the local (here Hongkong and Singapore) but, within such locales, between (1) the migrant domestic workers of different national backgrounds, (2) the unions and the NGOs and (3) different kinds of electronic media connecting but also separating all the above. They do not, however, deal with more nationally/ethnically homogenous communities of domestic workers as might be found in Lima, Peru.

14 Rather more interesting – and certainly more inspiring – would be

a comparison with the Charter of the Forests (1217), discussed by Peter Linebaugh (2008).

15 For the context within which such a declaration could be issued, see the contribution to the present volume of Anagnostopoulos and Evangelindis.

16 For a general position concerning these see Waterman (2012).

17 See here, Peter Beilharz (1992) on *Labour's Utopias: Bolshevism, Fabianism, Social Democracy*. By 1992, these had all collapsed or where collapsing.

18 Erik Olin Wright's 'Real Utopias' Project, www.ssc. wisc.edu/~wright/ RealUtopias.htm, seems, at time of writing, to be in large part a 'Real Reformism Project' – and confined largely to the (post-)industrialised capitalist nation-state as its significant unit of analysis. Wright's new book on class (Wright 2015) considers, as advancing worker 'economic' interests, the following: Worker Cooperatives, ESOPS (employee-majority stock ownership), the Social Economy and Solidarity Financing. Neither singly nor collectively (nor in combination with 'political' activity, defined as what relates to the nation-state) do these measures seem conceived as more than making national capitalism more humane.

19 I mention here only the Networked Labour Society/Culture site of Orsan Senalp, the Labortech site of Steve Zeltzer, Walton Pantland's Cyberunions and the P2PFoundation site of Michel Bauwens (see 'Reference and resources'). I give the names of those who set these up because they were originally and mostly still are the creations of individuals, with all the problematic implications for collective self-management. I give the names also to show that these are all men. And mostly European.

20 A Gallup Poll in the US, 2014, suggested that the average hours of a fulltime worker were 47:

> 42 per cent of respondents reported working a standard 40-hour week with a mere 8 per cent working less than that. Twenty-one percent of Americans now work between 50 to 59 hours with 18 per cent taking their weekly quota to 60 hours plus. (www.forbes. com/sites/ niallmccarthy/2014/09/01/a-40- hour-work-week-in-the-united- states-actually-lasts-47-hours/)

There are, of course, lies, damned lies and hegemonic statistics. So this poll might conceal more than it reveals. It does not, of course, count hours of household and other unpaid carework, mostly that of women.

21 Given the millennia that have passed, and the varied translations available, I have chosen a source for the complete verse with the wording I find the most relevant (https://en.wikipedia. org/wiki/Hillel_the_Elder):

> If I am not for myself, then who will be for me?
> And being for my own self, what am 'I'?
> And if not now, when?

References and resources

13th Feminist Encounter (2014) 'Political Manifesto for the Emancipation of Our Bodies. Latin America and the Caribbean XIII Feminist Encounter for Latin America (XIII EFLAC)'. Here in English: www. dropbox.com/s/opeh5ej6c1fldgr/ Manifesto13thEncuentroEnglish%20 2014%20.docx?dl=0&preview=Manife sto13thEncuentroEnglish+2014+.docx.

Argentinian Housewives (2002) 'Manifiesto a las mujeres de nuestra patria y de América Latina' (Manifesto for the Women of Our Country and Latin America). http://anterior.rimaweb.com.ar/opinion/manifiesto_mujeres_arg.html.

Australia-Asia Worker Links (2010) 'We Need a Global Labour Charter'. http://aawl.org.au/content/we-need-global-labour-movement-charter.

Beilharz, Peter (1992) *Labour's Utopias: Bolshevism, Fabianism, Social Democracy*, London: Routledge.

Bloch, Ernst (1954–1959) *The Principle of Hope*, vols 1–3. https://en.wikipedia.org/wiki/The_Principle_of_Hope.

Breman, Jan (2013) 'A Bogus Concept', *New Left Review*, 84: 130–138.

Burgmann, Verity (2016) *Globalisation and Labour in the 21st Century*, Abingdon: Routledge.

Carlsson, Chris (2008) *Nowtopia: A New Politics of Work*. www.processedworld.com/carlsson/nowtopia_web/.

Charter of the Forest (1217). https://en.wikipedia.org/wiki/Charter_of_the_Forest.

ConnessioniPrecarie (2015a) *Towards a Transnational Social Strike: Call for a Transnational Meeting in Poznan – 2/3/4th October 2015*. www.connessioniprecarie.org/2015/07/14/towards-a-transnational-social-strike-call-for-a-transnational-meeting-in-poznan-234th-october-2015/.

ConnessioniPrecarie (2015b) *Factory without Society: Around Some Problems Concerning the Transnational Social Strike*. www.connessioniprecarie.org/2015/08/04/factory-without-society-around-some-problems-concerning-the-transnational-social-strike/.

Cruise O'Brien, Conner (1968) *The United Nations: Sacred Drama*, London: Hutchinson.

Cyberunions: Building an Open Source Software Libre Labour Movement. https://cyberunions.org/.

Dencik, Lina and Wilkin, Peter (2015) *Worker Resistance and the Media: Challenging Global Corporate Power in the 21st Century*, New York: Peter Lang.

Digital Humanities Network (2015) 'Researching Global Labour Movements: Where Do Digital Methods Fit In?' www.digitalhumanities.cam.ac.uk/events/globallabourmethodsworkshop.

Dinerstein, Ana (2014) 'The Dream of Dignified Work: On Good and Bad Utopias', *Development and Change*, 45(5): 1037–1058.

Drasi (2013) 'For the Regeneration of a Social-Labour Movement from the Base for Emancipation'. http://blog.p2pfoundation.net/for-the-regeneration-of-a-social-labour-movement-from-the-base-for-emancipation/2014/01/15.

Equal Times (2013) 'C189: "The Work That Makes All Work Possible" Finally Recognised by Int'l Law'. www.equaltimes.org/c189-the-work-that-makes-all-work#.Vp_yp8qBG9Z.

Fairbrother, Peter, Hennebert, Marc-Antonin and Lévesque, Christian (2013) *Transnational Trade Unionism: Building Union Power*, London: Routledge.

Forman, Erik (2015) 'Breaking the Negative Dialectic: Theses for a Unionism beyond Capitalism'. www.academia.edu/19588871/Breaking_the_Negative_Dialectic_Theses_on_a_Unionism_Beyond_Capitalism.

Geras, Norman (2000) 'Minimum Utopia: Ten Theses', in *Socialist Register: On Necessary and Unnecessary Utopias*, pp. 41–52. London: Merlin Press.

Globalcommonstrust. http://globalcommonstrust.org/?page_id=20Global.

Global Migrants Action (2011) *World Charter of Migrants*. http://globalmigrantsaction.org/sn_displayfull.php?row_ID=173.

Harrod, J. and O'Brien, R. (eds) (2002) *Global Unions?: Theory and Strategies of Organized Labour in the Global Political Economy*, London: Routledge.

Haworth, Nigel and Ramsay, Harvie (1984) 'Grasping the Nettle: Problems with the Theory of International Trade Union Solidarity', in Waterman, Peter (ed.) *For a New Labour Internationalism*, pp. 60–87. The Hague: ILERI Foundation.

Heerma van Voss, Lex (1988) 'The International Federation of Trade Unions and the Attempt to Maintain the Eight-Hour Working Day (1919–1929)', in van Holthoon, Frits and van der Linden, Marcel (eds) *Internationalism in the Labour Movement 1830–1940*, pp. 518–542. Leiden: Brill.

Industrial Workers of the World (IWW) (1905/1908) *Manifesto and Preamble*. www.historyisaweapon.com/defcon1/iwwpreamblemanifesto.html.

International Committee on the Rights of Sex Workers in Europe (2005) 'Sexworkers in Europe Manifesto'. www.sexworkeurope.org/sites/default/files/userfiles/files/join/manbrussels2005.pdf.

International Domestic Workers Federation. www.idwfed.org/en.

ITUC. 'Decent Work, Decent Life'. www.google.com/search?q=ituc+decent+work+decent+life&ie=utf-8&oe=utf-8#.

Katayama, Sen (1914) *Japanese Manifesto*. www.marxists.org/archive/katayama/1914/09/japanese_manifesto.htm.

Kleiner, Dmytri (2010) *The Telekommunist Manifesto*. http://telekommunisten.net/the-telekommunist-manifesto/.

Labortech. www.labortech.net/.

Lievens, Jean (2011) *Manifesto for a Socialist Alternative*. http://p2pfoundation.ning.com/profiles/blogs/manifesto-for-a-socialist-alternative-introduction.

Linebaugh, Peter (2008) *Magna Carta Manifesto: Liberties and Commons for All*, Berkeley, CA: University of California Press.

Marx, Karl and Engels, Frederick (1848) *Manifesto of the Communist Party*. www.marxists.org/archive/marx/works/1848/communist-manifesto/.

Munck, Ronaldo (2013) 'The Precariat: A View from the South', *Third World Quarterly*, 34(5): 747–762.

Mustill, Ed. (ed.) (2013) *The Global Labour Movement: An Introduction*, London: Labour Start.

Ness, Immanuel (2014) *New Forms of Worker Organization: The Syndicalist and Autonomist Restoration of Class Struggle Unionism*, Oakland, CA: PM Press.

Networked Labour Society/Culture. www.facebook.com/Networked-Labour-460360007334523.

P2PFoundation. http://p2pfoundation.net/Main_Page.

Parliamentary Committee of the Trades Union Congress (1914) *Manifesto to the Trade Unionists of the Country*. http://fair-use.org/trade-union-congress/manifesto-to-the-trade-unionists-of-the-country#p5.

Plekhanov, G.V. (1884) *Programme of the Social-Democratic Emancipation of Labour Group*. www.marxists.org/archive/plekhanov/1883/xx/sdelg1.htm.

Pons-Vignon, Nicolas (ed.) (2011) *There Is an Alternative: Economic Policies and Labour Strategies beyond the Mainstream*, Geneva: International Labour Office. www.ilo.org/wcmsp5/groups/public/@dgreports/@dcomm/@publ/documents/publication/wcms_155448.pdf.

Post, Charles (2016) 'Rethinking Precarity and Capitalism: An Interview with Charlie Post'. *Alternate Routes*. www.alternateroutes.ca/index.php/ar/article/view/22401/18183.

Puri Declaration of the All India Union of Forest Working People (2013). http://ntui.org.in/what-we-do/nrega/affiliate-updates/all-india-union-of-forest-working-people/.

REDD (2012) 'Peoples' Summit for Social and Environmental Justice against the Mercantization of Life, in Defence of the Commons. . . . Living Well / Healthy Full Life'. www.redd-monitor.org/2012/06/22/indigenous-peoples-terra-livre-declaration-at-rio-20-rejects-redd/.

Selwyn, Ben (2015) 'Elite Development Theory: A Labour-Centred Critique, *Third World Quarterly*. www.tandfonline.com/doi/full/10.1080/01436597.2015.1120156.

Serrano, Melisa, Xhafa, Edlira and Fichter, Michael (eds) (2011) *Trade Unions and the Global Crisis: Labour's Visions, Strategies and Responses*, Geneva: International Labour Office. www.ilo.org/wcmsp5/groups/public/---dgreports/---dcomm/---publ/documents/publication/wcms_163855.pdf.

Socialist Register (2000) *Necessary and Unnecessary Utopias*, London: Merlin Press. http://socialistregister.com/index.php/srv/issue/view/436#.Vp1asMqBG9Z.

Standing, Guy (2014a) *A Precariat Charter: From Denizens to Citizens*, London: Bloomsbury.

Standing, Guy (2014b) 'Why the Precariat Is Not a "Bogus Concept"', *Open Democracy*. www.opendemocracy.net/guy-standing/why-precariat-is-not-%E2%80%9Cbogus-concept%E2%80%9D.

Tovar, Carlos (Carlin) (2007) *Manifiesto del siglo XXI: La gran fisura mundial y cómo revertila*, Lima: Fundo Editorial UNMSM.

Tristan, Flora (1843) *The Workers' Union*, Chicago, IL: University of Illinois Press. www.academia.edu/5282386/Flora_Tristan_The_Workers_Union_1843_.

Waterman, Peter (2005) 'From Decent Work to the Liberation of Life from Work'. www.struggle.ws/anarkismo/peterwork.pdf.

Waterman, Peter (2007) 'The Networked Internationalism of Labour's Others: A Suitable Case for Treatment'. www.choike.org/documentos/waterman_others2007.pdf.

Waterman, Peter (2009) 'Needed: A Global Labour Charter Movement'. http://interfacejournal.nuim.ie/wordpress/wp-content/uploads/2010/11/Interface-1-2-pp255-262-Waterman.pdf.

Waterman, Peter (2012) 'An Emancipatory Global Labour Studies Is Necessary: On Rethinking the Global Labour Movement in the Time of Furnaces', *Interface: A Journal for and about Social Movements*, 4(2). www.interfacejournal.net/wordpress/wp-content/uploads/2012/11/Interface-4-2-Waterman.pdf.

Waterman, Peter (2014) 'The International Labour Movement in, against and beyond, the Globalized and Informatized Cage of Capitalism and Bureaucracy'. www.interfacejournal.net/wordpress/wp-content/uploads/2014/12/Issue-6_2-Waterman.pdf.

Waterman, Peter (2015) 'Bringing Manifesto(s) Back in' (Original Draft). www.dropbox.com/s/e7siqsfy7lyo3m9/CambConfManif Pap240815%20%20%20%20Words.docx?dl=0.

Waterman, Peter and Dave Spooner (2015) 'The Future and Praxis of Decent Work', *Global Labour Journal*, 6(2). https://escarpmentpress.org/globallabour/article/view/2338.

Webster, Edward, Lambert, Rob and Bezuidenhout, Andries (2012) *Grounding Globalization: Labour in the Age of Insecurity*, Chichester: John Wiley.

World Federation of Trade Unions (2013) 'All in the Streets – October 3, 2013'. www.wftucentral.org/all-in-the-streets-october-32013/.

World March of Women (2004) Women's Global Charter for Humanity.

Wright, Eric Olin (2015) *Understanding Class*, London: Verso.

Zapatistas (2005) The Sixth Declaration of the Lacandon Jungle. https://en.wikisource.org/wiki/Sixth_Declaration_of_the_Lacandon_Jungle.

ABOUT THE CONTRIBUTORS

Anne Alexander is a research fellow at the Centre for Research in the Arts, Social Sciences and Humanities (CRASSH) at the University of Cambridge. She has published widely on Middle Eastern politics, social movements and digital media, and is the author of a biography of Gamal Abdel-Nasser (Haus, 2005).

Aris Anagnostopoulos holds a PhD in social anthropology from the University of Kent, and previously trained as a historian at the University of Leicester. His post-doctoral work is in the interdisciplinary field of archaeological ethnography. He currently serves as assistant director of the Irish Institute of Hellenic Studies in Athens, is a post-doctoral fellow with the Initiative for Heritage Conservation, Greece, and holds an honorary lectureship at the University of Kent.

Marco Aparicio Wilhelmi is a doctor of public law, and currently professor in the University of Girona, Spain. His research interests are indigenous peoples' and migrants' rights, demand-making for social rights and Latin American constitutionalism. He works with various organisations in defence of human rights.

Mostafa Bassiouny has more than a decade's experience as a reporter and editor in the Egyptian and regional press. He was industrial correspondent for the newspaper *Al-Dustour* between 2005 and 2010, reporting on the mass strikes by textile workers in Mahalla al-Kubra in 2006 and 2007, and the uprising which rocked the town in 2008. He reported on the overthrow of Ben Ali in Tunisia in January 2011 before returning to Egypt to participate in the uprising against Mubarak. Between 2011 and 2014 he was head of news for liberal daily *Al-Tahrir* and is currently Egypt correspondent for the Lebanese daily *Al-Safir*.

Henry Chango Lopez is from Ecuador but has been living in the UK for most of his adult life. Henry is an outsourced porter at the University of London and has been an active trade unionist for the past five years. He is currently vice-president of the IWGB trade union.

Mary Compton is a past president of the UK National Union of Teachers, a lifelong teacher and education activist. She founded and edits the website www.teachersolidarity.com and has written numerous articles on the issue of global education 'reform' and the resistance to it. She co-edited the book *The Global Assault on Teaching Teachers and their Unions: Stories for Resistance* (2008).

Walid Daou is a school teacher and trade unionist, member of the Socialist Forum, a revolutionary socialist organisation that issues a quarterly electronic bulletin 'Al-Manshour' (The Pamphlet http://al-manshour.org), and co-publishes the *Al-Thawra Al-Da'ima* (Permanent Revolution http://permanentrevolution-journal.org/) magazine with fellow revolutionary socialist organisations in the Arab and Maghreb region. We stand with the revolutions in the region and the world, against dictatorial regimes and against the Zionist occupation. We stand against capitalism, all imperialisms, racism, sectarianism and gender discrimination. We aspire to build a revolutionary party in Lebanon and achieve social justice, secularism and equality.

Angelos Evangelinidis studied political science and history in Panteion University. He holds two master's degrees, one from Panteion University in political science and another from University of Athens in media and communication. His research interests are political sociology, social movements and media activism. He is currently a PhD student in the Department of Southeast European History and Anthropology in the University of Graz, Austria.

Thomas Grisaffi is a social anthropologist currently working as a post-doctoral research fellow at the Institute of the Americas (University College London). His main research focus is the political ascent of the Chapare coca growers union in Bolivia. His thematic interests include democracy, citizenship, the illegal cocaine trade, social movements and community radio. Thomas' research has been supported by the Leverhulme Trust, ESRC and the SSRC/Open Society Foundations.

Lucy McMahon is a lecturer at the Human Rights Consortium at the School of Advanced Study, University of London. Her PhD thesis explored the 2013–2014 protests in Brazil. She also works for the Traveller Literacy and Advocacy Project and as a translator for Rio On Watch.

Virginia Manzano gained her PhD in social anthropology from the University of Buenos Aires, Argentina. She is an adjunct researcher in the Council for Scientific and Technical Research, Argentina (CONICET), and professor of political anthropology at the University of Buenos Aires. Her research interests are the dynamics of collective organisation around work and urbanisation.

Salvador Martí i Puig is a doctor of political science, and currently professor in the University of Girona, Spain. His research interests are social movements, political conflict, processes of change and comparative politics, especially in Latin America. He collaborates with various solidarity networks internationally.

Jason Moyer-Lee is a 30-year-old American. He came to London to study at the School of Oriental and African Studies, University of London where he obtained his PhD. Jason got involved in cleaners' disputes and became active in the IWGB trade union of which he is currently president.

Mohamed-Salah Omri (University of Oxford, UK) is a scholar of modern Arabic literature and Tunisian cultural politics. His publications include *Nationalism, Islam and World Literature* (2006), a special issue of *Comparative Critical Studies* (2007), 'A Revolution of Dignity and Poetry' (2012) and 'Towards a Theory of Confluency – *Tarafud*' (2014).

Irene Peano is a precarious militant researcher. She currently holds a postdoctoral position at the University of Bologna, where her research project deals with forms of resistance to the regime of mobility control and the exploitation of migrant labour, with a special focus on the agro-industrial context and on its reproductive articulations. She received her PhD in social anthropology from the University of Cambridge, for a project on the bonded sexual labour of Nigerian migrants.

Peter Waterman worked for international Communist organisations in Prague (mid-1950s, later-1960s), before leaving the 'Communist World and the World of Communism'. He settled in The Hague, working at the Institute of Social Studies (1972–1998) on Third World and international trade unions and social movements, and their (computer) communications. He is pensioned but, so far, unretiring.

INDEX